Differentiated Instructional Management

Differentiated Instructional Management
Work Smarter, Not Harder

Carolyn Chapman • Rita King

CORWIN PRESS
A SAGE Company
Thousand Oaks, CA 91320

For information:

Corwin Press
A SAGE Company
2455 Teller Road
Thousand Oaks, California 91320
www.corwinpress.com

SAGE Ltd.
1 Oliver's Yard
55 City Road
London EC1Y 1SP
United Kingdom

SAGE India Pvt. Ltd.
B 1/I 1 Mohan Cooperative Industrial Area
Mathura Road, New Delhi 110 044
India

SAGE Asia-Pacific Pte. Ltd.
33 Pekin Street #02–01
Far East Square
Singapore 048763

Printed in the United States of America.

Library of Congress Cataloging-in-Publication Data

Chapman, Carolyn.
  Differentiated instructional management: work smarter, not harder / Carolyn Chapman and Rita King.
    p. cm.
Includes index.
ISBN 978-1-4129-2500-6 (cloth)
ISBN 978-1-4129-2501-3 (pbk.)
  1. Individualized instruction. 2. Cognitive styles in children. 3. Mixed ability grouping in education. I. Chapman, Carolyn, 1945-
II. King, Rita. III. Title.

LB1031.C465 2008
371.2′52—dc22   2007029938

This book is printed on acid-free paper.

07 08 09 10 11 10 9 8 7 6 5 4 3 2 1

Acquisitions Editor:	Hudson Perigo
Managing Editor:	Cathy Hernandez
Editorial Assistants:	Gem Rabanera and Lesley Blake
Production Editor:	Libby Larson
Copy Editor:	Gillian Dickens
Typesetter:	C&M Digitals (P) Ltd.
Proofreader:	Sally Jaskold
Indexer:	Maria Sosnowski
Cover Designer:	Lisa Miller
Illustrations:	Tammy Kay Brunson

CONTENTS

ACKNOWLEDGMENTS

A SPECIAL THANK YOU TO JIM CHAPMAN, CAROLYN'S HUSBAND, for his continued support, encouragement, constructive ideas, and his unbelievable patience. And to Sam, Rita's dog, for sitting and waiting patiently by the computer on many occasions for walks.

The teachers in Elko, Nevada; Plainfield, Indiana; and Beaufort County, South Carolina used many of the strategies and activities. Their feedback and encouragement is deeply appreciated.

Liz Bennett's educational expertise and creative mind continues to support and inspire us.

We are always in awe of Douglas Rife and the staff at Corwin Press who are there for us with their expertise and support. Faye Zucker understood our vision and helped us get this book well on its way. Kylee Liegl burned the midnight oil on many evenings adding her touches and editing expertise. The editing skills and support of Cathy Hernandez and Libby Larson guided our final steps.

Corwin Press gratefully acknowledges the contributions of the following reviewers:

Linda S. Prichard, Elementary Instructional Specialist, Rutherford County Schools, Murfreesboro, TN

Laura B. Harper, Adjunct Instructor and Supervisor of Student Teachers, Trevecca Nazarene University, Nashville, TN

Karen Nina Klingerman, Coordinator of Professional Development and Literacy Programs, Bensalem Township School District, Bensalem, PA

Valorie M. Catalano, Director, Chautauqua County Teachers' Center, Jamestown, NY

Steve Hutton, Area Consultant, Kentucky Center for Instructional Discipline, Villa Hills, KY

Michael L. Fisher Jr., Critical Thinking Specialist, Starpoint Middle School, Lockport, NY

Jane Ching Fung, Educator, Alexander Science Center School, Los Angeles, CA

ABOUT THE AUTHORS

Carolyn Chapman continues her life's goal as an international educational consultant, author, and teacher to make a difference in the minds and hearts of educators and learners. She supports educators in their process of change for today's students. She has taught in kindergarten to college classrooms. Her interactive, practical, energetic, motivating presentations provide professional development opportunities that focus on challenging the mind to ensure success for learners of all ages.

Carolyn walks her walk and talks her talk to make a difference in the journey of learning in today's classrooms. She inspires educators to put excitement and quality in effective learning. She is renowned for her expertise in a number of different areas, including differentiated instruction, multiple intelligences, and brain-compatible learning.

Carolyn has authored and coauthored many bestselling educational publications on differentiated instruction, literacy, and multiple intelligences. The books include:

Differentiated Assessment Strategies: One Tool Doesn't Fit All, Differentiated Instructional Strategies for Reading in the Content Areas, Differentiated Instructional Strategies for Writing in the Content Areas, Differentiated Instructional Strategies: One Size Doesn't Fit All, Test Success in the Brain Compatible Classroom, Multiple Assessments for Multiple Intelligences, Multiple Intelligences Through Centers and Projects, If the Shoe Fits . . . How to Develop Multiple Intelligences in the Classroom, and *Activities for the Differentiated Classroom.*

Each of these publications demonstrates Carolyn's desire and determination to make an effective impact for educators and students. She may be contacted through the Creative Learning Connection Web site at www.carolynchapman.com, e-mail at cchapman@carolynchapman.com, or by calling (706) 597-0706.

Rita King is an international trainer, keynote speaker, consultant, and author. She conducts training sessions for teachers, administrators, and parents. She served as the principal and director of the teacher-training program in Middle Tennessee State University's laboratory school. In this capacity, she taught methods courses and conducted demonstration lessons. Educators relate to Rita because of her background as a teacher and administrator and her experiences in PreK–12 classrooms. She has been recognized as an Exemplary Educator by the state of Tennessee. Rita's doctorate degree is in Educational Leadership. Her undergraduate and doctoral studies were directly related to education and teacher training.

The books Rita has coauthored are bestsellers. They include:

Differentiated Instructional Strategies for Reading in the Content Areas, Differentiated Instructional Strategies for Writing in the Content Areas, Differentiated Assessment Strategies: One Tool Doesn't Fit All, and *Test Success in the Brain-Compatible Classroom.* She coauthored training manuals for Creative Learning Connection's Train the Trainer courses.

Rita's sessions give educators and parents innovative, engaging activities to develop students as self-directed, independent learners. Her areas of expertise include differentiated instruction, classroom management, coaching, mentoring, and test success.

Participants enjoy Rita's practical, easy-to-use strategies, sense of humor, enthusiasm, and genuine desire to lead each learner to success. She may be reached through the Web site for King Learning Associates, Inc. at www.kinglearningassociates.com, by phone at (615) 848-8439, or via e-mail at kingrs@bellsouth.net.

INTRODUCTION

OH, THE MANY HATS WE WEAR DAILY AS EDUCATORS. HOW MANY roles must we assume in order to meet the unique needs of our students? We know that one style does not fit everyone because each individual comes to each learning experience with a unique bank of prior knowledge and experiences. We consider the learner's needs and choose the most appropriate style for each activity or event.

In these daily activities, we wear a variety of hats for each occasion. We are aware of the need for them to be appropriate, so we search for the right one!

Hats are worn for specific jobs and special occasions. For example, police officers, firefighters, and members of the armed services wear uniform hats. Educators wear uniform hats, too, as they carry out federal, state, and local mandates and standards. The established standards provide a framework for expectations and responsibilities in each grade level. It is important for educators to become familiar with the uniform hats needed for their state, district, and school. They must keep these accessible at all times to carry out mandates. While these hats are passed to teachers from outside the classroom, the way a teacher chooses to wear them while teaching the standards is usually in their control.

Differentiated management challenges educators to wear a variety of management hats daily as they adapt to the students' unique needs. Most teachers have a large collection of comfortable hats—or favorite instructional approaches. Often, a teacher's favorite, and most comfortable, instructional hat does not coordinate with a particular student's strengths or preferred method of learning. When this occurs, the teacher must wear an uncomfortable hat in order to reach that learner.

Responsive educators must go to great lengths to find the right hat for each student's learning styles. For example, when a struggling student is a visual learner and visual/spatial approaches are the teacher's weakness, that teacher needs to put on a glitzy hat and move into uncomfortable, visual strategies to help the learner.

STRATEGICALLY PLANNING DIFFERENTIATED MANAGEMENT

According to Gregory and Chapman (2007), differentiation is a philosophy. To make sure all students are learning every day, teachers choose to differentiate instruction. For this to happen, teachers purposely plan to meet each learner's varied needs. This is not an easy task.

The differentiation movement is making educators more aware of the need to reach the diverse needs of the population in a classroom. This idea has been discussed for centuries, but today, more than ever, educators are doing a better job of meeting this goal. They are improving because they have more assessment tools, instructional techniques, models, strategies, and resources. This belief is creating more multidimensional classrooms than ever before. But with so many activities and assignments going on simultaneously, teachers need well-planned management strategies to be successful.

WHAT ARE DIFFERENTIATED MANAGEMENT STRATEGIES?

Differentiated management strategies organize and customize instruction to provide the very best learning opportunities for each student. Routines and rules are carefully selected and designed to meet learners' changing needs.

Teachers who are taking the first steps into differentiated instruction need to begin with small steps, choosing one or two strategies or activities to implement at a time. Teachers currently using differentiated management techniques can adapt the ideas to tweak their skills, reaffirm their beliefs in present approaches, add novel strategies, or a new twist to old ways of doing things. The checklists, charts, outlines, activities, and suggestions in this book can be used to plan and organize differentiated instruction.

The keys to successful use of differentiated instructional management include the following:

- Maintaining a learning environment that is comfortable and stimulating
- Assessing students' individual needs before, during, and after learning
- Using the assessment data to plan strategically with the most beneficial models, techniques, and strategies
- Selecting and organizing instructional activities for the total group, individuals, partners, and small groups
- Instilling each student's desire to learn and improve

TEACHER JUDGMENT: CHOOSING THE APPROPRIATE HAT FOR THE OCCASION

Teacher judgment is a key to selecting the appropriate hat to wear for each instructional event. For example, when assessment data is analyzed, the teacher makes decisions about how to use the results. Here are some questions to address in selecting the hat to wear for the student's best interest.

- What is the best strategy to use so this individual can learn this concept?
- Do I need to assume the role of a facilitator or teacher?
- Does the student need to work independently or with a partner?
- Will I need to rewind or fast forward the curriculum for this student?
- Do I need to continue with grade-level instruction for this learning segment?

Effective instructional management decisions are based on the teacher's ability to select the standard and the content information to reach and teach each learner. Selection, organization, and pacing of instruction for the student's uniqueness are determined by many factors, including the learner's . . .

Knowledge base	Cultural background	Learning styles
Strengths and needs	Special needs	Preferences
Cognitive ability	Personality	Interests

ANALYZE SELF AND PURPOSE OF DIFFERENTIATING

Teachers need to take a look at themselves before deciding to differentiate their instruction. They need to decide what they currently are doing well to meet the unique needs of learners in their classroom, what can be done better, and why they feel they should work toward building a differentiated curriculum. The following checklist will answer some of these questions.

Fill in the answers to the questions below to see how ready you are to implement differentiation strategies into your classroom. Keep this survey so you remember the areas to improve.

Y = YES! I do this!

N = NEED! I need to improve in this area.

To differentiate, a teacher needs to . . .

1. _____ Know standards and students.

2. _____ Teach with knowledge, passion, and "with-it-ness."

3. _____ Use assessment data to guide planning for the diverse needs of the students.

4. _____ Give students more control of learning to make the information their own.

5. _____ Customize individual and small group assignments that fit using the most effective resources for the individual student's need.

6. _____ Establish flexible grouping to engage students in meaningful activities that teach the standards.

7. _____ Provide choice.

8. _____ Reteach to zap gaps.

9. _____ Provide enrichment and enhancement opportunities for learners according to their knowledge base.

10. _____ Create an optimal learning environment.

Introduction.1	
Stages	*Implementation Thoughts and Reactions to Buy-In*
Stage 1: Not interested *I don't need a new hat.* [Complete denial]	☐ My old hat is very comfortable. ☐ I don't have the time or energy to try anything new. ☐ This new style will soon pass.
Stage 2: Discovering *Trying on the new hat.* [Investigation]	☐ I'll just try it on to see how it fits. ☐ I may keep wearing my old hat. ☐ I can try this one again later. ☐ Others like this style, but do I need it? ☐ I feel uncomfortable when wearing it.
Stage 3: Wearing the hat *This hat works on certain occasions.* [Buy-in]	☐ Wearing it more often because it is working for you ☐ Seeing how to make it fit into your daily routine ☐ Feeling confidence ☐ Wearing it for specific occasions and times
Stage 4: Favorite hat *This is my best hat!* [Preferred approach]	☐ Wearing it as your most comfortable hat ☐ Wearing it with pride and encouraging others to wear it ☐ Keeping it in an accessible place ☐ Other people see it working for teaching and learning in my classroom

ANALYZING MANAGEMENT STYLE

Each teacher has a personal management style that is reflected in daily teaching. Some are more comfortable in quiet rooms, while others need the buzz of active learning. A teacher's personality is reflected in the management style implemented in the classroom.

Some students respond to their teacher's style, while others may be very uncomfortable in the learning environment. It's important for the teacher to look around and make sure all the students are comfortable. This is when "knowing your students" becomes so important. If a student thrives on movement but is never allowed to get the wiggles out by getting up and taking a quick walk around, comprehension will ultimately suffer.

Think about your personal teaching style. What management strategies support your own . . .

☐ Learning style?
☐ Personality?
☐ Intelligences?
☐ Tolerance levels?

ANALYZING TEACHING STYLE

The following Likert scale can be used as an informal self-analysis of teaching styles. Teachers may find that, when they fill it out or think about it, their approaches fall between the two extremes. That's okay. It can be used to move in the right direction.

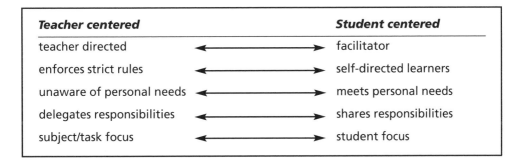

Teacher centered		Student centered
teacher directed	←——————→	facilitator
enforces strict rules	←——————→	self-directed learners
unaware of personal needs	←——————→	meets personal needs
delegates responsibilities	←——————→	shares responsibilities
subject/task focus	←——————→	student focus

OUR GOALS IN WRITING THIS BOOK

We wrote this book to assist teachers with the complex task of managing differentiated instruction. We know the body of knowledge related to differentiated instruction continues to grow as researchers share information about how the brain learns. Brain imaging is not available to classroom teachers so we have to take the findings of brain specialists to identify the best practices for individual learners.

Our beliefs for effective teaching and learning are based on the latest brain research that guides our work. We believe effective differentiating teachers

- Provide management tips and strategies to design and maintain an organized, productive learning environment for each student.

- Present models as blueprints for planning and organizing differentiated instruction.

- Present management techniques and ideas to effectively incorporate flexible grouping strategies as needed.

- Add to the repertoire of strategies for differentiated instruction.

- Assist in the process of gathering and managing assessment data before, during, and after learning to guide instruction.

- Provide planning suggestions and tools that can be used to strategically manage differentiated instruction and lead each student to success.

We encourage readers to adapt our ideas and suggestions to manage differentiated instruction. Choosing the right hat at the right time to "Put on the Ritz" gives each student optimal learning opportunities.

READY FOR THE CHANGE!

As teachers get comfortable with the idea of differentiation, they need to examine whether they are ready to implement the change within their own classrooms.

> Where do you fall in your readiness to make the change in your classroom? Take a look at the following figure and see which describes you. Are you ready for a change?

Introduction.2	
Teacher Position	*Reactions and Actions Toward Change*
Holding back	☐ You are fearful of the new idea. ☐ You think, "I don't believe this could ever be for me." ☐ You do not perceive differentiation as a valuable use of your time. It would not be worth the time and energy you would need to put into it. ☐ You are required to teach using a mandated program or method. The changes needed to differentiate are out of your control.

Ready to move forward	☐ Obtain support with colleagues or other educators who believe in the value of differentiation.
	☐ Examine and appreciate your beliefs and opinions.
	☐ Confront your fears and barriers to change.
	☐ Explore and learn about new possibilities.
	☐ Keep in mind that change comes gradually Begin to change and adjust the instructional techniques and strategies that are in your comfort zone.
	☐ Ask yourself questions similar to the following:
	  ○ Which strategies and activities do I want to keep?
	  ○ What is the easiest adjustment or change I can make to move forward?

A Preview of the Book

Each strategy, technique, and guideline was carefully selected. The management tips were narrowed to five-star summary statements. We hope they give our readers star power to work smarter, not harder.

This book does not address discipline. As a matter of fact, we avoided this "D" word. We believe that appropriate management strategies minimize and eliminate behavior problems, so we addressed the "D" of differentiation instead.

Below is a chapter-by-chapter description, making it easy for teachers to read through and know what to expect and where to go for specific topic discussions.

Managing the Differentiated Learning Environment

The environment plays a vital role in what and how much students learn. This chapter explores ways to improve the classroom environment to increase student learning. Both the physical and emotional climate of the room is important to the community of learners who call it home. In this section, teachers will learn to put on their chef's hat in order to cook up a recipe for affective and cognitive success in their classrooms.

Managing Differentiated Models

When a special activity, event, or unit of study is coming up in a classroom, teachers can pull out their formal planning hats! By choosing the best framework for the instruction, the goals of the lesson will be met in an engaging way, and students will learn.

Teachers are challenged every day to fill in the gaps for the students who do not have the proper background to be ready to learn the standards and the information that will be taught. Students who know the information need to be challenged. This chapter will help teachers know just which model to choose to meet the needs of everyone in their class, so everyone learns every day.

Managing Grouping Strategies

Like the baseball or football coach, a teacher needs to continually assess his or her students' skills, how they're improving, and what they still need to work on. When a teacher puts on a coaching hat, she or he is required to determine how students' needs will best be met. Do they need to work on a specific skill with a small group? Should they work alone to move further ahead while the rest of the class receives additional instruction in an area they have already mastered?

When a teacher remembers to keep grouping flexible and add variety to his or her grouping strategies, students stay engaged in learning. This chapter explores various flexible grouping strategies and discusses how to use them in the classroom, while managing several different activities going on at the same time.

Managing Instructional Strategies

Pulling from their treasure box of hats, teachers have many different choices in how they approach their teaching. This chapter will discuss some of the many varied strategies for meeting the unique needs of the different learners.

Teachers can learn to put on their magician's hat and pull out the perfect strategy to engage all students in the "act" of learning. They will have a classroom of students who are focused and ready to learn. When students are learning in appropriate leveled activities, they learn happily.

Managing Differentiated Assessment

Teachers are sometimes like detectives trying to solve a case. They need to compile the data to draw conclusions about their case—or class. Because of the differentiated movement, teachers are putting on their detective hats and assessing before, during, and after the learning. Assessment reveals needed information about what a learner knows and doesn't know. It provides valuable insight into student needs and assists teachers in planning well-rounded and meaningful lessons.

Both informal and formal assessments provide teachers the tools to plan strategically to meet the unique needs of the learners. Teachers assess students with many formal assessment tools. Many take hours of preparation. Some informal tools such as response cards or signals can provide immediate information needed to show how to plan for individual needs.

This chapter is designed to help teachers put on that detective hat, assess their students in meaningful ways, and use the data to solve the mystery of what each student needs to learn in order to be successful.

Managing Plans for Differentiated Instruction

Once teachers have the tools and elements necessary to create a differentiated environment in their own classrooms, they need to don their captain's hat and chart a course for the adventure of meeting the varied needs of their students. This chapter brings together those elements and helps teachers plan deliberately and for specific purposes. It allows teachers the freedom to choose the right hat for the occasion.

UNDERSTANDING THE BOOK FORMAT

The following format is followed with each model and strategy to keep the book consistent and easy to follow.

What is _____?	This provides a working definition and description of the model or strategy presented.
What are the instructional benefits?	This presents a rationale for using the model, tool, or strategy to meet the diverse needs of students.
Teacher's role	The necessary steps for implementing the model or strategy are outlined.
Demystifying	The information in this section can be used to explain this model or strategy to your students, parents, or colleagues.
Student's role	This explanation of the student's role can be adapted and presented to your students as they take an active part in learning.
Five-star management tips	The suggested techniques and approaches are presented to begin using the model or strategy right away.
Examples	The sample situations provide practical suggestions for the models and strategies.

MANAGING THE DIFFERENTIATED LEARNING ENVIRONMENT 1

IN A DIFFERENTIATED CLASSROOM, ALL ASPECTS OF THE environment are designed to provide each student with the most positive, productive, and nourishing learning experiences possible. The affective and physical environments are consciously established and maintained. Like a chef, a teacher needs to prepare the right recipe for the appropriate situation. Wearing the chef's hat, the teacher chooses the perfect ingredients to make learning a treat while nurturing each student's unique needs and tastes.

The affective realm includes the student's attitude toward learning and feelings about personal relationships with peers and the teacher. A positive classroom environment feeds the brain's ability to receive, process, and apply information. The physical realm includes the arrangement of desks, furniture, books, and materials. The appearance of posted information and displays has a major impact on the learner's perception of the physical environment.

Any classroom can be a comfortable, inviting place to learn. This was evident to us in a recent visit to a small, but cozy, high school classroom. We asked students why they were so anxious to get to this class. They said, "We hurry because we like our teacher. We feel at home." This teacher had established an extremely positive climate for learning in one of the smallest classrooms we have visited.

An inviting and comfortable learning culture that supports the unique needs of a student fosters personal and academic success. Finding the right recipe to manage the complexities of the learning environment in the differentiated classroom is a challenging but rewarding task.

MANAGING THE AFFECTIVE ENVIRONMENT

The affective environment sets the tone or climate for learning. Students need a safe, inviting place that gives them a sense of home when they enter the room. The teacher must manage the classroom to be sure it stays safe and is comfortable and risk free. Students need to feel honored and encouraged to try new things. When all individuals feel that others support and genuinely care about their success, the climate is ideal. Intentionally create a warm, inspiring environment that causes students to think, "I know I am going to be comfortable and learn here." Strategically plan all aspects of the classroom climate to create, develop, and maintain positive attitudes for learning. Remember, the affective environment produces feelings associated with learning that are carried by most students for a lifetime.

PRESENT EVIDENCE OF YOUR EXPECTATIONS

Learners usually want to live up to the teacher's expectations, particularly when they feel the teacher cares about them. In the play *My Fair Lady,* Professor Higgins demonstrates the lasting impact of personal investment and high expectations. He transforms a coarse-speaking girl of the streets into a lady with beauty and formal grace. The professor verbalizes and demonstrates his expectations for her success while guiding the transformation. Likewise, your students need to know that you see their potential, and they need to hear encouraging words.

> Treat people as if they were what they ought to be, and you help them become what they are capable of being.
>
> —Johann Von Goethe

Present evidence of your expectations:

- Display phrases, sayings, and rules that support and encourage learners.
- Show interest in each individual's personal life and outside achievements.
- Verbalize high achievable academic goals for the class and for individuals.
- Display personal goal statements that students can use or adapt.
- Use verbal and visual reminders.

Establish Rules and Routines

To create that safe learning environment, a teacher establishes manageable rules and basic routines. Provide opportunities for students or groups to assist in developing these guidelines. When students have a role in creating the rules and routines, they are more likely to follow them. Include your expectations in the rules for successful differentiated instruction. Be sure the rules are written in positive terms and posted so each student understands the behavior you want to observe.

Guidelines for introducing rules and routines:

- Display the rule or routine in a visual format and explain its purpose.
- State and model each step or procedure.
- Call on students to role-play, demonstrate, and restate it.
- Establish consequences for breaking rules and follow through with them.
- Review the rules and routines periodically during the first few days of implementation.

Model Expectations for Rules and Routines

Rules and routines must be in place in differentiated classrooms to ensure that things run smoothly. It is crucial to emphasize and demonstrate your expectations of proper behavior. Give students opportunities to role-play or create simulations to practice each new rule or routine after introducing it. Also give them opportunities to ask questions and express concerns. Yes, this takes time at the outset, but it saves time in the long run because students will internalize the new expectations during the presentations and discussions, and it won't be necessary to repeatedly restate the rules and routines. Students have fewer questions and feel more confident while engaging in activities when they know and understand the guidelines.

The experiences and personalities of some students make them natural followers and pleasers, while others tend to break rules to test boundaries. Whatever the cause, give extra guidance to individuals who have difficulty following the expected rules and routines.

Be Consistent and Persistent in Enforcing Rules and Routines

Students want to know what to expect. They need consistent rules and routines written in language they understand. Avoid changing a rule or consequence unless it is absolutely necessary.

- Practice rules and routines until they are understood and established.

- Carry out consequences immediately following infractions.

- Be consistent with identified consequences. Failure for a teacher to "follow through" creates uncertainty and deteriorates any respect students have for the teacher. Be persistent in applying the rules to all learners in all situations.

- Explicitly state your expectation that students follow rules and routines the first time. Do not give second chances as options.

   Note: Students often receive second chances in their homes and after-school activities. It may take them a while to conform to the "first time" expectation. When students receive second chances, they do not perceive the teacher as being consistent and persistent. Second chances tell learners it is okay to ignore the rule or routine the first time. Consider what could happen if students formed the habit of waiting for a second chance and you had to say, *"Stop! Don't cross the street! A car is coming!"*

- Explain why quick responses are important and how they save time for learning. Use banners, posters, and other visuals to challenge students with the "first-time" expectation. Examples: *Say it one time! Save time—do it right the first time!*

Make Manners Mandatory

Manners are an essential part of establishing an environment where all learners feel honored and respected. Remember, the classroom is the only environment where some students learn how to use manners and extend common courtesies.

- Introduce the concept of manners by explaining that the first syllable, *man-*, is derived from a Latin word that means "hand." People who show their manners are reaching out a hand to others to assist and to show their respect. Let students know you expect them to be kind, courteous, and helpful every day to create a special learning team.

- Make it clear that negative comments and "putdowns" about classmates are not tolerated. Guide students in a brainstorming session to create a list of common negative statements or "put-downs." Lead a discussion about how statements such as this make the receiver feel. Post this reminder: *If you can't say something kind or nice about someone, don't say anything.*

- Explain the importance of using positive comments, so everyone is comfortable as they learn. Guide the class through a brainstorming session to gather a list of "put-ups" or praise statements. Display these positive words and phrases on a poster or chart. Encourage students to add to the list throughout the year.

Way to go!	*Good try!*
You can do it!	*You deserve a pat on the back!*

- Discuss the importance of the interpersonal relationships in a differentiated classroom. Emphasize the value of respect and cooperation. Post a list of words and phrases that reflect the manners you expect such as "thank you" and "excuse me."

- Earn the respect of students. Expect them to respect you and others.

Realize That Body Language Speaks—and Make It Speak for You

Body language is a valuable management tool in a differentiated classroom. The quiet, unobtrusive movements replace verbal comments and actions that interrupt learning. Use it to give individual and group feedback. Be aware of its effectiveness when various groups and individuals are engaged in thinking.

Facial Language

Facial expressions are a universal language. Seasoned teachers rely on them as management tools. Use facial expressions to set the tone for learning as students enter the room and throughout the day. Collect a variety of expressions that are comfortable for you and practice them in front of the mirror to be certain they get the right message across.

Here are a few examples:

- Wink = *pleased; happy; attention*
- Frown = *disappointment; disapproval; sadness*
- Arching or raising the eyebrows = *surprise; disbelief*
- Turning the head side to side = *disapproval; warning*
- Smile = *approval; praise*

Facial language can be learned through the observation of family members, actors, colleagues, and friends. Practice the "Don't even think about it!" look. As soon as the learner or group responds appropriately, replace "the look" with the "I am proud of you!" expression.

Hand Language

Use hand language to support and strengthen verbal and facial language.

- Thumbs up = Approval or Good job!
- Palm toward the student = Wait . . . or Stop!
- Pointing to a student with the index finger = I see you!
- Moving the index finger forward and back to you = Come here.
- Forming a circle with a finger and thumb = Okay or Great!

Know your students and be aware of their body language. Familiarize students with the quiet signals they need to recognize and respond to in various situations. Identify specific body language to use as signals for struggling students.

Positioning Language: Be on the Move!

In a differentiated classroom, the teacher is on the move meeting individual and small group needs. Strategically plan and assess your moves with and among students.

- Face the majority of the class when working with individuals or groups.
- Use nonverbal or body language to emphasize messages.
- Teach students how to work independently and in small groups while you monitor and assist others.
- Continuously vary your walking pattern.
- Analyze your movement with a videotape or ask someone to record your patterns of movement on a classroom map.

Use positioning as a management strategy. Students who struggle or need special attention may need frequent teacher proximity. Off-task students usually return to work when the teacher simply moves in their direction. Proximity combined with body language can be a means of giving quiet feedback.

- Place yourself on eye level with the learner while assisting and coaching.
- Position yourself so you and the student have the same view of an object, book, or paper you are reviewing or discussing.
- Stand in front of and above the student's eye level when giving a strong directive or correction for disruptive behavior.
- Avoid placing yourself in a dangerous position directly behind or above a student without announcing or indicating your presence.
- Position yourself at a distance when a student is addressing the class. Move to the opposite side of the room, if possible. A student usually addresses comments in the teacher's direction, even when the presentations are for the class. When the teacher or other adults stand at a distance, a student speaks louder, making it easier for everyone to hear.

Make Words Work

Your statements set the tone for learning. Negative comments create emotional barriers to learning, so screen and control your thoughts before speaking. Create a mental file of positive words and phrases to replace unnecessary, negative comments.

Use Praise Statements

- You've got it!
- I knew I would see your best work on . . .
- You will be successful because . . .
- I can't wait to see you . . .
- I am proud of you each time you . . .

Give verbal rewards in specific terms to reinforce expectations. Students who receive praise often repeat their actions simply to please the teacher or to re-create the feelings that come with success.

Use Humor

> The wheels of creativity can be greased with humor.
>
> —Goleman, Kaufman, and Ray (1993)

When students list the characteristics of effective teachers, they seldom fail to emphasize a sense of humor. Laughter leads to positive feelings about the experience and cements learning.

In his explanation of how the brain learns, David Sousa outlines the benefits of using humor to enhance learning:

- More oxygen enters the bloodstream and fuels the brain.
- An endorphin surge increases enjoyment and attention.
- The experience creates a positive climate, bonding, and community spirit.
- Retention increases because the emotions are involved.
- Mental health is improved as stress is relieved and attitudes improve.*

Here are a few effective ways you can inject a bit of humor into your lessons.

- Introduce a segment of learning with a joke that relates to the study.
- Use a funny cartoon related to the topic.
- Offer students opportunities to use humor in activities and assignments.

Jokes	Riddles	Video clips	Puns
Cartoons	Role-playing	Silly songs	Surprises
Caricatures	Stories	Props	Celebrations

---

*From Sousa, D. 2006. *How the brain learns* (3rd ed.). Thousand Oaks, CA: Corwin Press. Used with permission.

Eliminate SCARcastic Humor and Remarks

Sarcasm is defined as "cutting of the flesh" because it leaves emotional scars. Recipients and classmates often laugh at sarcastic comments, but they seldom forget the remarks or the way the words made them feel. Years later in social gatherings and reunions, they recall the comments and talk about the pain and agony that lingers.

Refer to this type of humor as "*SCAR*casm" to emphasize the impact of this type of negative humor.

Pressures to teach many standards and skills in a little time can lead teachers to use sarcastic remarks when frustrated with a learner who is not meeting expectations or maintaining the pace of instruction. Just remember, if *SCARcastic* comments are used, the student will not absorb the information any faster. In fact, quite the opposite might happen: It might take the student even *longer* to learn the skill than if no remark had been made. SCARcastic remarks frequently create barriers to learning. Become consciously aware of statements such as the following:

- You are this age and you don't know how to _____?
- Let me just show you ONE more time.
- The answer is the same now as it was the last time you asked.
- Your brother was good at math.
- I don't know why this is so hard for you.

If you feel yourself getting frustrated, remind yourself to replace negative thoughts and comments with encouraging statements similar to these:

- Let's talk about what you have right and see what you need next.
- You got this one right so tell me how you did it.
- Now tell me what you do next.
- Because you understand _____, you will be able to _____.
- Let me show you how to "Zap this gap!"

Realize the Impact of Vicarious Learning

In differentiated classrooms, students often learn indirectly or vicariously by hearing and seeing the teacher interact with others. For example, if the teacher reminds one student to place a dollar sign in front of her answers in money problems, the students who overhear this statement may check their work to see if they have dollar signs in place.

Make only positive comments or reminders in public. If a statement is intimidating or embarrassing, students who overhear it will have negative reactions when they see the teacher coming their way. If negative comments are necessary, make them in private.

Answer questions with positive statements and praise or pats on the back. This makes other students eager to add comments and ask questions.

Establish Open Communication

When students are comfortable talking to adults in their lives, they are more equipped to take risks and fail. Only when they are open to failure will they learn. It is important that the students feel that they can talk to the teacher about both positive and negative issues.

Honor Student Contributions

Be approachable, so students can make statements or ask questions. Praise them for coming to you or for making contributions. When you need uninterrupted time, tell the students so they won't be confused or hurt if you have to turn them away.

Use the following suggestions to demonstrate that you are approachable:

- Smile
- Be attentive and project the "I care about you" attitude.
- Make comments to encourage creative and critical thinking.
- Correct with dignity and respect. Avoid expressing frustrations and anger.
- Expect and praise concentration, hard work, and persistence.

Listen With Intent

Listen actively. Be aware of your expectations as a listener. Honor the individual who is talking.

- Use direct eye contact with the student who is speaking. Avoid multitasking.
- Be an active listener by nodding when appropriate, asking clarifying questions when necessary, and showing that you care about what is being said.
- Establish open communication and stay neutral. Students should not feel that it is "the teacher's way or the highway."
- If you do not agree with a student, respect the student's opinion. Avoid saying "I disagree." Say, "I hear what you are saying" or "I value your thinking."
- Provide opportunities for students to participate in open discussions. With teacher guidance, students learn valuable lessons in respecting the views of others and in forming their opinions.
  - Avoid expecting incorrect answers from low-ability students. Listen carefully because they may prove you to be wrong.
  - Students who are expected to know the answers should feel comfortable in raising a hand to say, "I do not know this." Honor them for speaking up.
  - Avoid making judgment calls with inappropriate remarks.

Build Rapport

Rapport is a genuine, caring, and harmonious relationship or emotional bond that exists between the teacher and the student, between the student and classmates. A learner who likes and respects the teacher usually wants to please and responds to praise eagerly.

In a positive differentiated classroom environment, students know they are honored and valued as members of the learning community. They feel that the teacher appreciates their unique strengths and weaknesses and has their best interests at heart when making instructional decisions.

Students who have good relationships with everyone in the class are more likely to feel confident and comfortable. They are more likely to ask questions and to explore new ways of thinking when the teacher

- Responds to their moods
- Recognizes important episodes in their personal lives
- Treats their errors as teaching opportunities rather than mistakes
- Accepts new and unique ways of processing information
- Celebrates each success

Be "With-It"

Students perceive a "with-it" teacher as someone who knows and understands their world. Use "with-it-ness" to build rapport with students who have unique needs.

1. Survey students often to know their current fads, interests, and favorite things to do. Remember, student interests are forever changing, so stay "with-it."

2. Watch their favorite television shows, play their favorite computer games, and learn about their sports. Play their music, if it is appropriate.

3. If possible, avoid burdening students with homework on special occasions associated with the school. They need to enjoy the social events and feel relaxed as they support school-sponsored activities.

4. Let students know you are interested in their personal lives. Express interest in their extracurricular activities such as ballgames, concerts, or other events. Refer to afterschool activities, interests, fads, and families in informal conversations.
   - I heard you had a good game last night! Tell me about it.
   - You have on my favorite shirt today.
   - You must be proud of your sister's . . .
   - The teacher in your afterschool class said you . . .
   - We are going to use your favorite CD during our study of . . .

5. Use the information gathered to
   - See what motivates, informs, and inspires your students so you have a better understanding of their backgrounds and value systems.
   - Make a connection with your students. If they know you truly care about and support who they are, they will work hard to please you.
   - Create opportunities for students to connect things and happenings in their world to content and skills for better retention.

6. Remember: "With-it-ness" demonstrates understanding and caring about what is important to them.

Give Extra Attention

Identify students who need extra attention. Maintain open communication with students and their parents so you know when someone is dealing with death, illness, divorce, poverty, physical handicaps, or other emotional problems. Sensitive and shy students often need opportunities to develop interpersonal skills and self-confidence. Let other teachers, administrators, and the support staff know when a student needs more time and attention. Roles such as the following provide opportunities to engage in more social interactions:

- Delivering messages
- Leading routine activities
- Collecting and dispensing materials
- Working with a partner to organize materials and supplies
- Tutoring or reading to classmates or younger students

Celebrate Success

Celebrate the success of a student or small group. Challenge individuals and groups to create their own celebration activity. The following are examples of classroom celebrations:

High fives	Chants	Banners
Pats on the back	Songs	Pennants
Cheers	Raps	Signs

WOW Your Students

How often do you enjoy hearing your students say, "I can't wait to see what you are going to do next," or "I don't want to go to my next class. May I stay with you?" One way to create these reactions is to give your students a "WOW" every day. According to Stephen Barkley (2005), a WOW learning experience

- Provides novelty
- Creates positive emotions
- Notifies the brain that something new and exciting is happening
- Primes the pump for learning*

Using Novelty

The brain responds to anything new or different. Use novelty to gain attention, enhance instruction, and intrigue learners. Design activities that are appealing and different to make each learning experience a pleasant, memorable event and to keep learners guessing about what might happen next. Interesting and exciting activities enhance retention because they hook a memory or emotion to the information.

---

*Reprinted with permission from Performance Learning Systems, Inc.©, an educational services company located in Allentown, Pennsylvania, U.S.A. and on the World Wide Web at www.plsweb.com. Copyright © 2005 Performance Learning Systems, Inc. All rights reserved.

- Greet students at the door dressed as a person or character in the lesson.
- Play a short, musical snippet that supports instruction when it is least expected.
- End the lesson with a snack that reinforces a fact or concept.
- Sprinkle confetti in the center of each group when the task is completed.
- Vary the exit strategies to celebrate the day's learning or to entice students to come back tomorrow.

Foster Self-Efficacy

Self-efficacy is the "I believe in me" feeling. At home and in school, students need to feel they are great and getting greater every day. Take advantage of any opportunity to provide support and build confidence so your students know they will succeed.

Develop a Sense of Ownership

Periodically ask your students, "What do we need to do to make this a better place to learn?" Give students a sense of ownership in the teaching and learning process by sharing responsibilities in preparing, organizing, and maintaining the environment and various aspects of daily activities. The roles benefit all students but especially those who need more confidence, feelings of success, and belonging. The tasks also create opportunities for students to get to know one another as they informally work together.

> Few things help an individual more than to place responsibility upon him, and to let him know that you trust him.
>
> —Booker T. Washington

Students can share responsibility by

- Labeling displays, materials, and artifacts
- Preparing bulletin boards and centers
- Designing games, puzzles, and activities for learning zones
- Collecting artifacts, models, and pictures to support instruction
- Organizing desks or furniture for an activity

As students assume roles that lead to the success of the learning team, they develop a sense of pride and internal commitment to the class goals. Struggling students often feel ostracized. They need to develop a sense of ownership and belonging to fuel their desire to learn.

Guide students to develop their ability to reason and become responsible for their own actions and their learning. Explain that it takes time to think. Teach learners to

- Identify the error and incorrect action
- Describe it in their own words
- Tell "how and why" the action occurred
- Describe how to correct or improve the mistake or inappropriate action
- State or write a personal improvement plan

This approach teaches students to reason through academic and social actions. Independent thinking serves as a skill throughout their academic careers and beyond.

Give Choices

Consider the many choices most students have in their daily activities before and after school. It makes little sense to strip them of this ability once inside the classroom. Providing choices fosters buy-in to instruction and helps develop independent thinkers and responsible learners.

Consider the students' ages, characteristics, and preferences in designing choice activities. Provide choices of seating arrangements, seating types, working teams, and activities.

Teach Resiliency

Struggling students often experience negative feelings and depression while striving to learn. They need to know how to bring themselves out of these negative mental states that often follow failure and disappointment. This ability is crucial in all aspects of life.

Remind students that

- Everyone faces obstacles.
- Mistakes and failures are opportunities to improve in disguise. When you can identify a learning gap, you can zap it!
- It is brave to admit when you need help.
- You can use your strengths to strengthen your weaknesses.
- Progress calls for celebration!

Introduce students, especially those who are struggling, to techniques they can use to become resilient. Give them real-world examples of triumphs over adversity.

- Read fables students can use for self-encouragement and discuss the lessons they present.
- Share personal stories of triumph over disaster found in newspapers and magazines. Examples: Michael Jordan was eliminated in tryouts for his high school basketball team. Patricia Polacco, a nonreader, became a famous author.
- Teach students sayings and jingles to internalize and use after failures and disappointments. Examples:

  If at first you don't succeed, try, try again.
  When life gives you lemons, make lemonade.
  You only fail if you don't get up the last time you fall.

- Play or sing songs with upbeat lyrics. Examples: Gloria Gaynor's "I Will Survive" and Frank Sinatra's "That's Life." Post the refrain. Here is an example from Aaliyah's song, "Try Again."

  And if at first you don't succeed
  Then dust yourself off and try again
  You can dust it off and try again, try again

Ask students to change the words to fit roles in their lives. Example: Change the words in "That's Life" to "I've been a winner, a loser, a student, and a clown. . . ."

- Have students identify sources of support, including classmates, friends, teachers, parents, and other adults.

Teach Stress-Reducing Strategies

All students need to know how to relieve stress at school and in their daily activities. Students who are identified as being at risk or struggling, academically or personnally, need to know how to apply these techniques independently.

Discuss the value of good stress and the negative impact of bad stress. Introduce students to stress-reducing activities. See the examples in Figure 1.1.

Motivate the Unmotivated

Unmotivated students often have had few successful experiences. This is the result of a lack of support and encouragement, inadequate role models, low expectations, and negative learning experiences.

Figure 1.1	
Stress Reducers	
Physical Exercises	*Relaxation Exercises*
• Jumping jacks • Running in place • Toe touches and reaching for the sky • Arm windmills • Shoulder shrugs and stretches	• Take a deep breath and exhale slowly. • Tense and relax specific muscles repeatedly. • Lie down. Listen to soothing music with eyes closed. • Stare at an object in a distant point. • Imagine a pen slowly drawing an outline around your body. Remove all other thoughts.
Mental Exercises	*Rest Spot*
• Take a mental mini-vacation to your favorite place. • Visualize and concentrate on your favorite person, pet, or scene for two or three minutes. • Use games and brain teasers. • Complete word games such as crosswords and acrostics. • Play number games such as Sudoku.	• Reserve a space that is used only for relaxation as a reward. • Use a beanbag, a rug, or a lounge chair. • Encourage students to go to the Rest Spot when they need to relax or regain self-control. • Use the Rest Spot to work alone or to think.

Find ways to unlock unmotivated minds. Thoroughly investigate various aspects of the learner, including academic, social, and emotional needs. Consider the individual's abilities, home life, and previous academic experiences.

Teachers usually become aware of unmotivated learners through informal observation. The following behaviors can be identified during regular classroom activities:

- Slouching in the seat often with arms folded
- Avoiding eye contact
- Talking back with negative statements. Examples:
  I am not going to work on . . .

  This is too hard.

  I can't do this!

  You can't make me . . .
- Lowering the head.
- Slow in following directions or contributing

Use the following ideas to motivate the unmotivated:

- Offer the learner a choice of activities that engage his or her strengths and interests in challenging and intriguing ways.
- Show the student how the information relates to his or her world. Help the student understand the personal value and purpose for learning the information.
- Identify the next steps the learner needs. Present instruction and activities in small chunks within his or her level of success.
- Respect and honor every student as an important team member with something to contribute to the learning community. Every learner must feel accepted as an individual by classmates and adults.
- Find ways for the student to contribute to the class. Praise the smallest successes.

MANAGING THE PHYSICAL ENVIRONMENT

The physical environment includes the classroom furniture, displays, storage areas, lighting, and the temperature. It also includes all peripheries—everything within the learners' visual range. Effective organization and the productive use of the physical environment has a positive impact on learning.

Managing Students' Personal Space

Every student needs a place of his or her own in the classroom. Teach students to respect the items that belong to their classmates such as coats, bags, extra books, and supplies.

- Provide each student with a place in the room that is identified as his or her personal space.
- Allow students to personalize their spaces with their names, drawings, and special objects.
- Ask students who share their personal spaces with students from other classes to remove personal items daily.
- Store student work in personalized portfolios, cubbies, lockers, folders, or boxes.
- Establish a rule that requires respect for personal items and space.

Designate Common/Group Work Areas

Explain how and when common meeting areas are used. Identify areas for class meetings, independent conferences, small group discussions, presentations, and learning celebrations.

Provide work areas for student conferencing, partner, and small group work. Identify locations for students to gather such as grouping chairs or desks together, sitting or standing in discussion huddles, or gathering around a table.

Designate Display Spaces

Establish areas for groups and individuals to display their work. Give groups opportunities to display summaries of their progress, timelines, flowcharts, drawings, booklets, flyers, and exhibits.

Post or display work related to the current study inside the classroom. Move the display to a hall area outside the room when the study ends. Refer to it to reinforce and review previously taught information. Provide various ways for students to post their individual work without adult supervision. Now the room is prepared for new learning.

For example, students can post their work on		
Walls	Shades	Bulletin boards
Doors	Clotheslines	Sides of filing cabinets
Cork boards	Chart stands	Chairs
Hallways	Cabinet doors	Window sills

Managing Student Materials

Some people use organizers, files, and lists so they know where everything is located. They don't waste valuable time looking for things. Other people do not need to have their surroundings as neat and organized. Students have a tendency to conform to the personal organizational style of the adult in the room. Here are some suggestions to assist with organizing classroom materials:

- Provide a place or a home for everything. Teach students to keep books, material, equipment, and personal items in their place. Post the well-known phrase, "A place for everything and everything in its place."

- Color-code each item to match its home or space.

- Organize materials by categories.

- Teach students to clean up. Use reminders such as "If I mess up, I clean up."

- Discard materials that are no longer needed.

Use attractive containers in centers, stations, zones, and labs:

Baggies	Storage tubs with lids	Crates
Boxes	Bags with handles	Buckets
Folders	Envelopes	Baskets

Managing Your Piles and Files

Many teachers spend valuable time looking for things. Survey your classroom. Ask yourself if your piles and files appear as clutter to students, parents, administrators, and visitors. Remember that perceptions are often more important than reality. If individuals see you as being disorganized, they may connect this with ineffectiveness. If an evaluator views clutter as a sign of ineffectiveness, an observation may be influenced by the perception.

Teachers are natural packrats. If you fit this description, make your clutter appear organized. You don't want an assistant or substitute to open your closet and say, "I won't be able to find one thing in this mess!"

Managing Tips for Pack Rats

Teachers who differentiate usually have more activities and materials than traditional teachers. The following suggestions are for the packrats (Count us in this group!). Use the tips to organize or appear organized:

- Honor your personal organizational style. If you need visible stacks of paper, use a cubby storage unit.

- Purchase inexpensive containers that are the same size, shape, and design. Dump your precious teaching junk into the color-coded containers and label them.

- Ask a colleague, volunteer, or a student to help you organize. Don't leave the chore for that individual. Be there so you will know how and where your prized paraphernalia is stored.

- Identify a personal space for items that are "Off Limits" to students. A cabinet, desk, shelf, or table can serve this purpose.

- Assign a student to assist with organization.

Managing Student Papers

Students need clear directions as to what to do with their paperwork. Provide guidelines for placement of completed assignments and products. Use these guidelines to create routines and rituals so students assume this responsibility.

- Use "In/Out" baskets, trays, folders, or containers. Display them in the same place daily. Avoid using the teacher's desk as an "In/Out" station.

- Find a place for materials needed for the day's or the week's assignments. At the end of the day, remove extra items. Gather materials for the next day in one place for easy access.

- Color-code folders by subjects or levels of tiered assignments. Consistently use the same colors for independent assignments or center activities.

- Assign a student to be a materials manager or assistant.

- Designate areas with answer sheets for students to check their own papers. Remember to have a fun writing implement such as a pen with feathers or green gel. No pencils allowed.

Some examples of where students can keep their work are as follows:

Complete Work:	basket	display area	booklet
Incomplete Work:	portfolio	notebook	file

Managing Noise Levels

In differentiated classrooms, groups and individuals engage in various activities simultaneously, so higher noise levels and more movement are expected. Use the following ideas to reduce noise levels and the amount of movement. (Also see Figure 1.2.)

- Provide supply carts or containers near student work areas for groups of students to share extra pencils, paper, crayons, markers, sticky notes, scissors, glue, and assignment materials.

- Create a clear walkway through the entire class so you can easily reach and assist each learner. Provide easy passages for students, too.

- Add quiet zone areas. Strategically plan activities so students who need to concentrate have an area away from the louder groups.

- Establish, teach, and practice movement transitions, such as how to efficiently move into groups for partner or small group assignments.

- Discuss appropriate voice levels for different kinds of activities. Display a poster with each noise level identified and explanations of what each one means and when it is used. Teach students to identify the appropriate noise level before they begin their individual and group activities. A sign may be placed in the station or center with the voice level displayed.

Organizational Tips for Sharing a Classroom With Another Adult

Teachers who work together in differentiated classrooms or inclusion situations must work cooperatively to create a positive learning environment. The way they honor and respect each other as they share the classroom, materials, and responsibilities is evident to students.

Teachers who share a classroom or a work area with a colleague need to consider each individual's organizational style. Be aware of the other person's natural tendencies and avoid overpowering or undervaluing these characteristics. Remember, creative individuals often are less organized. Analytical thinkers usually are organizers, so they may have communication barriers with pile-gathering thinkers.

Communicate your organizational needs to adults who work with you. Discuss the physical space and ways to honor the organizational style of each person.

If more than one class shares the room with different teachers, divide the display areas into assigned sections for each class. Provide places for students to display work when it is completed. This develops a print-rich environment. If space is available, rotate the displayed work of each class throughout the year.

Managing Time

Consider the value of time in each learning experience. Be aware of time that may be wasted or lost. For example, plan activities for students who finish work early. Develop routines and rituals that are easily repeated by students. Teach the class that time is a valuable resource to use wisely. See Figure 1.3.

Managing Class Time

Emphasize the value of time in lessons, activities, and transitions. Establish and teach routines for daily activities. Time each class activity over a week's period so you realize the amount of time for each routine activity. Clear, concise directions are key to managing class time.

- Have instant activities ready for difficult moments.
- Have focus and sponge activities ready to use as needed.
- Turn routines and responsibilities over to students whenever possible.
- Establish ways to distribute or obtain materials. Have materials and resources available for each activity or assignment.
- Give quality assignments appropriate for each student's knowledge base, based on assessment data gathered before, during, and after the learning.

Managing Personal Time

- Be a list maker and prioritize items. Check off or mark through completed tasks. Place activities, due dates, appointments, and other important events on a desk or wall calendar. Beware of crowding too many expectations or overlapping tasks into one time frame.
- Meet time guidelines and due dates by recording the deadline warning a few days prior to the actual due date on the calendar.
- If asked for a commitment, respond with "I will get back to you" to give yourself time to check your calendar. Be sure the time needed is valuable for you.
- Arrive at school early to prepare for the day and organize your thoughts.
- Schedule time for yourself and for planning.

Figure 1.2

Voice Level	What Does It Mean?	When Is It Used?
0	No talking	Taking tests When receiving directions Independent work time While someone is presenting or speaking to the class During lecturettes During announcements
1	Whisper	When others are concentrating on their work Sharing ideas or responses with a partner
2	Low voice	Working with a partner or small group Engaging in activities with a classmate
3	Talking voice	When there is no danger of interrupting the thinking of other people
4	Speaking voice	Projecting your voice to be heard by everyone Giving directions to the group Sharing with the group Responding to someone from a distance
5	Loud voice	Playing outside Gym activities Games Celebrations

SETTING THE TONE

The way you present yourself and your expectations has a major impact on the way students respond to you each day of the year. Make each student feel excited about being a unique member of your class every day with every action and comment you make.

Earn your students' respect. Demonstrate or show them that you know your subject. Let them see and feel your passion. Make it clear why they need to listen to you and that you will listen to them. Smile and care! Show the class that you are not a teacher from the black lagoon but someone who truly cares for each one of them as individuals.

Demonstrate your genuine interest in each student's success in school and in life. State your desire for each individual to be a happy, productive citizen in the class and in life.

Show that you are dedicated to helping them learn the subject and skills they need. Be sure they leave each day knowing they are going to enjoy learning with you tomorrow.

Entering and Preparing for Class

When you are prepared for your students, they know that they are important to you. Make sure you take time to arrive early and think the day through, getting all of the necessary supplies before your students arrive. Plan well to make each moment of learning a worthwhile experience.

Greeting Students

Observe how students enter a room. Do they joke and laugh or meander? This can be relevant for learning. The entrance of individuals of any age provides valuable information. Make mental notes as you meet and greet your students at the door.

The teacher's presence and actions as students enter the classroom set the tone for learning. This time can be used to interact with students who have unique needs. Here are some greetings that make entrances more inviting:

- Smile and call them by name
- Share a high five or pat on the back
- Notice and comment on changes such as new clothes or a new haircut.
- Share a welcoming handshake
- Use a kind, personal comment or question that shows you are excited about seeing each one of them

Remember the value of informal, social interactions. Give students opportunities to say "hello" and socialize before class formally begins. During this time, they can gather materials or supplies and prepare for the day.

Jump-Start Each Day of Learning

Jump-start the learners' day using a variety of strategies and approaches. Most classes need to begin the year with structured activities. When students become accustomed to routines, select activities to encourage creativity, stimulate higher order thinking, or showcase talents and interests.

Place a focus or bell-ringing challenge in the same spot each day. After the students meet and greet and check for needed materials for class, they begin the assignment.

Bell-Ringing Activities

- Go on a scavenger hunt and find _____ in the text.
- Work the brain challenge activity.
- Write three things you recall from yesterday.
- Share your homework with a partner.
- Make a list of important facts from yesterday's learning.

Plan activities that create an initial routine to begin the day and promote order. Select or design each activity with the students' individual needs in mind. For example, in the following activity, each student has a specific role that develops communication skills, increases confidence, and develops responsibility.

Example:

Select five students to serve as the news team.

- First student—local or school news
- Second student—state news
- Third student—national news
- Fourth student—weather report
- Fifth student—leads the pledge and moment of silence

Since all students are engaged on the news team or as audience members, the teacher can use this time to conference with students, prepare the lunch count, take the roll, or prepare for the first lesson.

Calling the Roll

Calling the roll consumes valuable time. After the first few days when the roll is finalized, use another quick, efficient method to check attendance. Use procedures similar to the following to save class time.

Example A: Clothesline Rolls

Share classroom management responsibilities with students. Adapt the following procedure to your grade level:

1. Hang a clothesline. Place a container for the clothespins nearby.

2. Place the students' names on clothespins. Provide time for the class to personalize their clothespins with miniature drawings that symbolize them such as their hobbies, interests, or pets.

3. Tell students to find their clothespin on the line and place it in the container as soon as they enter the room.

4. Record absentees by taking the names from the remaining clothespins.

5. Assign one student to place all pins on the line after attendance is recorded.

Figure 1.3	
Time Killers	*Time Savers*
Repeating directions and expectations	• Train students to listen the first time • Give one or two directions at a time • Call on one or two students to repeat the directions • Role-play or create simulations • Give a visual or verbal signal to let students know they need to listen to directions
Passing out papers	• Establish a routine with designated distributors • Color-code baskets or small tubs for groups or individuals to obtain papers or materials • Give the papers to three or four students to distribute • Arrange papers in seating order
Collecting papers	• Provide privacy by asking students to fold their papers and place their name on the outside • Designate a container for papers • Identify a "materials" person • Ask students to leave completed papers on the desk

Example B: Clothespin Rolls

Write the name of each student around the outer edges of a chart or poster in bright colors and various fonts. Ask students to place a clothespin or colorful clip on or next to their names when they arrive. Keep the clothespins or clips in a box that is easy to access.

Example C: Learning Students' Names

1. Guide students through steps to personalize a name tent. Give students directions similar to the following:
   a. Fold the index card in half to create a name tent.
   b. Write the name you want me to call you in large, colorful letters on each side of the name tent.
   c. Draw several symbols that represent your hobbies and interests on each side of the name tent.

2. Designate one or two students to distribute the name tents.

3. Observe the name tents at empty seats to record absences.

Example D: Name Tags

Prepare name tags for students to use the first few weeks. Students pick up and return their name tags to a designated area.

Example E: Check-In

Display a grid with names listed on the left-hand side and dates listed on the top row. Students place a checkmark beside their names under the date when they enter the room.

Managing Lesson Closures and Classroom Exits

In differentiated classrooms, students often are working in small groups or as individuals when it is time to bring closure to the lesson. Maintain a focus on learning as students complete activities or prepare to exit the classroom. Practice the selected routine. Planned, structured procedures create organized closures and exits.

Wrap Ups

Wrap ups are closures for lessons and activities. Avoid interrupting students during their tasks and related discussions. Use a signal to let students know they have five more minutes to wrap up or bring activities to closure. This lets students know their work and conversations are valued. Use another signal to end the activity.

Example A: Sharing Aha's of the Day

Students return to their seats and write a review of the activity. If time permits, call on a few students to share the most important points.

Example B: Ticket Out the Door

Tell students to write three facts they learned on a sticky note. Ask them to place their notes on the facing of the door as they exit.

Example C: Exit Statements

End each learning session on a high note.

- I am proud of the things you learned today.
- I like the way you worked together to learn.
- You won't believe what we are going to do tomorrow that will add to the things you learned today.

Perceptions of Organized Chaos

A differentiated classroom may appear to be in a state of chaos to individuals who are accustomed to traditional classroom settings. They observe the teacher serving as a learning facilitator who is monitoring, guiding thinking, assisting, modeling, observing, encouraging, and questioning small groups and individuals. Visitors often enter the room and say, "Where is your teacher?"

Differentiated classrooms have multidimensional environments because . . .

- Students simultaneously engage in various activities.
- The noise level is higher with constructive busy noise.
- Students move from one area to another as they work on individual, partner, or small group tasks.
- Conversations related to various tasks may be heard from students working in different areas of the room.
- Individuals and small groups are engaged using easily accessible manipulatives, materials, books, reference tools, and computers.

Figure 1.4

Managing the Complex Differentiated Classroom Environment	
Characteristics of the differentiated classroom environment	Identify the hats you need to manage the learning environment.
Classrooms are multidimensional. *Collect a large variety of hats for the complex roles you fill.*	Identify specific hats you may need to meet the needs of the unique individuals in each class. Keep your hats handy. Add to your collection of hats by • Borrowing from colleagues and administrators • Pulling ideas from a book, CD, or video • Joining an online chat group with teachers on your grade level or subject area • Joining professional organizations related to your field • Reading professional journals • Viewing others who wear the hats you need

(Continued)

Figure 1.4 (Continued)

Managing the Complex Differentiated Classroom Environment

Students engage in a variety of different activities simultaneously. *Be prepared to wear more than one hat at one time.*	Establish clear, concise guidelines for independent and group work and movement. Make materials accessible. • Place supplies near the groups. • Assign one student in each group to obtain materials. • Maintain a supply shelf or area for student use. • Design activities and assignments that need little or no teacher direction. • Identify quiet signals and reminders that do not interrupt teaching and learning.
Teacher attention is used wisely and selectively with individuals and groups. *Know when to change hats and when to leave them on the hat stand.*	Use teacher judgment to decide which events need • To be ignored • Immediate attention • Delayed attention Teach students how to respond to the most common events such as changes in group or individual assignments.
Events often are unpredictable. *Have hats ready for unexpected happenings during instruction.*	Predict the unexpected. Provide directions to students for events and emergencies that require your immediate, undivided attention: • An assigned student finds another teacher or notifies the office • Listen intently to directions • Post emergency plans
Little privacy exists. *Remember that the hats you wear are reflections of you.*	Spotlight the success of struggling individuals or groups for the school and community. • Realize that perceptions of observers often become their reality. • Share positive events. • Invite special guests. • Make positive comments about students in the lounge and community. • Design the environment to reflect current learning. • Carefully choose at least one colleague to serve as a confidant. • Reprimand in private. Praise in public. • Be genuine and show your passion for making a difference.

SELECT YOUR HATS FOR THE ENVIRONMENT

As stated previously, differentiated classrooms are multidimensional, complex places. Use the following chart to identify the hats you may need to manage the many aspects of your classroom. Adapt and add to our suggestions as you prepare the optimal learning environment for your students. See Figure 1.4.

Assess Your Differentiated Management Skills

Assess your differentiated management skills for optimal learning environment. Use your responses as a guide to improve.

1 = Never   2 = Occasionally   3 = Frequently   4 = Always

- All individuals know they are vital working members of the class family.
- Rituals and rules are established and carried out with equality for all.
- The room has specified areas for materials, movement, and independent and group work.
- Expectations for a respectful and caring learning community are stated and modeled.
- Respect and honor are earned and given to adults and students.

CONCLUSION

When teachers keep in mind the environment they create for students, the learners in their class are better able to succeed. A teacher needs to remember that when he or she wears the chef's hat, he or she is responsible for creating a safe, comfortable environment where students are free to take risks. Like the chef, a teacher needs to use the right ingredients so each student is nourished and enjoys the experience. Keep this hat handy as you evaluate, manage, and re-create your classroom environment.

WHAT IS A MODEL?

A man or woman may wear a formal hat for just the right touch to an occasion. This type of hat is chosen because it not only fits the occasion but also adds the personalized touch to an outfit. Likewise, a model—a blueprint for organizing instruction—is selected for the specific learning event. It offers the finishing touch and oomph for planning a lesson. It provides a pattern with steps to follow. A theory or belief serves as the foundation for each one.

The differentiated models presented in this chapter were selected and designed to assist teachers in planning for specific learner needs. Each one can be adapted to the unique needs of a class, small group, or individual.

The models are frameworks for managing instruction in a differentiated classroom. Each model can be used to organize strategies and activities. When the teacher becomes familiar with the models, it is easier to select the one that coordinates with the students' identified needs.

The first model presented, the adjustable assignment model, is recommended as the master plan or map for differentiated instruction. When used effectively, everyone benefits from the outlined details because this information identifies each student's knowledge level in relation to the new learning. The remaining models are guides for carrying out instruction.

It takes time to know the standards. Also, much time must be given to selecting the appropriate model for the learner's need. Matching the planning model with the needs of students is like wearing the right hat with the right outfit. The same hat does not fit all occasions, and the same model does not fit all student needs!

ADJUSTABLE ASSIGNMENT MODEL

What Is the Adjustable Assignment Model?

The adjustable assignment model is a planning tool that was designed by Gayle Gregory and Carolyn Chapman (Gregory, 2006). It uses a grid with special features to plan assignments according to the diverse needs of students. It was adapted from Carol Ann Tomlinson's tiered model (Tomlinson, 2006).*

A formal or informal preassessment identifies each student's background knowledge and experiences in relation to the upcoming standard, information, concept, or skill. A preassessment tool is selected because it gives the needed information and consumes the least amount of time.

The first step in completing the grid is to analyze the preassessment data to discover the students' background knowledge or experiences in relation to the upcoming standard, information, concept, or skill. The teacher analyzes the results to identify what each learner knows and records this information in the area of the grid that matches the student's knowledge level: beginning, approaching mastery, or high degree of mastery. This information includes the concepts or skills the students possess at the current time.

In the second step, the teacher lists what the learners on each level need to know next. This list determines the entry points for instruction.

In the third step, the teacher identifies the most effective instructional strategies and/or activities for each level and lists them for each group, so all students learn. The adjustable assignment model is a keystone of differentiated instruction because the learners' needs guide strategic planning.

What Are the Instructional Benefits of Using an Adjustable Assignment?

An adjustable assignment is a planning tool designed to assist the classroom teacher with the complex task of designing instruction that meets the needs of individuals and/or multiple groups.

- Lessons are designed and customized for the learners based on their knowledge level.
- Students are not bored with information learned previously or frustrated with lessons that are too difficult.
- Students who need to "zap gaps" in their knowledge of a topic or skill receive the instruction they need.
- Students who demonstrate readiness for a grade-level topic or skill receive instruction on the approaching mastery level.
- Students who know the information have opportunities to extend their knowledge in the current area of study.

Teacher's Role

- Introduce adjustable assignments to the class.
- Discuss the value, purposes, and organizational procedures of using adjustable assignments.

---

*Adapted from Tomlinson, C. A., Kaplan, S. N., Purcell, J. H., Leppien, J. H., Burns, D. E., et al. (2006). *The parallel curriculum in the classroom, book 2: Units for application across the content areas, K–12.* Thousand Oaks, CA: Corwin Press. Used with permission.

- Discuss the varied experiences and knowledge levels students will bring to each new topic or skill.
- Emphasize the value of learning basic information, knowing the grade-level standards, and expanding knowledge.
- Use ongoing assessment to identify students who need to move to a more productive level during a unit of study.

Demystifying Adjustable Assignments

Introduce adjustable assignments to students by discussing the term *knowledge base*. Explain that each student's knowledge of a topic or skill varies because it is based on background, interests, and attitudes formed during past experiences. Ask students to identify their level of expertise in several sports and hobbies such as water skiing, soccer, swimming, cooking, and carpentry.

Remind students that all experts begin on the lowest level of knowledge and experience. Discuss the journeys their movie stars and sports heroes take to success. Emphasize that it takes desire and practice to move to a higher level.

Compare the levels for adjustable assignments with the levels on computer and video games. Students of all ages understand levels of difficulty because they play games that move them from the beginning and average levels to the highest degree of expertise and speed. Give examples of adjustable assignments they may encounter.

Student's Role

- Each time a new topic or skill is introduced, think about the past experiences you have had that relate to it. Ask yourself about the knowledge you have that will help you in this new study and what else you need to know about it.
- Realize that assessment results are based on your experiences and what you know, not on how smart you are.
- Be honest and do your best on each preassessment for the teacher design plans to help you.
- Know when you need to zap a gap, ask a question, or move on to a higher challenge level.
- Respect and honor classmates who are working at a different pace or level.

**FIVE (STAR) MANAGEMENT
TIPS FOR ADJUSTABLE ASSIGNMENTS**

Remember that an adjustable assignment model is a planning tool designed to address the needs of students on multiple knowledge levels. It is best used when it is deemed to be the most effective way to identify learners' needs. It takes more time to develop plans for more than one level, but the extra efforts benefit each student in the long run.

1. Use a large sheet of chart paper to create the planning grid.
2. Work with a team whenever possible to generate more valuable ideas.

(Continued)

(Continued)

3. Use the adjustable assignment model to plan for two or three groups. It is difficult to plan, organize, and manage effectively for more than three groups.

4. Use color-coded materials for each level. Use a different color for Levels 1, 2, and 3. Students in each level may receive an independent, partner, or small-group assignment.

5. Use a word or phrase that builds confidence with each color-coded level. In the following color-coding samples, notice how each color represents a stage of growth in knowledge. Give students opportunities to select the color and a phrase for their level.

Level 1 (Beginning Level) GREEN—I am growing. Zap the Gaps

Students in the beginning level have little or no prior knowledge and experiences related to the topic or skill. They need to master the basics or procedures that prepare them for the grade-level information. Develop intriguing activities to zap gaps in learning early in the unit of study.

**FIVE (STAR) MANAGEMENT TIPS FOR LEVEL 1
ADJUSTABLE ASSIGNMENTS**

1. Target the most important knowledge or skills the student must have to understand the grade-level standard.

2. Present Level 1 assignments as activities for "zapping the gaps."

3. Develop choice activities by placing specifically planned activities in a design or grid. This provides students with options to work on their areas of need and be successful. They don't feel isolated when they work with choices.

4. Design an agenda with a list of specific assignments and activities to fill holes in learning. This gives the student opportunity to back up and learn a skill or knowledge that was missed. Place the agenda in the student's green folder.

5. Build time in your teaching plan to provide basic, personalized instruction for individuals in this group while other students engage in Level 2 and 3 assignments.

Use Curriculum Rewinding to Zap the Gap

Curriculum rewinding takes instruction back to the basic information or skills a student failed to learn. It is needed when a preassessment uncovers a gap or hole in the fundamental information or skills the student failed to learn. The teacher analyzes the student's needs and rewinds the curriculum to the point where the learning gap occurred. This requires planning instruction that teaches the basics or foundations for a skill or concept.

All grade-level and subject area teachers are responsible for student progress. They must rewind the curriculum as needed. Too often, teachers feel responsible for their subject and fail to realize their responsibility to assist students who need to fill in missing pieces. This often occurs when the learning gap is unrelated to the subject or the teacher's expertise. For instance, if a science experiment requires measurement and a student cannot use or read the appropriate instrument, the teacher must rewind to teach the learner how to use the measurement tool.

Rewinding often requires specific instruction in skills below grade level. The educator is professionally obligated to find ways to assess each student's needs and improve the specific skills or ability to learn. If several learning gaps are evident, the teacher selects those that are the most critical for understanding grade-level material.

Teach students to be aware of their own learning gaps. Guide them in understanding the value of going back—or rewinding—to master skills they failed to learn.

Consider the following scenario that demonstrates the need to rewind the curriculum:

The teacher plans to teach two-digit addition. A pretest reveals that several students are not ready for this skill because they do not know the addition facts.

Questions to consider include the following:

- What skills do these students need?

- How am I going to assess the students?

- What do I need to do to see that they learn how to add single digits?

- Do I have programs or lessons to meet their needs?

- Do these students need to go to another classroom to learn and practice addition facts?

At some point in planning the unit for these students, time is built in for them to learn addition facts. These sessions and tasks replace assignments given to the rest of the class.

Hitting the Rewind Button: Tips for Zapping the Gap

- Use a preassessment to discover the student's skill level or knowledge base in the topic.

- Identify a gap in learning as soon as it occurs.

- Explain the need to rewind to basic or fundamental skills or information.

- Zap the gap by strategically choosing instructional strategies and activities for the learner. Use an instructional approach that is different from the approach that led the student to failure.

Reasons for Learning Gaps

Here are some common reasons for learning gaps:

- The student was never exposed to the needed information.

- The teacher exposed the student to the skill, concept, or information, but it was not understood or processed.

- The information was learned for the moment or for a test. The student did not have opportunities to take the skill to the level of mastery or automaticity.

- Memory cues or hooks were not used to store and retrieve the information.

- The student did not have opportunities to make meaningful, personal connections to the skill or topic.

It is frustrating and disappointing when teachers realize that students are not prepared for the new information or skill. It is easy to dwell on the various reasons for the learning gaps. Students benefit when this valuable time and energy is used to design plans and activities that fill the gaps.

- Present students with ways to identify and zap their own gaps. This includes reference materials, computer programs, peer assistance, and other instructional tools such as informative tables, charts, and posters.

Level 2 (Approaching Mastery) YELLOW— I am a ray of sunshine. Grade-Level Ready

Students in the approaching mastery level are ready for the grade-level information and need to work with the new standard, concept, or skill. This group demonstrated on a pre-assessment that they possess the background information needed to be successful.

If all students came to class on this level, there would be no need to differentiate. We know this does not occur in the real world. Do not lose these individuals in the shuffle. Teach and nurture this group.

Level 2 learners need instruction that extends their current, bright rays of knowledge. Select activities to excite and stimulate their minds.

★ ★ ★ ★ ★

FIVE (STAR) MANAGEMENT TIPS FOR LEVEL 2 ADJUSTABLE ASSIGNMENTS

1. Design activities in the Level 2 or yellow folder to reinforce and provide practice with grade-level standards, competences, and concepts.

2. Place the agenda or assignment on the board because Level 2 learners usually make up the majority of the class.

3. Continue to move this group forward in learning. Avoid holding these students back to teach peers.

4. Occasionally give these students choices to generate interests as they learn and practice an activity.

5. Remember that boring or busy work does not produce a payoff for anyone!

★ ★ ★ ★ ★

Level 3 (High Degree of Mastery) RED— Fired Up! Ready for the Challenge!

Students on Level 3 know the grade-level information and become bored or unmotivated with instruction. They do not need the explanations and practice lessons except for quick reviews. Productive activities and assignments are planned for these learners to expand their knowledge and skills in an area related to the current topic. These opportunities are designed to engage their minds in creative, challenging tasks and higher level thinking skills.

FIVE (STAR) MANAGEMENT TIPS
FOR LEVEL 3 ADJUSTABLE ASSIGNMENTS

1. Preassessment is crucial. It identifies the student who knows the upcoming information. Use fast-forwarding when it is obvious that the learner would be bored with the planned instruction and activities.

2. If a student proves he or she knows the information, valuable learning time is wasted when the learner is asked to complete the class assignment. An alternative assignment is needed.

3. Ask the learner, "What do you want to learn next related to our topic of study?" Involve the student in selecting and planning activities.

4. Do not expect students working with Level 3 tasks to complete Level 2 assignments. The time should be used productively to expand their knowledge and improve thinking skills.

5. Be cautious about assigning Level 3 students as peer tutors. Often the information and skills have become automatic for these learners. It is difficult for them to explain the fundamentals because they have moved beyond the basics. When students on this level are asked to explain an operation or skill, they often say, "I can't explain it. I just do it."

Fast-Forwarding the Curriculum

Curriculum fast-forwarding provides the student with opportunities to learn new information and skills related to the current topic or skill. The teacher analyzes the student's strengths and needs and fast-forwards the curriculum to new areas for research and exploration. This requires planning instruction to teach skills and facts beyond the required grade-level expectations.

Place the curriculum on fast-forward when the preassessment results reveal that the students know the information. For example, students do not need to study coin value if they can give you correct change from a five-dollar bill for a $2.79 purchase.

When the preassessment indicates that a student knows and understands the grade-level information, challenge the learner to select one of the following fast-forwarding strategies.

1. Run quickly through the tape while viewing the scenes.

Move through the new information quickly to review. Observe to check for understanding of each segment. The students who give correct answers may go through the introduction and explanations with a small group or total group to review the information. They move to a new segment while classmates work in practice sessions.

Example:

The learners are asked to identify the subjects and predicates in five sentences. The students who respond with correct answers and explain one example move on to the next learning level.

2. Turn off the picture and fast-forward quickly to a specific point.

Move to a new level after a preassessment when there is no need for the learner to review. The student skips a level and moves immediately to the new learning.
Examples:

- A coach is teaching the skill for dribbling a basketball. Students who know this skill practice passing the ball.

- A math teacher is teaching the process of multiplying with one-digit numbers, and the students participate in the initial explanations. The independent assignment is made for a small group to work with two-digit multiplication while another group practices with one-digit multiplication.

3. Fast-forward through familiar scenes of a recorded show or movie.

Skip the first level, topic, subject, or grade because the student knows the introductory information. The learner moves to a higher level within the current study.
Examples:

- A child in second grade iss socially, emotionally, and academically ready to move to fourth grade instead of third.

- A student knows basic Spanish and moves to Spanish II.

- Two students are comprehending, fluent readers. During independent reading time, they become poetry pals to work with poems they choose.

MANAGING CURRICULUM COMPACTING

What Is Curriculum Compacting?

Many educators place gifted and talented students in special classes or pull-out programs to work with challenging activities using higher order thinking skills such as problem solving and critical thinking. The students do not remain in the classroom and become bored.

Curriculum compacting has evolved in the past few years. Mandates now require schools to use full inclusion. This presents more challenges to classroom teachers because they are required to meet individual student needs within the classroom walls.

In differentiated instruction, curriculum compacting is implemented with students who are beyond the high degree of mastery level. They are exempt from grade level instruction. Their needs can be addressed through projects, agendas, academic contracts, personal discoveries, and investigations that intrigue the mind. Each assignment is designed to provide a productive, challenging learning experience.

Curriculum compacting may involve a major change in placement and assignments such as skipping a grade or a subject exemption. A new placement is rarely needed, but it can be the most beneficial experience of a student's academic life.

What Are the Instructional Benefits of Curriculum Compacting?

- A student who knows the upcoming standards and skills has an opportunity to be exempt from the mastered unit or subject. The learner's time is used wisely with an alternative assignment or placement.

- It provides productive learning time for the student who knows the information and skills.

- The student engages in high-interest activities that challenge the mind.

- When learners engage in selecting the activities and have responsibilities for completing assignments with little or no adult instruction, they have opportunities to become self-directed learners.

- Curriculum compacting removes the cap on a learner's potential.

Teacher's Role

- Identify the students who need to be exempt from the upcoming standard or skill.

- Brainstorm ways to provide alternative, productive assignments for the learners. Select the most productive strategy.

- Identify the purpose, timeline, activities, and assessment technique. Assign roles and responsibilities for each individual.

- Explain, discuss, and obtain approval from other teachers, administrators, parents, and the students involved in the alternative assignment or placement.

- Create buy-in. This is critical for everyone involved.

Demystifying Curriculum Compacting

Introduce curriculum compacting by leading a discussion similar to the following:

If you prove that you know and can use the information and skills that are going to be in an upcoming study, you will have opportunities to participate in more challenging adventures that come with new learning.

Student's Role

- Prove that you need an alternative assignment by doing your best on the preassessment.
- Analyze your knowledge of the upcoming study. Let the teacher know if you have an area of weakness or questions related to it.
- Take advantage of the learning opportunity in the new environment and situation.
- Move and work with your special assignment without disrupting classmates.
- Realize that a curriculum compacting experience is a privilege.

FIVE (STAR) MANAGEMENT TIPS FOR CURRICULUM COMPACTING

1. Use curriculum compacting as an option for a student who knows the upcoming information and skills. Be sure the learner will benefit from an alternative assignment or placement rather than a Level 3 extension or enrichment activity.

2. Analyze all gathered data, including observations and input from other teachers, to make major placement or assignment changes.

3. Design a special, new assignment that is the most valuable use of the learner's time. Select activities to challenge the mind so optimal learning takes place.

4. The teacher who designs instruction in the learner's new placement or assignment is responsible for the grade.

5. Do not require the student who engages in alternate assignments to complete work missed in the regular program.

Examples of Curriculum Compacting

Example A: Subject Placement

A first-grade student who is working on a higher level with a subject is placed in a second-grade class for daily instruction in that area.

Example B: Alternative Assignment

A group of fluent, comprehending readers receive alternative assignments while the other students receive direct instruction. The high-performing readers form a learning community for a novel study group. This may take place within a class or with students from different classrooms.

Example C: Exemption

A high school student is exempt from the senior English program. He attends a university English class and receives college credit.

MANAGING THE PROBLEM-BASED MODEL

What Is the Problem-Based Model?

The problem-based model provides students with an opportunity to select and solve an identified problem. It may focus on the classroom, school, community, state, national, or international concerns. The teacher guides students in choosing a problem they can investigate and solve with little adult assistance. The responsibilities, roles, and assignments are identified and assigned to individuals and/or small groups. For example, during a study of an endangered species, partner teams engage in a data-gathering session to investigate the causes for the problem. Each team creates a list of causes and presents it to generate a class list.

What Are the Instructional Benefits of the Problem-Based Model?

The problem-based model engages students in authentic activities that may evolve into a service project for the school or community. Problem-based tasks are designed to teach standards, skills, and concepts. This approach teaches students to be critical and creative thinkers. As they participate, they realize that there are several steps to finding solutions. Students learn that problem solving often uses a process that extends over a period of time.

This instructional approach easily adapts for use with the total class, small groups, or individuals in all curriculum areas. Each step in the process presents valuable learning opportunities. Students have a sense of pride in their accomplishments when they see the results of their efforts. Figure 2.1 presents ideas to explore in problem-based learning:

Teacher's Role

- Introduce and carry through the steps in the problem-based model with guidelines and a time frame. See Figure 2.2 on page 47.
- Assume the role of facilitator and guide. Ask questions during each stage of the process to stimulate thinking and discussion.
- Set aside time for students to carry out their assignments, report progress or findings, and share stumbling blocks and successes.
- Give students opportunities to present their findings, recommendations, suggested solutions, and results to administrators, legislators, parents, or other appropriate groups.
- Guide reflective discussions about the process and celebrate success throughout the procedure.

Demystifying Problem Solving

Explain to students that every day, problems are solved by working teams in the business world and in daily situations. Discuss the importance of learning how to address and solve minor and major problems throughout their lives in any situation. Take students through the problem-solving steps by guiding their thinking to solve a problem in their world.

Examples:

- In the middle of a party, the host announces that pizza is ready for them on the patio. Everyone runs to the area, pushing and shoving as they grab slices of the treat.

Figure 2.1

Classroom	School	Community
• Obtain donations for a game station, research nook, or reading corner. • Learn to recycle. • Establish rules for a classroom citizen. • Select a Yuk Spot to beautify. • Organize a "Say No to Drugs" campaign.	• Design an outdoor trail. • Develop a new study area such as a station or lab. • Establish a schoolwide recycling program. • Improve the cafeteria's menus. • Raise funds for a new piece of equipment.	• Beautify or clean up a park or corner lot. • Go to local commissioners to state a case for change. • Adopt a grandparent. • Conduct a food drive. • Stop pollution in a local creek or lake.

State	National	International
• Identify a law that needs to be changed. • Examine ways to improve factory pollution. • Adopt an animal or plant in a state park. • Identify a state law that needs to be changed. • Compare your school with another one in the state. Analyze the results.	• Raise funds for an endangered species. • Study the reasons gas prices rise and fall. • Examine shortage of a product and the consumers' role. • Investigate ways to help a community or school that is dealing with a major disaster. • Identify a problem facing poor families. Write letters to politicians addressing the problem.	• Identify steps for world peace. • Explore solutions to global warming. • Investigate a possible disaster and set up a preparedness plan. • Identify items needed by soldiers on battlefields. Collect the items and send them with personal notes. • Participate in a fundraising project for a specific cause.

The pizza is gone before some guests enter the patio. What steps could be taken to solve this problem during the next party?

- A grocery store establishes a recycling program with designated containers for customers to drop off plastic or glass products. Discuss why the store provides this service and the problem this solves. If a local store does not have a recycling program, this can be an ideal place to begin a community-based, problem-solving project.

Student's Role

- Participate in the brainstorming process to select a problem.
- List the steps needed to carry out the tasks.
- Volunteer for the part of the task that you will complete.
- Do your part in your role and tasks to solve the problem successfully.
- Prepare a presentation of the data or results. Reflect and celebrate!

Figure 2.2

1. Identify the problem.

2. Brainstorm possible solutions for the problem.

3. Reach consensus on the best ways to solve the problem.

4. Create a plan with procedures to carry it out.

5. Assign investigative roles, responsibilities, and assignments, such as researchers, interviewers, recorders, and designers for charts or posters.

6. Identify a reporting tool.

7. Carry out the identified plan.

8. Discuss and explore results. Present findings.

9. Assess and celebrate accomplishments.

★ ★ ★ ★ ★

**FIVE (STAR) MANAGEMENT TIPS FOR USING
THE PROBLEM-BASED MODEL**

1. Analyze the current study to identify standards and skills that can be taught in a problem-solving activity.

2. Introduce the model using a high-interest problem in the classroom, school, or community that will lead to visible results.

3. Introduce the problem-based learning approach by discussing the importance of knowing how to solve problems in daily activities and various careers.

4. Model and guide students through the planning steps so they understand the process.

5. Involve the learners in every step of the problem-solving process. Remember that students need to carry out the plan, but the teacher approves each step.

★ ★ ★ ★ ★

Examples of the Problem-Based Model

Example A: Problem Solving in the Classroom

Students identify a reading corner that needs improvements so it will be comfortable and inviting. They find people who donate a rocking chair, beanbag, rug, lamp, and large pillows. They display books and book characters in the area.

Example B: Problem Solving in the School

Students identify a section of the school grounds to improve. The area is covered with dirt. They want to get rid of the mud and dust that interferes with their outside activities, so they select this problem to tackle. The teacher approves this problem-solving project.

The group brainstorms and comes to consensus on ways to develop the area. They decide that planting grass and plants will solve the problem. The students outline a plan that includes assigned roles and data-gathering techniques. The students conduct a parent and community survey to find volunteers to donate grass seed, fertilizer, and shrubs. The school's parent organization agrees to prepare the area.

Example C: Problem Solving in the Community

The teacher leads a brainstorming session for students to create a list of local problems that affect them. The group selects one problem to solve from the brainstormed list: A busy intersection near the community recreation center needs a traffic light. The teacher invites the city traffic engineer to share the steps needed for approval of the light.

The teacher and volunteer parents take students on a bus to an area, a safe distance from the intersection. They observe the vehicles as they pass through the intersection during the specific time period. The students gather data and create graphs to report the information. Selected graphics and a data summary are placed in letters to the local newspaper and community leaders. Within two months, the new traffic light is installed.

MANAGING THE PROJECT-BASED MODEL

What Is the Project-Based Model?

A project is an assignment that takes a student into an in-depth study to learn more on a topic of interest. A project may be assigned to a total class, small groups, partners, or an individual student. It is geared to the age and interest of the student so the whole assignment requires little adult supervision.

What Are the Instructional Benefits of Using the Project-Based Model?

A project is an excellent way for students to learn more about an area of interest from the content standards. Projects provide exciting opportunities to actively engage more students in learning.

Students enjoy creating a project and can learn the process as they learn the content information. As a project develops over a period of time, they learn to carry out a plan using a timeline, accept responsibility, develop independence, pace their work, and make decisions. These skills are valuable for a lifetime.

The project-based model honors the different ways students learn. They have opportunities to select interest areas that use their strengths and intrigue their individual minds. The options provided allow students to learn through their favorite modalities, genres, styles, or intelligences. The learners also have choices in the ways they present the products or project information.

Teacher's Role

- Identify the grade-level standards, content topic information, and skills to address.
- Select the grouping strategy:

  Total Group   Alone   Partners   Small Groups

- Prepare the requirements, including the guidelines, purposes, expectations, assessment tool, and timeline.
- Provide choices for the research format, the presentation, and display.
- Present the project information to the group for success.

Demystifying Projects

Explain the term *project* as an activity or product created by following a plan. The verb form of the word *project* means to predict results. Specific steps or procedures are outlined and followed in a project to obtain the desired results. Challenge students to discuss familiar projects such as cleaning out a closet, painting a room, or cleaning a yard.

Lead students through a class, independent, or small group simulation of tasks in a project. Walk them through the planning process, procedures, and timeline for designing a product. Remember to identify your inside thinking for each step.

Student's Role

- Select a topic from the list.
- Identify areas of interest to explore and commit to the project assignment.
- Become familiar with the guidelines, expectations, and assessment tools.
- List and gather materials.
- Complete the project process to the final product, following the timeline.

FIVE (STAR) MANAGEMENT TIPS FOR MANAGING PROJECTS

1. Compile the project topic list around the current standards and content topics. Give students an opportunity to choose their projects.

2. Assist students by providing a Project Packet similar to the following to guide their project plans. Model and guide students through each step so they understand the process.

> Project Packet:
>
> - Purpose and guidelines
> - Timeline, checkpoints, and due dates
> - Assessment tools to use before, during, and after
> - Procedure checklist for project partners
> - Presentation and display options

3. Schedule accountability checkpoints or conferences for project partners or groups to share findings along the way. During these sessions, students go through the process, review the information, go over the procedures, and analyze what they are learning.

4. Remember, projects are a wise use of class time when individuals or small groups engage in tasks that directly relate to the current topic and content standards or skills. Ask students to emphasize the steps and procedures they used in the learning process during their presentations.

5. Schedule information celebrations for students to demonstrate or present the final product as evidence of their learning.

Examples of the Project-Based Model

Example A: In-Class Project

The teacher divides the class into cooperative groups during a social studies unit. Each group chooses a project from a teacher-made list.

1. The teacher introduces the project purposes, directions, and timeline of the assignment.

2. Each person is assigned a person, event, place, or artifact from the social studies unit.

3. Periodically give an assignment that fits each student's project similar to the following:

- What significant role does _____ play in history?
- List five characteristics or attributes about _____.
- Research _____ from five sources including the textbook.
- Teach students the research card format. Ask students to use it to take useful notes from their reading material.

4. Establish a log or journal for personal comments. Identify specific times for journal entries.

5. Create a display about _____.

6. Present the key points learned to the class using a choice board activity. See Figure 2.3.

Figure 2.3			
Project Choice Board			
Prepare a Web page news report	Design a poster	Role-play	Design a PowerPoint presentation
Interview	Be a stand-up comic	Create a song	Create a brochure

7. Conference with students about their experiences. Discuss the thinking process used in the project.

Example B: Home-School Projects

After guiding students through the project process, assign some activities for completion at home and others to complete during class time. The same procedures are followed that were presented for the in-class project.

Example C: Home Project

Use the same procedures as those listed above. The entire project is completed at home. On the due date, the student brings the project to class. Remember, project partners may be assigned to work together. They meet periodically to discuss the stage of their progress. They share their accomplishments, needs, and what they are learning during the project work.

MANAGING THE MULTIPLE INTELLIGENCE PLANNING MODEL

What Is the Multiple Intelligence Planning Model?

The multiple intelligence planning model is based on the work of Howard Gardner at Harvard University. The intelligences are verbal/linguistic, musical/rhythmic, logical/mathematical, bodily/kinesthetic, visual/spatial, naturalist, intrapersonal, and interpersonal. According to Gardner, intelligence is the ability to solve a problem, to create a problem to solve, and to contribute to one's culture. Use Figure 2.4 to incorporate the students' intelligences in strategies and activities.

What Are the Instructional Benefits of Using the Multiple Intelligence Planning Model?

The multiple intelligence planning model is a management tool that serves as a guide to label the targeted intelligences for instruction to meet the diverse needs of each student. The student has a better chance of grasping knowledge and understanding when his or her strongest intelligences can be used to learn a standard, skill, concept, or information.

- The targeted intelligences can be labeled in each planned activity.
- Everyone has all of the intelligences. Everyone can become more intelligent.
- Everyone has at least three or four areas of strengths that can be strengthened and used to learn more. An individual's weaknesses are identified so they can be strengthened.
- The intelligences addressed in activities are labeled, not the students.
- The planning model guides teachers to incorporate the learner's strongest intelligences in learning new skills.

Teacher's Role

- Plan using the multiple intelligences. To reach more students, use a blending of the intelligences in the plan.
- Label each activity addressed in a lesson with a targeted intelligence and one or two supporting intelligences.
- Observe students as they work and interact with others to identify the intelligences they use in daily activities and interactions.
- Establish learning zones and independent tasks that provide choices around the intelligence targets to reach the learners' diverse needs.
- Plan and use intelligences that are not in your comfort zones, if they are conduits to reach the learner. It is natural for you to use your strong and most comfortable intelligences. Remember, the students' strengths and your strengths may not be the same.

Figure 2.4

Multiple Intelligence Planning Model

Steps for Implementation	*Directions*
1. Name the topic or unit.	List the content standards, information, skills, and/or concepts to be learned.
2. Assess students to find out what they know.	Use the most effective formal or informal tool to identify the learner's prior knowledge, background, attitude, and interests.
3. Brainstorm a list of strategies and activities related to the topic.	List all the activities and strategies that teach the content standards, information, skills, and concepts. Record each thought in writing to create a quantity of ideas.
4. Write the lesson plan.	Analyze the preassessment data and select the "best" activities from the brainstormed list to teach the information needed by this individual or group of students. Write each activity in the order you plan to teach it. Create a smooth flow or transition between instructional segments.
5. Label the targeted intelligence and the supporting intelligences for each activity.	Identify one "intelligence" as the target of the activity. A task usually engages more than one intelligence, so identify one or two supporting intelligences. Use the abbreviations: V/L = visual/linguistic L/M = logical/mathematical M/R = musical/rhythmic B/K = bodily/kinesthetic V/S = visual/spatial N = naturalist Intra = intrapersonal Inter = interpersonal
6. Tally the targeted and supporting intelligences. Check overkills and omissions.	Design a form or checklist similar to the following to monitor how often the learner engages in a targeted intelligence and one or more supporting intelligences. <table><tr><td>V/L</td><td>V/S</td><td>L/M</td><td>M/R</td><td>B/K</td><td>N</td></tr><tr><td>卌I</td><td>IIII</td><td>卌</td><td>III</td><td>卌</td><td>III</td></tr></table>
7. Identify the grouping arrangements.	Label the flexible grouping strategy using the TAPS acronym. T = Total group A = Alone P = Partner S = Small group

(Continued)

Figure 2.4 (Continued)

Multiple Intelligence Planning Model

Steps for Implementation	Directions
	Examples:
	When the activity begins with a total group and then learners work alone, label it TA.
	When the activity begins with students working in cooperative groups and then each student writes an individual summary of what was learned, label it SA.
8. Tally the use of the grouping scenarios.	Check for an effective blending of different grouping scenarios. If overkills and omissions are evident, refer to the brainstormed strategy and activity list.
9. Teach the unit. Use ongoing assessment to monitor and guide the plan.	Constantly monitor and assess students and the plan. Revamp and readjust the plan according to the student's needs. Remember to refer to the brainstorming list for activity alternatives.

Total Group	Alone	Partner	Small Group
THL II	THL III	III	IIII

Demystifying the Multiple Intelligence Planning Model

Tell the students that Howard Gardner, a Harvard professor, named eight ways that people are intelligent or smart. In the chart (see Figure 2.5), the intelligences are listed with suggested words and phases you can use to help students understand each one. Adapt our descriptors for your learners, as you introduce an intelligence and discuss the many ways the students are smart.

Student's Role

- Learn the different ways that you are smart.
- Identify the intelligences that are your areas of strengths. Remember, you learn best in these intelligences.
- Use your strengths to overcome your weaknesses. For example, if you are strong in musical/rhythmic intelligence and have difficulty memorizing facts, place them in the form of a jingle, rap, or rhyme.
- Honor the intelligences of your classmates.
- Remember that the intelligences change and grow with your knowledge and experiences.

Figure 2.5	
Intelligence	*Describes someone who is smart in . . .*
Verbal/linguistic	Reading Writing Listening Talking Linking information Making connections
Musical/rhythmic	Dancing Playing an instrument Singing Composing Creating poetry, rhymes, or jingles Identifying tonal patterns Developing rhythms and beats Chanting and rapping
Logical/mathematical	Placing thoughts or things in order Discovering and using patterns Using numbers to create and solve problems Using the world of technology Using manipulatives
Bodily/kinesthetic	Moving the body using large or small movements Using eye and hand coordination Making large (gross) or small (fine) body movements
Visual/spatial	Using the mind's eye to see lines, color, and space Designing Building Using graphics and pictures
Naturalist	Knowing about nature Working with nature Exploring areas of science
Intrapersonal	Working alone Being independent Feeling comfortable with one's own thoughts and feelings
Interpersonal	Working successfully with others Socializing with other people

FIVE (STAR) MANAGEMENT TIPS FOR USING THE MULTIPLE INTELLIGENCE PLANNING MODEL

1. Follow the planning model and meet the needs of more students. Each individual has three or four intelligences that are strong areas. More needs are met when individual ways of learning are addressed.

2. Remember to label strategies and activities, not students. Consciously label the targeted and supporting intelligences when planning activities and strategies.

3. Instructors are human, so they often use their strongest intelligences or strengths to teach. Later they wonder why students did not learn the information.

4. Make learning interesting, challenging, and exciting with multiple intelligence planning. For example, if students are struggling to remember a procedure and they are strong in the bodily/kinesthetic and musical/rhythmic intelligences, guide them in chanting the information as they move to a simple exercise such as jumping jacks.

5. Design the plan to incorporate a blending of the ways students are grouped to give opportunities for the interpersonal learner who needs to work with others and the intrapersonal learner who needs time to process and work alone with information. A teacher is usually dominant in the intrapersonal or interpersonal intelligence. Avoid planning around your preference. Plan to meet the student's needs or strengths.

Examples of the Multiple Intelligence Planning Model

Example A: Individual Unit Planning

A teacher follows the planning process presented in the model to design the upcoming unit of study.

Example B: Team Unit Planning

A grade-level team follows the process to plan an upcoming unit of study. The team members brainstorm activities and strategies that use the various intelligences. Each teacher assesses his or her own students and decides which activities and strategies to use in their personal plans. As the unit progresses, the reference list of brainstormed possibilities is available for new learning opportunities.

Example C: Lesson Plan Analysis

The teacher uses a two- to three-week section of lesson plans that has been taught and labels the target intelligence for each activity and assignment. Each intelligence addressed is listed and tallied as it is used. This helps the teacher recognize omissions, overkills, and the intelligences addressed properly to meet the students' needs.

MANAGING THE TRIARCHIC TEAMING MODEL

What Is the Triarchic Teaming Model?

Robert Sternberg's triarchic theory of intelligence emphasizes using three ways of thinking to adapt and shape the environment. He states that the successful intelligences are analytical, creative, and practical. He recommends that a problem-solving team be composed of members who are strong in different intelligences. The group can engage each member's strengths and approach the task from the various perspectives.

What Are the Instructional Benefits of the Triarchic Teaming Model?

- Students can become familiar with three ways of being smart, interacting, and communicating in a group.
- The teacher and the students can identify their strong areas of communication.
- Each student has a distinct role using an analytical, creative, or practical point of view.
- When students use their strongest intelligences, they are comfortable during the learning process.
- More productive teams are created using the Triarchic Model.

Teacher's Role

- Define Sternberg's three intelligence areas so you and the students understand the attributes for each area. Refer to the chart.

- Identify each student's area of strength in working with a group.
  a. Conduct a student survey to discover the students' intelligences and identify members for a problem-solving team.
     1. Study the words and phrases listed for Sternberg's intelligences on the chart.

     2. List the three intelligences. Prioritize these by placing the number 1 next to the intelligence that reflects the best way for you to contribute to a problem-solving team. Select another intelligence that you would use. Place the number 3 beside the area you would use least.
     ____ Analytical
     ____ Creative
     ____ Practical

Figure 2.6		
Analytical	*Creative*	*Practical*
• Compare • Contrast • Identify the parts • Evaluate each section • Analyze the benefits	• Imagine_____. • Use _____ to invent • Find a new way to _____ • List your ideas about. . . . • Suppose. . . .	• Using this skill or information to make your life easier. • Finding the most helpful way to use _____. • Shape • Adapt

Write and discuss reasons for the order of your selection with a partner. Turn in the survey results to the teacher. Use the data to form compatible working teams.

   b. Observe each learner as he or she makes contributions in a group situation to identify his or her strengths.

- Place students in groups with at least one representative for the analytical, practical, and creative areas.

- Observe the groups working together through several tasks.

- Adjust groups as needed from observation notes and performance.

Demystifying the Triarchic Model

Explain the meaning of *tri-* and *arch*. Draw three arches. Write one intelligence in each arch to illustrate Sternberg's theory. Define the intelligences.

Student's Role

- Learn the significance and the meaning of Sternberg's three intelligences: analytical, practical, and creative. Realize the value of having a team member who is strong in each area.

- Identify your area of strength when contributing to a group.

- Recognize and respect classmates who think in different ways.

- Be an active group participant during all assignments and activities while sharing ideas from your point of view.

- Analyze and reflect on your personal and group performance by answering questions similar to the following.
  - What contributions did you make to the group?
  - What worked? Why?
  - What will make the group more successful next time it meets?

**FIVE (STAR) MANAGEMENT TIPS FOR USING
THE TRIARCHIC TEAMING MODEL**

1. Know the student's strongest intelligences for the most effective placement for team or group work.

2. Remember, each student has at least three or four strong intelligences to contribute to a team.

3. Plan team activities that engage the learner's strongest intelligence. A student usually contributes automatically to a group when working through the lens of his or her strengths.

4. Create teams with five or fewer members.

5. Assign a representative of the analytical, practical, and creative intelligence to each group.

Examples of the Triarchic Teaming Model

Example A: Assigned Problem-Solving Triads

Groups are assigned to triads with students who are strong in each of the triarchic intelligences: analytical, practical, or creative. Each group is assigned a problem to process and solve. The group works through the problem and shares conclusions. Team members make entries in their individual journals recording their roles and the thinking process used by the triad team.

Example B: Student-Selected Project Teams

The groups form three teams of their favorite role in a team situation:

Team A: Analytical   Team B: Practical   Team C: Creative

One member from each team joins together to form a triad to complete a project. Students choose their teammates.

Example C: Random Assignment Team

Students complete a survey to identify their individual strengths as a team player: analytical, practical, or creative. The results are given to the students. Three areas of the room are labeled by displaying one intelligence on a large card in each space. Students line up in front of the word that matches their strength. The students in each line number off. Example: 1, 2, 3, 4, and so on. The 1s form a group, the 2s form the second group, and so forth. The teacher gives the groups a problem, project, or cooperative task to complete.

MANAGING THE ACTIVITY ANALYSIS MODEL

What Is the Activity Analysis Model?

The activity analysis model is a guide to strategically selecting and thoroughly planning an activity for an individual or group of students. The outline presented in the model is designed to serve as a planning guide for the teacher so the most appropriate activity is selected for each learning experience.

The preassessment data identifies students who need to learn a specific skill. The teacher considers each activity that could be used to teach the skill. The lead-in questions and statements can be used to make quick but in-depth analyses of each step in the decision process that is needed to select and organize each activity. This model guides the teacher to select the most effective activity for an individual or a group.

What Are the Instructional Benefits of Using the Activity Analysis Model?

The activity analysis model is a guide to making more accurate decisions when selecting instructional activities. In a differentiated classroom, this decision process is more complex as the teacher plans activities for the needs and strengths of individuals and small groups. This model provides a format that is practical and easy to use during each planning session.

This tool guides the teacher to select activities that are appropriate for an individual or specific group of learners. It helps teachers avoid activities that become busywork, assignments that do not teach the needed information or skills, and assigning the wrong activities to the wrong students.

Too often, teachers use their favorite activities because they are accessible, familiar, and easy to use. The analysis helps teachers avoid this natural tendency because the question outline leads to a strategic selection process to provide each learner the very best learning experiences.

This model holds the key to solving the dilemma of deciding which standards and skills to identify for instruction and which activity to select for a specific group or individual. It can serve as a guide in choosing between two or three activities for one time slot.

Demystifying the Activity Analysis Model

Let students know that much of your planning time is used to select the very best activities for the class, for individuals, and for small group lessons. Explain that each activity is carefully selected or designed to help them become successful in using the skill or information. Use the following metaphor to guide the discussion:

> When I am trying to find the right activity for you, it is like selecting a hat for a special occasion. It must match the outfit and be comfortable. In the same way, I find the activity that matches the way you learn and fits the lesson you need so you will be comfortable as you engage in each learning experience.

Teacher's Role

- Identify the activity to teach the standard, concept, or skill.
- Use the suggested questions in the chart to analyze the activity's effectiveness.

Figure 2.7

WHAT are you going to teach?	• Identify the standards, concepts, skills, or information. • Select the unit or topic. • Select assessment tools to use during and after the activity. The results serve as a guide for instruction.

WHO needs it?	• Use the preassessment data to identify the students who need
	  o A specific segment of instruction
	  o More or less instruction
	  o To use an extension or enrichment activity
	  o To work alone
	  o To work with others
	• Decide how to assess during learning and evaluate progress to identify immediate needs.
	• Assess at the end of the learning to identify students who have needs that can be addressed in the upcoming plans.

WHEN are you going to teach it?	• Identify the best time to schedule instruction for the activity. • Decide when to teach each part of the lesson. Establish the order for each instructional segment. • Identify the best time to take an individual or small group aside for a special assignment or direct instruction. • Integrate the new learning in various areas of the curriculum, if possible. • Be aware of the need to revamp or readjust during instruction.
WHERE will the student(s) work productively?	• Identify the best learning scenario for the student using the TAPS acronym: **T** = Total group **A** = Alone **P** = Partner **S** = Small group • Identify the best area for the student to work such as a Learning zone Center Station Lab • Identify the best place for the student to complete the tasks: At a table On a desk In a chair On a rug
HOW will the activity engage the student?	• Decide if the student learns best engaging in a student-focused activity or a teacher-directed activity. • Select the most effective group design for the student: Multiage Knowledge base Ability Interests Random Cooperative team Peer tutoring • Identify the type of assignment for the activity: Homework Anchor task Choice board Agenda Contract Project

- Strategically decide if this is the best activity to teach, reinforce, or enrich the information. Can it be integrated with other content, seasonal, or real-life events?
- Identify who needs the activity.
- Place the activity in the plan, being aware that it may need to be changed or adapted for the learner.

Student's Role

- Realize that the teacher carefully designs or selects each activity for you to learn the information or skills. Be sure you understand the directions and expectations before you begin an activity.
- Always do your best to master the skill or information in each activity.
- If you need assistance in completing an activity, ask someone to help you, unless the directions tell you that you can't ask questions.
- List your suggestions for improving the activity. Make a special note that tells why the activity was too easy or too difficult for you.
- Review your tasks to see if you can improve them before you finish the activity.

FIVE (STAR) MANAGEMENT TIPS FOR USING THE ACTIVITY ANALYSIS MODEL

1. Dig into the preassessment data to discover who needs the new standard or skill, what content to use, when to teach it, where the students will work productively, and how to teach it.
2. Analyze an activity to see if it is the most effective way for the group or individual to learn, review, or extend knowledge of the information.
3. Remember every assignment does not need to be the same for every student.
4. Realize that all students may not be ready to learn the skill at the same time. Some students may waste valuable time completing the activity so they need an alternate activity.
5. Use the chart when you need to analyze the worthiness of an activity as the most valuable opportunity for learning.

Bonus Tip

Be aware of unexpected events and unusual objects that can be molded into the most valuable learning activities or teachable moments. For example, a big snow presents an opportunity for students to learn about friction while riding sleds or watching drivers as they try to control their vehicles on the icy roads.

Become a scavenger while shopping and traveling. You may find the most valuable visuals and manipulatives for an activity in unexpected places. Ask business owners for discarded displays, signs, and objects that can make an activity more inviting for the students.

Examples of Uses for the Activity Analysis Model

Example A: Analyzing an Activity

The teacher uses the chart presented in the model to analyze the benefits of an activity. An activity is selected to consider for a group of students ("Who"). It is chosen to teach specific content information ("What"). The "When," "Where," and "How" sections of the model chart are applied to analyze the activity. When the process is complete, the right decision can be made for the learners.

Example B: Activities for Student Agenda

The preassessment data reveals that two students ("Who") know the upcoming skill. After considering the options as to "What" these students need, the teacher decides they can expand their knowledge of the skill ("What") using some enrichment activities in an agenda. Student-focused activities are selected because the two students are responsible, self-directed learners ("How"). They work independently and as partners while the remaining students work with the grade-level skill ("When").

The teacher selects activities to engage each learner's strongest intelligences: The first student is strong in the visual/spatial, musical/rhythmic, and interpersonal areas ("How") so his activities include producing an illustration and creating a rap using the facts. The second student's strongest areas are verbal/linguistic, visual/spatial, and interpersonal. The tasks on her agenda include reading an article related to the skill and designing a graphic organizer for the facts. They share their work with each other and prepare a short presentation for the class.

The two students choose the most comfortable place to work independently and move to another chosen area to share and prepare their presentation ("Where").

Example C: Small Group Activity

The informal preassessment reveals that three students ("Who") have not learned the prerequisite procedures for the upcoming skill ("What"). The teacher knows that the students must master these procedures quickly to be successful in the study, so teacher-directed instruction ("How") is planned for these learners while the other students are engaged with center activities ("When"). The group is gathered at a table for the lesson ("Where"). The teacher reintroduces the procedures and guides them through appropriate practice sessions. A choice board ("How") is presented with activities specifically designed for the learners to individually demonstrate mastery of the prerequisite skills.

MANAGING THE STUDENT-DIRECTED LEARNING MODEL

What Is the Student-Directed Learning Model?

The student-directed learning model empowers each learner. The goal of the model is to teach each student to be productive while working and learning with a partner, in a group or independently. The student feels empowered with a sense of control in how to work. The goal of the model is to teach all students how to be in charge of or take responsibility for their learning.

In a differentiated classroom, students work independently or in groups with little or no adult supervision. When students become self-directed, self-regulated learners, the teacher spends less time giving reminders, repeating directions, keeping students on task, and answering trivial questions.

What Are the Instructional Benefits of the Student-Directed Learning Model?

Responsibilities for learning are turned over to students. The teacher becomes a learning facilitator.

The model develops learners who

- Know how and where to find resources or assistance as needed
- Become self-initiators
- Are reflective thinkers. They know how to listen and analyze the ideas of others to make the best decisions
- Occupy their time wisely when activities or assignment are complete
- Know how to take responsibility for their own learning

Teacher's Role

- Give clear, specific guidelines, parameters, and time frame.
- Turn over more responsibilities to the students.
- Present options whenever appropriate.

  Examples: materials, sources, activities, assessment tools, presentation formats

- Use fewer commanding verbs and directives, such as *list, move, sit,* and *write,* because the learners make decisions, take control of their actions, and carry through with their responsibilities.
- Explain the value and purpose of each activity so students realize its importance in their learning process.

Demystifying the Student-Directed Learning Model

Use a metaphor similar to the following to introduce the student-directed learning model:

In self-directed learning, the teacher's role is similar to the builder and the student's tasks are similar to the role of the subcontractor who receives a special assignment and a timeline. For example, the electrician and plumber receive copies of the blueprint with specific directions and a deadline. The different tasks are completed independently. The plumber cannot complete the electrician's work. The electrician cannot complete the plumber's tasks. In the same way, specific tasks will be assigned for individuals and groups by the teacher.

In our class, the directions guide you to complete the various tasks independently or with classmates. During these tasks, you will work with very little assistance.

Student's Role

- Ask yourself questions similar to the following:
  o Why do I need to learn this information or skill?

  o What can I do to learn this information so I can use it automatically?

  o What can I do to be a better learner?

- Be sure you understand the directions or guidelines before you begin.

- Use your time wisely to complete the task assigned with little or no assistance from the teacher.

- Check your work.

- Ask yourself questions similar to the following for reflection and growth:
  o What did I learn?

  o What parts were easiest for me?

  o What parts were difficult for me?

  o What do I need next?

**FIVE (STAR) MANAGEMENT TIPS FOR USING
THE STUDENT-DIRECTED LEARNING MODEL**

1. Use the assessment data to identify the more effective activity for the independent assignment. This assignment should not bore or frustrate the learner but provide a needed, challenging learning opportunity.

2. Model or demonstrate each addressed skill. Give the student opportunities to practice one before it becomes an expectation in a student-directed task assignment.

3. Remember that this task is for a student to perform with little or no adult supervision! Keep yourself in close proximity while you work with other students.

4. Whenever possible, assign more than one task using a menu or agenda. This allows the students to work at their own pace, select the task order, and tailor the work to their own specific needs.

5. Establish checkpoints or times for reflections and self-assessments.

Examples of the Student-Directed Learning Model

Example A: Homework

A self-directed learner who is working on homework realizes that help is needed, but no adult is available to assist.

The student knows the options to consider, such as the following:

- Use trial and error
- Revisit notes
- Review the textbook material
- Read the highlighted handout notes
- Call a study buddy

Example B: Class Assignment

A student is working on an agenda, special assignment, or project using the guidelines, directions, task expectations, and a timeline provided by the teacher. The learner assumes responsibilities, including

- Pacing
- The order and approaches to the tasks
- Finding the best solutions to the problems
- Using the self-assessment tools
- Making corrections

Example C: Studying for a Test

A student is studying for a social studies test and realizes the importance of knowing historical events and dates in the chapter. He knows several memory tools to use, such as rehearsal, graphic organizers, and mnemonic devices. He selects the best strategy to learn the needed facts.

MANAGING THE TEACHER-DIRECTED LEARNING MODEL

What Is the Teacher-Directed Learning Model?

The teacher-directed learning model is a structured approach to teaching a specific skill or procedure for mastery. The teacher becomes the information disseminator. Bruce Joyce and Marsha Weil (2004) identify five steps in the approach as the orientation, presentation, and structured, guided, and independent practice.

This instructional method is a common practice in classrooms today because many teachers feel pressured to cover a large amount of material to prepare students for standardized tests. Direct instruction is not "the way" to teach, but it is one way. The steps used in this approach to instruction are valuable procedures for tutors to follow.

What Are the Instructional Benefits of Using the Teacher-Directed Learning Model?

This model is most effective when used with individuals or small groups who need to master specific skills or procedures. The students benefit from this approach because

- The teacher guides students who are struggling to master information, steps in a skill, a basic skill, or concept.
- Lessons are structured with the teacher presenting and pacing instruction for the learners.
- Teacher-student interactions occur during each instructional segment.
- The teacher is able to provide immediate feedback, encourage, assist, reinforce efforts, and give suggestions for improvement.
- Individuals or groups of students are led through an introduction and practice sessions with the teacher directing the work. In the second stage of practice, the teacher guides and assists as needed. When students demonstrate knowledge and understanding, they practice independently.

Teacher's Role

- Use a preassessment to identify students who need to master a specific skill or procedure.
- Use a lecturette that provides information in a way that makes the content come alive.
- Give students an overview of the steps they need to complete to master the skill or procedures.
- Select practice activities on the students' level of success to actively engage them in each step.
- Assess, monitor, and adjust to the needs of students in each step.

Demystifying the Teacher-Directed Learning Model

Use a lecturette similar to the following to introduce the teacher-directed learning model:

> Sometimes I will work with the total class, with a small group or with you individually to explain a skill or something you need to know. I will guide you through each step. I will work with you until you can do it by yourself.

Student's Role

- Gather the supplies you need for the lesson.
- Listen carefully to the teacher's directions and explanations.
- Ask questions, if you need more explanations or assistance.
- Connect your past experiences to the new information during the lesson.
- Use notes and memory hooks to remember the information.

**FIVE (STAR) MANAGEMENT TIPS FOR
THE TEACHER-DIRECTED LEARNING MODEL**

1. Use an orientation that presents the purpose of the lesson with a connection to the learner's prior knowledge and experiences.
2. Present the new vocabulary words, phrases, and terminology.
3. Explain the new skill or concept by demonstrating its use. Use artifacts, illustrations, or models.
4. Provide structured, monitored practice with assistance as needed.
5. Assign practice activities the student can successfully complete independently.

Examples of the Teacher-Directed Learning Model

Example A: Using Color and Manipulatives

A student does not know how to use context clues. The teacher introduces the use of synonyms as one way to unlock the meaning of words. The teacher leads the student through sentences that contain examples. The teacher gives the student a small plastic disk to place next to the unknown word and a colored pen to mark the synonym. The teacher monitors and guides the activity. When the student demonstrates understanding, the teacher provides an assignment or activity as independent practice with the skill.

Example B: Using Demonstrations and Movement

A small group does not know how to measure the perimeter of objects. The teacher introduces the term, discusses practical applications of the skill, and demonstrates how to measure the perimeter of several different shapes. The students measure the perimeter of objects in the room with the teacher's direction and assistance. They receive independent practice activities.

Example C: Using Visuals and a Beat

A music student cannot say the names of notes on the music staff. The teacher uses a large diagram of a music staff to introduce notes on the lines. A rap is used as a memory strategy to repeat and recall the names of the notes on sight.

MANAGING THE NESTED ACTIVITY MODEL

What Is the Nested Activity Model?

The nested model is Heidi Jacob's design for integrating curriculum (Chapman, 1993). Since it is a decision-making device for selecting the most appropriate instructional activity, we have named this model the nested activity model. This planning tool analyzes an activity to see if it is a valuable use of instructional time. There are many standards and skills to teach. This planning tool outlines and highlights all objectives addressed in one activity such as the standard, social skills, multiple intelligences, and thinking skills.

What Are the Instructional Benefits of Using the Nested Activity Model?

The nested activity model is a planning strategy that assists in making the most effective activity choices for a particular time slot. A commonly heard, valid complaint of teachers is, "There is never enough time to teach all of the information." The nested activity analyzes the value of a chosen activity. Lessons are usually multifaceted, teaching more than one standard, skill, or intelligence at one time. When teachers realize everything one activity can teach, they become consciously effective while designing and making wise activity choices.

Teacher's Role

- Realize that the purpose of the nested model is to analyze an activity selection in order to make the most accurate curriculum decision for a particular time slot.
- Place the categories that fit your personal, local, or state requirements in the model form. Some examples are standards, benchmarks, competences, thinking skills, or social skills.
- Select an activity and analyze it.
- Remember that this model can also be used to compare two activities for a time slot to see which one offers the optimum benefit for this group of learners.
- Keep your nesting notes for reference when making a curriculum decision for this particular activity.

Demystifying the Nested Activity Model

When students are experiencing an activity designed with a nested format, guide them in filling in the grid. This helps learners recognize the many facets of the activity. They realize that many experiences are included in one learning activity.

Demonstrate nesting by placing the word "movie" in the center of a circle. Draw nested circles around it. Fill in related terms such as stars, plot, setting, and so on.

Student's Role

- Identify the different ways you are learning during an activity.
- Analyze the personal benefits of each activity.
- Make a journal entry to answer the question, "How many things did I learn from this activity?"
- Describe the different ways the skill or concept is presented.
- Identify your strengths and needs in using the skill or concept.

**FIVE (STAR) MANAGEMENT TIPS FOR USING
THE NESTED ACTIVITY MODEL**

1. Use the nested activity model as a planning tool to analyze the value of an activity. If it does not meet the learner's needs, it is not a wise choice. This analysis eliminates activities that are time wasters and fluff. The organizer identifies the most effective use of an activity for a time slot.

2. Try this one: Use the nested activity model to compare two activities. Decide which one best meets the needs of this particular group of students at this time.

3. Be selective! Differentiate! An activity that meets the needs of one group may not be needed for another group.

4. Remember it is all about what the students learn from an activity and its instructional benefits.

5. Use the data gathered to identify the students who need the activity and the students who would not benefit from using it.

★ ★ ★ ★ ★

Examples of the Nested Activity Model in Action

Example A: Original Nested Model

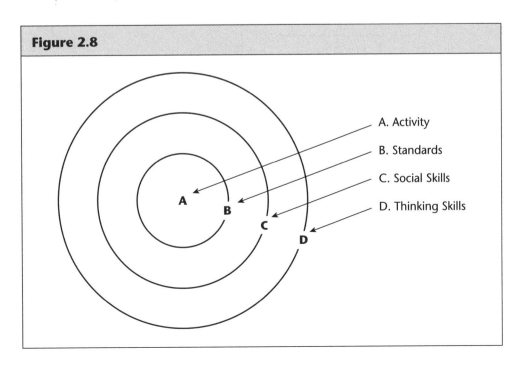

Figure 2.8

A. Activity
B. Standards
C. Social Skills
D. Thinking Skills

Example B: Nested Box Plan

Place the activity in the center box.

1. Identify the categories to analyze the activity.

2. Draw a nested box for each category. Determine the number of boxes by the number of categories you are exploring.

3. Write each category outside the nested boxes. Draw an arrow from each category to a box.

4. List the items addressed for each category in the corresponding box.

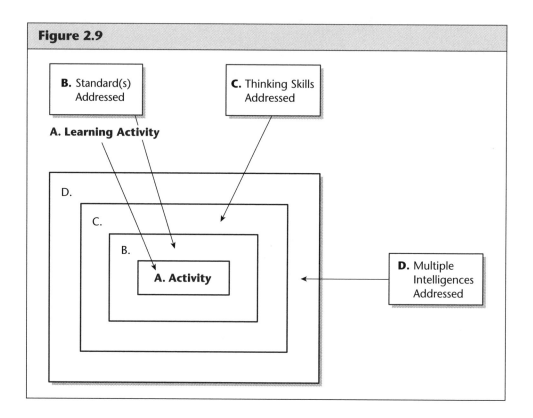

Figure 2.9

B. Standard(s) Addressed

C. Thinking Skills Addressed

A. Learning Activity

D.

C.

B.

A. Activity

D. Multiple Intelligences Addressed

Example C: Adapting the Nested Model to a Chart

1. Identify an activity.

2. Choose categories that coordinate with individual needs to address for the boxes. (See Figure 2.10.)

3. Analyze each category to be sure each one fits requirements in your school, district, or state.

4. List the standards, skills, concepts, or information the activity teaches in each category. If a category is lacking, add something to address the need in the activity.

5. If the activity does not meet the student needs, do not use it. Replace it with one that is beneficial.

Figure 2.10				
Activity _____				
Standards, Benchmarks, Competences	Objectives or Skills	Social Skills	Multiple Intelligences	Thinking Skills

MANAGING THE THREADED MODEL

What Is the Threaded Model?

The threaded model is a Heidi Hayes-Jacob planning tool for integrating the curriculum. A specific standard, skill, or concept is identified as the target for instruction because of its importance, misunderstanding, or weakness. The selected target becomes the focus of planning in each subject or topic in all curriculum areas.

The threaded model may be used as a planning tool in a self-contained classroom or across grade levels. It may be used by the resource specialist and classroom teacher, grade-level colleagues, an inclusion team, a total school, a district, or a state. Each task is designed to develop a weak area into an area of strength. The threaded model gives students opportunities to view the same standard, skill, concept, or information through different lenses in various subjects and situations and to use it in various ways.

What Are the Instructional Benefits of Using the Threaded Model?

This model provides opportunities for more than one teacher or subject area team to address the area of need for one or more learners. This organizational planning tool can be used to analyze how and when the targeted skill or concept is presented in each subject or class.

Teachers often feel like they are alone on an island because of their isolation within the four walls of their classrooms, and they feel that they have to do it all with little or no assistance. The threaded model gives teachers a tool that benefits students when plans are created and carried out to intentionally teach targeted standards and skills.

- In planning sessions, each educator shares ideas, vocabulary, and creative approaches to address the identified need.
- Teachers work together across grade levels in an elementary school or across subject areas in a middle or high school, making conscious efforts for everyone to address the need.
- More students learn because of the team effort and the major focus on a targeted area.
- Students see different uses, interpretations, and views of the information.
- If students do not fully understand the standard, skill, or concept in one lesson presentation or activity, they have several more opportunities to take ownership of it.

Teacher's Role

- Identify the learners' weakness or need. Share it with an individual or team who teaches or works with the student(s).
- Plot various ways to address the need in each subject or topic.
- Commit and devote time to being sure the weakness is addressed in the instructional plans so the students have several opportunities to reach understanding and master it.

- Share your accomplishments with your partner or team. Listen to experiences of other team members. Identify the next steps for advancement.

- When the skill is mastered or becomes automatic, use the threaded model to focus on another weak area.

Demystifying the Threaded Model

Debut the threaded model with a discussion of the phrase "threading it through." Adapt the following introduction to the model:

> The standards, skills, and information you need to learn will be used in different ways in all of your subjects or classes. They will appear in different ways, so watch for the threads.
>
> Everyone learns in different ways. By threading a skill through your activities and topics, you have more opportunities to grasp and use the information in many ways.

Student's Role

- Analyze what you understand and do not understand about the targeted skill, standard, or concept.

- Realize that your needs or weaknesses will be addressed in different subjects so you can see it through many lenses.

- Ask questions for clarification. Be ready to share your concerns and to make comments.

- Learn from each experience.

- Be a detective. Look for the new skill, standard, or concept in other subjects and classes.

FIVE (STAR) MANAGEMENT TIPS FOR USING THE THREADED MODEL

1. Target an area that needs more work by analyzing test data, grade-level performance, previous trouble spots, or teacher concerns. This leads to the realization that the learners have a specific need or weak area that must be emphasized because it has not been mastered by most students. Concentrated focus on a weak area can develop it into a strong area.

2. Use the threaded model in a self-contained classroom by addressing the same standard, skill, or concept in different lessons, activities, and subject areas.

3. Use the threaded model with a team. Each member has a role in improving the identified need. The team must be committed to changing the targeted weakness into a strength.

(Continued)

(Continued)

> 4. Remember, if a student does not master a skill in one way, there are more planned opportunities to understand and master it in other subjects or activities.
>
> 5. Survey students to discover their hobbies, fads, and other areas of interest. Connect the targeted learning experiences to the students' interests to intrigue them to learn the information.
>
> ★ ★ ★ ★ ★

Examples of the Threaded Model

Example A: Threading in a Self-Contained Classroom

1. Analyze test results to identify the weakest area to target.

2. Thread the targeted need through each subject area during the next week. This gives the students many opportunities to overcome the weak area.

Example B: Threading Across Grade Levels

The assessment results reveal that students need more emphasis on reading and interpreting the data. In most academic areas and on standardized tests, graphs are presented for the reader to interpret the represented information.

The team identifies ways to address the graphing skill.

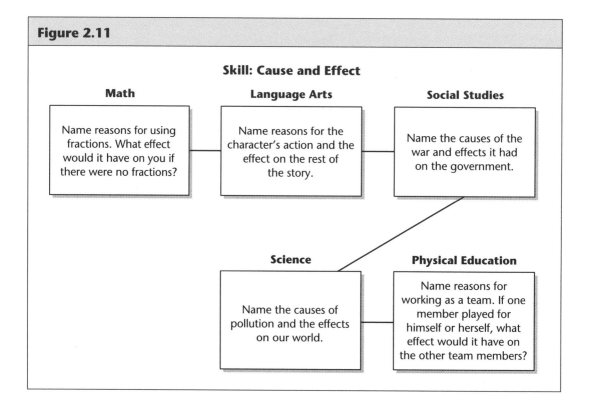

Figure 2.11

Skill: Cause and Effect

Math
Name reasons for using fractions. What effect would it have on you if there were no fractions?

Language Arts
Name reasons for the character's action and the effect on the rest of the story.

Social Studies
Name the causes of the war and effects it had on the government.

Science
Name the causes of pollution and the effects on our world.

Physical Education
Name reasons for working as a team. If one member played for himself or herself, what effect would it have on the other team members?

Example: Threading Schoolwide

- Interpret the data daily about the graphing.
- Use three types of graphs: bar graphs, line graphs, and pie charts.
- Show the graphs three ways: human, picture, and symbolic.
- Emphasize the following terms:

more than	less than	total	compare	plot
show	explain	contrast	analyze	examine
interpret	design	construct	summarize	identify

- Stimulate thinking with probing questions such as the following:
  - What does this graph tell or show?
  - How do you know?
  - Where is the data placed on the bar graph? Why?
  - Are they the same?
  - What does the data prove?
  - What did you learn from this?

The grade-level team identifies "how to use graphs and interpret the data" as an area of need to target over a nine-week period. Threading gives each team member responsibilities for teaching the graphing and interpretation skills. The students' skills become stronger because the graphing need is emphasized by each teaching team member.

Prekindergarten: During calendar time each morning during the month, add information to create a weather bar graph.

Kindergarten: During calendar time each morning, add to a weather bar graph. At the end of the month, students collect all the pictures that symbolize the daily weather and construct a pie chart.

First grade: In a science class, students construct a line graph to compare the growth of two plants over a period of time.

Second grade: During a math study, students create a bar graph recording their favorite ice creams, books, or sports. They make a pie chart using the data.

Third grade: The football team's scores from last season are compared with this year's scores on a line graph. The vertical lines on the graph are used to represent the game number, and the horizontal lines represent the scores of each game.

Fourth grade: The teacher gives an assignment for students to go on a scavenger hunt for a week and collect graphs. Each student brings the collection to a group-sharing session for discussion, interpretations, and discoveries. Each group shares their favorite graph and how it is used with the class.

Fifth grade: In a graphing station, students interpret the data on graph samples from newspapers, magazines, brochures, and the Web. Each learner selects one graph sample, places it in a journal, and writes an interpretation of it. The student signs the explanation. Another student reads the journal entry and adds more data. The teacher checks the explanations for correct or incorrect interpretations.

MANAGING MASTERY LEARNING

What Is Mastery Learning?

Mastery learning engages the student in activities and practice sessions with one skill until it is learned thoroughly. It is used with a student who needs to learn a skill.

The term *mastery* indicates that the student learns the information and is able to use it successfully. The teacher uses assessment data to identify a skill, fact, or concept that the student has failed to master. The learner is guided through specific teacher-directed activities that include an introduction, modeling, guided practice, and student-focused assignments until mastery is evident.

A learner at the mastery level is able to explain "inside" thought procedures to tell how the problem was solved. The student is able to respond, "This is the way I got the answer. First I . . . , then I. . . ." This is a metacognitive activity, where students are required to think about their thinking. Students on the mastery level are ready to move into a higher level of automaticity. Give students opportunities to move past the mastery level whenever possible. This is more likely to occur when students make personal links and have opportunities to use the new learning and in their own way.

What Are the Instructional Benefits of Mastery Learning?

- A specific goal or level of mastery is identified and shared with the learner.
- Time is provided for the student to practice using information, or a skill needed as a base for future learning.
- The tasks are within the learners' level of success so they do not get frustrated and give up. When learners master information or a skill, they will not be overwhelmed with future tasks that build on this basic knowledge.
- Students receive constructive feedback so they never feel lost. They become more perseverant as a result.
- Mastery generates intrinsic motivation as the teacher leads students successfully through each step or procedure. The feelings that accompany success often create a desire to learn more.

Teacher's Role

- Use an assessment to identify the student's current ability or knowledge of the topic or skill.
- Identify an obtainable goal or level of success.
- Give assignments in small chunks or tasks within the student's level of success.
- Provide specific, corrective feedback often.
- Celebrate successes when the goal or level of mastery is attained.

Demystifying Mastery Learning

Explain that mastery learning is used so students practice using information or a skill until they take control of it and own it. When this happens, they can use it independently without assistance. Here is a suggested dialogue to use in introducing mastery learning to students:

> When you were learning to ride a bicycle, you learned to ride with training wheels while someone helped you balance. You then learned to ride by yourself with the special wheels. Later you mastered riding the bicycle by yourself without the extra wheels or assistance.
>
> In the same way, you may need to have extra assistance and take special steps to learn some of our skills or information. When you master something, you understand it and can use it whenever you need it.

Student's Role

- Know what you know.
- Practice it until it comes easily, and you never have to second-guess yourself.
- Ask yourself, where does it fit in with previously stored information?
- Explore how to use the information.
- Decide what you need to learn next.

FIVE (STAR) MANAGEMENT TIPS FOR MASTERY LEARNING

1. Analyze the assessment data to identify specific skills, concepts, or information the student must know or master.
2. Select the most efficient, effective procedures or steps to teach the information to the individual learner.
3. Use the students' strengths to strengthen their weaknesses.
4. Remember the adage, "If you do not use it, you lose it"? Link, spiral, and review so students continue to apply the mastered skill or information.
5. Assess knowledge before, during, and after for strategic planning.

Examples of Mastery Learning
Example A: A Student Needs to Master Vocabulary or Sight Words

- Seven of the most common sight words are placed on flash cards.
- A sentence, picture, or definition of the word is placed on the back of the card.
- A tutor is assigned to teach the seven words to the student.
- When the seven words are pronounced correctly, a timer is used to increase speed.
- When the student reaches the mastery goal, the next seven words are presented.

Example B: A Small Group of Students Needs to Master Steps to Work a Problem

- The steps are presented orally using a visual such as a poster or chart.
- The students echo the teacher as the steps are stated. This continues until the students can state the facts automatically with confidence.
- The teacher provides a practice session in which the students' work is monitored, so immediate feedback and assistance can be provided as needed.
- The students receive a short assignment for independent practice so they can demonstrate mastery.
- Students create a rap or dance using the steps to showcase their mastery of the skill.

Example C: A Student Must Show Mastery of a Rule and Be Able to Apply It

- Introduce the rule by showing how it is used and explaining why it is important.
- Demonstrate its use in various examples.
- Monitor and assist the student as he or she applies the rule in independent tasks.
- Ask the student to use his or her learning styles and strongest intelligences to present or display an example of the rule and its use.
- Listen to the student as he or she explains his or her step-by-step thinking while applying the rule.

CONCLUSION

We strongly recommend that you become familiar with the steps for using the Adjustable Assignment Model. It is designed to simplify the difficult task of organizing and managing lessons for students who are on different knowledge levels.

Like matching the right hat to the right occasion, it is important to know how each model benefits differentiated instruction. Just as the hat enhances an outfit, the selected model can be tailored for the student's learning event.

MANAGING GROUPING STRATEGIES 3

JUST AS A BASEBALL COACH GIVES INFORMATION TO AN ENTIRE team, a teacher gives information to a classroom of learners. The team is brought together to receive general directions, to discuss the techniques and statistics of the opposing players. They also receive performance feedback and pep talks.

Wearing a baseball hat, a teacher can act as the coach of his or her classroom. Students can be brought together when they need to receive directions, learn new skills, or practice before a test.

Just as players sometimes work alone to practice their batting skills, students may work alone to gain more confidence with a specific skill. Players and students may also work in small groups or with a partner based on their current needs.

One crucial and complex management task in the differentiated classroom involves making grouping decisions. Since instruction is student centered, the savvy differentiator continuously considers the most beneficial grouping scenarios.

Many questions must be answered during the planning process for grouping:

- Which preassessment tool will be the most effective in guiding grouping decisions? Will it be administered to the total group, individuals, partners, or small groups?

- What is the most beneficial instructional approach to reach the student with the needed information?

- What is the best way to arrange the room for group instruction for each activity? How will the room be designed for materials and transitions?

- Who needs to be in each group?

- How much time must be allotted for group work?

When students need to actively process information, dividing the class into small groups according to their needs can be a highly effective strategy. The groups need specific direction with appropriate monitoring to engage productively.

As the teacher becomes a coach, facilitator, or guide on the side, students engage in various types of group and independent work. The student must have clear directions, have all necessary materials, and understand the purpose of the assignment. When learners know how to carry out activities with little or no adult supervision, the teacher is free to assess and monitor other students or provide direct instruction for groups or individuals.

Teachers who are taking their first steps into differentiated instruction are advised to become familiar with the playbook of various grouping scenarios and the occasions when each is most effective in enhancing instruction. This will ensure that the most appropriate approach to grouping can be selected and adapted for the students' needs during specific periods of study.

MANAGING FLEXIBLE GROUPING

What Is Flexible Grouping?

Flexible grouping gives students opportunities to learn information in a total class, alone, with a partner, or with a small group. The teacher selects the grouping strategy or scenario that will provide the best learning experience for each participant in an activity based on the assessment data.

After determining the need for a partner or small group activity, the teacher decides if students are grouped according to knowledge base, ability, or interest. Other alternatives include random groupings, peer-to-peer tutoring, multiage teams, or cooperative learning situations.

Grouping scenarios are fluid because students move in and out of the groups as needed based on continuous assessment. For example, if several observations reveal that a student is excelling on the beginning level of a skill, the learner moves to a group that is working on more challenging tasks.

What Are the Instructional Benefits of Flexible Grouping?

- Flexible grouping decisions are made with ongoing assessments to meet the identified academic, social, and emotional needs of each learner.

- The teacher can zero in on the specific needs of each group to maximize learning for every student.

- Groups may be created with common interests and abilities. This allows students to feed off of each other's experiences and excitement. They are more likely to contribute when they do not feel overshadowed by classmates.

- When individuals engage in a variety of grouping designs, they learn to work independently and cooperatively with a variety of personalities.

- Groups are formed to strengthen strengths and/or weaknesses.

Teacher's Role

- Familiarize yourself with each grouping option and its benefits in order to make the most efficient and advantageous planning decisions possible.

- Preassess in order to identify each learner's needs and create appropriate groups.

- Plan instruction with a blending of activities that engage learners in a total group, alone, with a partner, or in a small group scenario.

- Be alert! Move individuals as needed into groups tailored for their needs.

- Avoid grouping ruts. Vary the grouping designs by making teacher-assigned and student-choice arrangements.

Demystifying Flexible Grouping

All students need to know what to expect in their classroom. If students are not familiar with flexible grouping, they need to understand the rationale for using it. Use an analogy such as the following to introduce flexible grouping:

> The baseball coach is using a practice session to improve individual and group skills. Two players are working on pitching and hitting the ball while other players practice passing the ball. One player is perfecting his catching skills. The remaining players are running and sliding into bases. During another special practice session, all players engage in a scrimmage game.
>
> In the same way, in our classroom, we work on skills individually and in small groups. Our scrimmage will take place when we have a practice session for a major test.

Student's Role

- Follow the guidelines and directions for the team work and assignments.
- Be an active, productive participant in all group tasks to gain information and increase brain power from each experience.
- Communicate! Listen to ideas respectfully and contribute to group discussions.
- Ask questions for clarification as needed.
- Move in and out of groups promptly when directed without disturbing classmates.

★ ★ ★ ★ ★
FIVE (STAR) MANAGEMENT TIPS FOR FLEXIBLE GROUPING

1. Identify the most effective grouping design for the learners. Decide how many students to place in each group from an analysis of the assessment data during the planning phase.

   Examples:

   Base Group: A group of students who sit at the same table or near each other move their seats together to form a cluster or place their desks together to work.

   Gender: Some groups work better when they are composed of all girls or all boys.

   Previous Relationships: After working together on several activities, members usually bond as a team. They get along socially and respect each other. They learn to use each other's individual strengths and talents to reach the group's goal.

   Student Selection: Students choose classmates they can work with to get the job done. *Example:* Choosing an energizing partner.

   Teacher Selection: The teacher places students together based on their needs. *Example:* Creating a cooperative learning group or a project team.

2. Observe group dynamics. If the members of a group get along socially, they are more likely to be successful in completing the assignment.

3. If group members do not want to work with a student, try this prescription: Hold a private conference with the learner to identify and discuss the reasons for the personal rejections. Develop a plan for improvement.

4. Move a learner to a more beneficial group when assessments, including observations, indicate that his or her needs have changed. For example, if one student is struggling with the skill being practiced in a group, this student needs to move to a new scenario in order to learn the skill.

5. Select reflection activities for groups and individuals to give feedback and learning summaries.

Examples of Flexible Grouping

Example A: Fast-Forwarding

Assessment data has shown that a small group of students has mastered the information being learned. During the independent work time, these students are given an alternative assignment to research a part of the topic of their interests.

Example B: Ready for Grade Level

A student has been meeting and doing the assignments with the readiness group. He understands the concept and now is given the assignments with the grade level groups.

Example C: Rewinding

From a checkpoint during the learning, it is evident that a group of the students still do not understand the information being taught. Specific assignments are given during independent work time to address the gap. Also the teacher brings this group together for in-depth explanation during a time when the other students are working on an independent assignment.

MANAGING TOTAL GROUPS

What Is a Total Group?

A total group activity involves the entire class. Though this tactic might seem counter-intuitive in a book about differentiation, it is an excellent means of reaching and engaging every learner in the classroom when used appropriately. The teacher analyzes each whole-group activity to be sure every student benefits from hearing or using the same information.

What Are the Instructional Benefits of Using Total Groups?

In the differentiated classroom, total groups are strategically planned. The sessions benefit the learners when they are designed for the following purposes:

- Sharing the same information all students need. This includes introductions, background information, or procedures needed in a skill or concept.
- Providing explicit guidelines, directions, schedules, and announcements.
- Engaging students in brainstorming opportunities that produce ideas to explore. Students can hear the views, ideas, and processing alternatives to learn information during discussions.
- Celebrating and enjoying learning experiences. Examples include playing team games, using drill and practice activities, hearing visiting speakers, presenting reports and demonstrations, or beginning and ending activities for the day.
- Administering grade-level assessments and evaluations.

Teacher's Role

- Plan each total group session strategically. Use this instructional arrangement when it is the most effective and efficient way to reach each learner.
- Divide lectures into manageable chunks or lecturettes for optimal comprehension.
- Actively engage all students during total group sessions.
- Intersperse opportunities for students to work alone, with a partner, or in a small group during a total group session.

    Examples:
    o Work independently to practice a newly introduced procedure.
    o Turn to a partner to restate and discuss a difficult concept or skill.
    o Brainstorm possibilities with a small group.

- Psyche your students up with your enthusiasm. Use novelty and your passion for a subject to capture and maintain students' interest and attention.

Demystifying Total Groups

Explain the purpose of total group sessions to your students using an analogy similar to the following:

> When audience members are observing a magician to learn a magic trick, they listen and watch carefully with eyes and ears open. They concentrate on the magician's directions and actions to uncover the mystery and repeat the performance.

During total group sessions, everyone needs to be engaged in the same way, giving their complete, undivided attention to the teacher.

Student's Role

- Focus your attention on the teacher. Ignore any distractions.
- Stay on task! Be an active learner in all aspects of the total group session.
- Ask appropriate questions at appropriate times.
- Link new information to your personal experiences and use memory hooks so you can recall it later.
- Take notes using symbols, shapes, colors, tabs, and graphic organizers to enhance your memory and use for future study.

FIVE (STAR) MANAGEMENT TIPS FOR MANAGING TOTAL GROUPS

1. Replace lengthy lectures with "lecturettes" or "mini-lectures." Be certain you are conveying information everyone needs to hear or see such as the following:
   - An introduction of vital segments of the grade-level material
   - Motivational hooks or focus activities for the lesson
   - A "how-to" demonstration or simulation
   - Directions for upcoming activities
   - Reviews, assessments, evaluations, and feedback sessions

2. Vary instructional strategies and activities according to different learning styles, modalities, and intelligences.

3. Actively engage learners in total group discussions. Establish rules for listening and responding similar to the following:
   - One person speaks at a time.
   - Respond when called on to contribute.
   - Speak so everyone can hear.
   - Listen to each person's contribution.
   - Be open to and respectful of the views of others.

4. Employ questioning techniques that make each individual accountable for a mental, written or oral response. Remind students to put on their thinking caps before questions are presented. Provide thinking time before calling on someone for a response. Establish note-taking procedures. The best questioners
   - Vary types of questions.
   - Give students novel ways to respond individually to questions.
   - Allow partners time to compose brief written or oral responses in the form of lists, phrases, or sentences.
   - Engage all students by requiring that each one give a visible response using dry-erase boards, signals, or response cards.
   - Ask students to whisper answers to a neighbor, agree upon the best answer, and prepare to give their response in unison with the class at the sound of a signal.

(Continued)

(Continued)

> 5. Vary ways to call for individual responses in total groups:
>
> | | | |
> |---|---|---|
> | Random selection | Volunteers | Secret number |
> | Alphabetical order | Birthdates | Seating arrangement |
> | Drawing a name | Signals | |
>
> ★ ★ ★ ★ ★

Examples of Effective Total Grouping

Example A: Beginning a Lesson

The teacher provides an intriguing introduction to the upcoming topic of study for the whole class. This may include a debut of important facts, new vocabulary words, a discussion of characters, or highlights to stimulate or excite minds for the new learning.

Example B: During Learning

After a period of time, working independently and in small groups, the teacher brings the whole class together to review, celebrate, and summarize the learned information. Then the teacher may introduce the next activity by setting the purpose, explaining directions, and establishing the grouping scenarios.

Example C: After a Learning Segment

Students are brought together to review and prepare for a posttest in the current unit. The teacher provides study tips and reviews important facts and concepts. The total class plays a game to review the information.

MANAGING STUDENTS WORKING ALONE

What Is Working Alone?

Working alone refers to a student who independently completes an activity or task. The student works in an assigned seat, a designated area, or a comfortable, self-selected place.

The teacher periodically monitors and assists the learner. If the teacher is engaged in direct instruction with a group, another adult or study buddy may serve as the teacher. If no assistant is available, the student is told how and when to interact with the teacher or other classmates.

A student who is working independently needs to be within the teacher's vision. Avoid placing a student in a totally secluded place that is unsupervised.

What Are the Instructional Benefits of Students Working Alone?

- Intrapersonal learners need quiet work periods. It takes time for them to think. They yearn for alone time to conceptualize and problem solve.

- Some students prefer to work with others but occasionally need assignments to complete independently. Working and learning alone is a life skill that everyone needs for success.

- When students work alone, they are able to show what they know, how they process information, and what they can accomplish on their own.

- When a student is successful during independent assignments, the time on task increases.

- The learner is able to work at his or her own pace.

Teacher's Role

- Give an individual assignment when a specific, unique need is identified.

- Use activities and assignments the student can complete with little or no assistance.

- Make materials and resources accessible to complete the task.

- Explicitly state how the student is to be held accountable for completing the assignment. It may be accomplished by simply making a statement similar to the following:
  o "Make a journal entry of your learning."
  o "Show me your work in our mini-conference."
  o "Complete the rubric form."
  o "Place completed work in the 'IN' basket for grading when you finish."
  o "Place your peer review in your portfolio."
  o "Check your work using the answer key. Correct it and place in your portfolio."

- Be sure the student understands the purpose of the assignment and each direction. Clear rules, rituals, and routines need to be established. See Figure 3.1 on page 90.

Figure 3.1

What if . . .	Options for the student	Suggestions for the teacher
I have a question.	• Raise your hand. • Place the question on a sticky note and place it in an assigned area. • Ask a study buddy.	• Establish rules and procedures for the student to ask questions during independent activities. • Realize that when a student asks too many questions, the individual did not receive clear, appropriate directions; seeks attention; or the assignment was too difficult.
I need some supplies.	• If the supplies are located in an area that is open to students, quietly go and obtain the needed supplies. • If not, then you have to ask the teacher for permission.	• Have needed supplies accessible and available for students. • Designate some closet, basket, or shelf areas with supplies available to learners.
My pencil point breaks.	• Obtain a pencil from a container of sharpened, extra pencils. • Borrow one from a neighbor or the teacher.	• Collect pencils from parents and neighbors. • Place containers of sharpened pencils around the room so a pencil is easily available.
I need to go to the bathroom.	• Use a hall pass. • Obtain the bathroom tag or necklace prepared for class passes.	• Establish bathroom rules and procedures. Be consistent and persistent with everyone.
I do not know how to work a piece of equipment.	• Ask appropriate questions or request a demonstration. • Ask for help from a peer, then the teacher. • Move to another assignment or spot to complete another task until the teacher is available.	• Make sure that students are taught and practice with adult supervision before given an independent assignment on a new piece of equipment. • Assign a knowledgeable student to be in charge to assist others.
I know a classmate needs help.	• Help by asking probing questions to pinpoint the problem. • Show and tell your step-by-step thinking.	• Establish guidelines stating when assistance can be given. • Explain and model how to assist others. • Realize that some students are better assistants.

Figure 3.1

What if . . .	Options for the student	Suggestions for the teacher
		• Remember, students who have an "aha" moment often are the best tutors because they know the steps and can exhibit their excitement.
I finished my assignment.	• Check over your work. • Move on to the next task. Return manipulatives or materials to their home or designated area. • Complete a self-assessment activity. • Find something to do on your own that will not distract others.	• Have alternative activities for students who have finished their work and are waiting for others to complete their work. • Teach students to review their answers. • Provide ways for students to check and correct their own papers immediately after completion.
I complete a task using manipulatives.	• Clean up the materials and return them to their proper places. • Then move on to your next assignment.	• Establish a significant spot for each manipulative. • Make cleaning up and returning the material to the designated spot a part of the assignment.

Demystifying Working Alone

Use a lecturette similar to the following to explain the purpose of working alone:

There are going to be times in your life when you have to work alone. When you work independently, you learn to stay on task, to have patience, and to complete assignments with little or no assistance. Consider the time an athlete spends working alone to perfect skills. For example, Michael Jordan practiced alone making four to five hundred hoop shots every day.

Student's Role

- Make sure that you understand the direction or guidelines before you begin. Ask appropriate questions, if necessary.
- Know where you can work.
- Gather the materials you need before you begin the activity.
- Stay on task! Do not disturb others or allow others to distract you.
- Check your work when you complete the assigned task.

★ ★ ★ ★ ★

FIVE (STAR) MANAGEMENT TIPS FOR WORKING ALONE

1. Use an individual assignment to address an identified need. The task should be designed to reinforce, practice, extend, or assess the learning.

2. Be sure the student understands the purpose of the assignment and directions to complete the tasks with little or no assistance.

3. Establish parameters that include
   - Options for places to work such as a rug, floor, table, or desk
   - Movement to other work areas
   - Obtaining the materials and resources necessary to complete the task
   - Talking to a study buddy
   - How and when to seek answers to questions

4. Teach the student how to check and correct the work.

5. Place the student engaging in independent tasks near the area where the teacher is working with other students. Proximity gives the teacher opportunities to use a signal such as "thumbs up" to encourage and support the learner.

★ ★ ★ ★ ★

Examples of the Effective Use of Working Alone

Example A: Agenda Assignment

A student receives an independent agenda assignment with three tasks to complete. The learner works at his or her own pace, selecting the order of the activities and moving freely to stations or areas to complete the tasks. The student selects two completed work samples to place in his or her portfolio or folder. One selection is checked and corrected. It is then placed in an assigned tray for teacher viewing.

Example B: Project Assignment

A learner has an ongoing, independent project assignment. The student completes a Web search on the computer to gather research for the selected topic. The topic information is gathered. During the next two independent work sessions, the student works at a desk reading, taking notes, and compiling valuable facts for the project.

Example C: Personalized Assignment

Analysis of a student's pretest data on a standard in the current study reveals a specific need. The learner works with materials to fill a gap or enhance learning. The student returns the materials to the storage space. The student makes oral or written reflection statements and makes a journal entry about the learning experience.

MANAGING PARTNER GROUPS

What Is a Partner Group?

A partner group consists of two students working cooperatively to complete a task or to reach a goal. They are placed together as a team to share ideas, cooperate, and assist each other. The students must be socially compatible to be successful partners.

What Are the Instructional Benefits of Using Partner Groups?

- Partner work actively engages more students in learning. For example, in some tasks, half of the class talks, while the other half listens. Then the roles are reversed.
- All students have opportunities to share ideas, revise, and work with someone.
- Learners experience the value of "two brains working as one."
- Every student receives immediate feedback, assistance, and encouragement.
- Some students work better with a partner than alone or in a larger group.

Teacher's Role

- Identify the appropriate assignment for partner teams.
- Vary the way partners are identified.
  - Assign partner teams according to academic need and social interaction.
  - Allow students to work with a friend. Establish the rule that only friends who stay on task and follow the rules have the privilege of working together.
  - Use random grouping techniques: draw names, have students count off, or create a search activity to form partner teams using a match game with one of the following categories: book titles with main characters, states with capitals, landmarks with cities, inventors with their inventions, or songs with the lyrics.
- Provide guidelines, rules, and regulations for productive, interactive learning. Model, practice, and role-play these guidelines.
- Teach students how to question each other to stimulate thinking while working together.
- Devise a personal reflection activity for partners to use in summarizing or listing what they learned together.

Demystifying Partner Groups

Teach your students that two heads are often better than one:

Every person has unique life experiences and different strengths and weaknesses. When working and learning with someone else, you have a bigger knowledge bank to draw from—two brains working as one to solve the same problem.

Working together, exchanging ideas, and sharing research, Orville and Wilbur Wright invented the first powered airplane capable of carrying a man, a feat that centuries of brilliant scientists and inventors working on their own had been unable to accomplish.

Orville and Wilbur Wright made history because they worked well as a team. They respected each other and valued each other's ideas. Remember that you have a right to your own opinion or way of doing something, but so does your partner. Successful partners value each other's contributions and discuss the pros and cons of each option before making a decision.

Student's Role

- Be an engaged listener with your eyes and body language.
- Use your individual strengths to assist your partner.
- Decide how to take turns and identify individual roles.
- Use questions that probe your partner's brain to think and improve the work.

Examples:
  o What are you thinking? Tell me more.
  o What steps did you use?
  o How did you come to that conclusion?
  o What do you need next?
  o How can we solve this together?

- Get to know your partner to form a respectful, productive working team as friends.

FIVE (STAR) MANAGEMENT TIPS FOR USING PARTNER GROUPS

1. Use partner teams wisely and purposefully. Prepare partner teams or small groups for specific assignments.
   - Select assignments and activities that enhance the current topic of study.
   - Be sure the partners receive thorough directions for the assignment so they can do it independently as a student-focused activity.
   - Give learners opportunities to ask questions related to the assignment.
   - Teach partners options for solving their own problems.
   - Make materials and resources accessible to minimize the group movement.

2. Establish energizing partners to work together throughout the day, class period, unit of study, or a grading period. Permit students to choose someone they can work with effectively or assign the partner teams.

3. Keep the same partners together long enough to cultivate mutual respect, trust, and team spirit.

4. Assign tasks that allow partners to choose a favorite place to work. If possible, let the team decide if they want to sit or stand to complete the tasks.

5. Ask students to write on their own papers even if they are discussing or checking answers with a partner. In this way, they learn to identify their own mistakes and take responsibility for making the corrections.

Examples of Effective Partner Grouping

Example A: Drill

Two students who need to learn facts use flash cards to drill and practice.

Example B: Reading Reflection

Students work together to complete a writing activity that summarizes their reading assignment. They brainstorm the information learned and compile the highlights.

Example C: Read, Share, Design, Report

Partners select or are assigned a topic in the current area of study to explore in depth. They design a display to share their findings with the class. They select an innovative way to present their findings.

MANAGING SMALL GROUPS

What Is a Small Group?

The meaning of the term *small group* probably appears to be obvious, but the word *small* is a relative term. A teacher who has a large class may consider 15 students as a small group, so there is a need for clarification here.

In a differentiated classroom, the most effective student-directed groups are composed of three or four members. The teacher-directed group is determined by the number of students who need to hear or work with the information. When the term *small group* is used in this resource, we are referring to the three- or four-person configuration.

What Are the Instructional Benefits of Using Small Groups?

- Because small groups are formed for cooperative activities or for learners to work on common tasks, students can engage in different, simultaneously occurring activities specifically designed for their needs.

- The teacher can introduce, review, or guide the practice of skills needed by more than one learner.

- Students who need support, immediate feedback, and encouragement are more easily monitored.

- When engaged in group work, learners are actively engaged in processing information for understanding and retention. Pathways to memory are created as they share, hear, and mentally manipulate the information during interactive activities.

- Each learner is given the opportunity to work, communicate, brainstorm, and be creative as a team member. Making decisions with others—learning how and when to compromise for consensus—is a valuable skill necessary to be successful in nearly all aspects of life.

Teacher's Role

- Use the assessment data to decide when the students need to be a part of a group to learn the standards and content in the most effective way.

- Strategically plan assignments that build a knowledge base and create curiosity: present a focus activity, provide an anticipatory set, or introduce small group activities.

    Find ____ facts related to _____.

    Use the experiment to explore _____.

    Discover the mysteries surrounding _____.

    Find out why we need to know about_____.

- Establish appropriate, beneficial roles that accommodate group needs and showcase individual talents. Introduce one way to select a group leader, recorder, reporter, and other necessary roles. Explain the purpose and responsibility of each role assignment. Continue to use this technique until students are comfortable with the different roles. When students understand two or three ways of selecting team members to fulfill the different roles, let each group choose the technique for assigning roles.

Examples:		
Use a spinner	Draw names	Ask for a volunteer
Use alphabetical order	Use birthdates	Take turns

- Provide groups with a clear purpose, expectations, and directions for the activity.

Example:

1. Name your group.

2. Review the assignment to be sure everyone understands the goal.

3. Discuss the best way to carry out the assignment.

4. Obtain needed materials and resources.

5. Establish individual roles.

6. Complete the assignment.

7. Share, reflect, and celebrate!

- Teach students how to transition in and out of groups efficiently and effectively or quickly and quietly (Q and Q).

- Allow enough time for each step of the process, presentation of the learning, and reflection. During the reflection period, individual members share cognitive and social aspects of the learning that occurred during the group work. Emphasize the steps in the process more than the product produced.

Demystifying Small Groups

By sharing responsibility, small groups can accomplish missions that individuals or partner teams might find overwhelming. Point out to your students that the average person is a member of many decision-making teams or committees in a lifetime, some of which involve problem solving as a group while others assign a different task to each member in order to achieve a common goal.

The following analogies may be helpful in explaining the benefits of two major forms of group collaboration:

In some groups, each member is assigned a different task in order to complete a large job. In a committee that is planning a large party on short notice, for example, one member may be responsible for choosing and purchasing decorations, another member may be responsible for hiring a band or DJ, a third member may be responsible for designing and printing fliers to advertise the party.

Small groups may brainstorm to solve a problem. Members of the president's cabinet, for instance, gather together periodically to discuss the pros and cons of laws the president is considering. Each member has a different specialty and unique viewpoint to offer. This helps the president consider all sides of an issue and determine the best course of action before making a decision.

Emphasize that each member has a different practical, analytical, or creative viewpoint to share with the group and that quality decision making and problem solving relies on respecting and thoughtfully considering each individual's contributions.

Student's Role

- Be a productive team member who contributes to the common goal.
- Stay on task to learn as much as you can from the experience.
- Carry out your role and assignments productively.
- Respect, assist, and encourage team members.
- Assess each step of the assignment to know what you are learning and how to improve.

FIVE (STAR) MANAGEMENT TIPS FOR TEACHER-DIRECTED SMALL GROUPS

1. Name the purposes of the day's learning. Hook students into wanting to learn! Present directions and explanations in language they understand.

2. Teach the content in varied ways, keeping each mind engaged and meeting the needs of the members of the group.

3. Provide immediate feedback. Assess continuously to know what the learners need next.

4. Avoid having more than three groups with you in a class period. We make this suggestion because it is difficult to plan and manage activities for more than three groups. When the teacher is engaged with too many groups, busy work assignments are often added to keep the students occupied. Plan to meet with different groups on different days.

5. Before leaving the group area:
   - Give an independent practice assignment as a follow-up activity.
   - Celebrate successes!
   - Lead a discussion to review the day's learning.
   - Ask students to state what they want to learn next.
   - Introduce highlights of the next small group meeting.

Design an effective combination of the various types of grouping, so both independent cognitive and social needs are met. The following activities in Figure 3.2 are suggestions for varying grouping scenarios for differentiation.

FIVE (STAR) MANAGEMENT TIPS FOR
STUDENT-FOCUSED SMALL GROUPS

1. Remember, group members must get along socially to complete an assignment successfully. Teach, model, and discuss the skills needed to be a productive team member.

2. Vary group formations to meet student needs and to add novelty to learning. Avoid creating groups with more than four students. If the group needs to make a decision, use an odd number of members so it will be easy for them to come to a consensus.

3. Establish clear, specific directions for the assignment with roles and duties for the group members so each student has a specific task. Assignments should require little teacher oversight and be customized for each group to suit the specific member needs, such as the following:
   - To review and practice essential information related to the skill or topic
   - To provide personalized, meaningful experiences
   - To build speed and accuracy
   - To move to mastery and automaticity
   - To apply information in a new way

4. In order to be a better facilitator and monitor during small group activities, try the following tips:
   - Be visible and stay in close proximity with students.
   - Keep moving among groups and avoid forming a walking pattern.
   - Use nonverbal body language to emphasize messages.
   - Position yourself on the opposite side of the group or behind it, when a student is addressing the group. A student usually addresses comments to the teacher. When adults stand at a distance, students speak to them.
   - Be careful about making promises to students that may be difficult to keep, such as, "I'll be there in a minute." In a differentiated classroom, you never know when a greater need will appear.

5. Avoid giving group grades. Assess learning during independent tasks. Group activities are best used for brainstorming sessions, producing products, making presentations, discussion time, reading, or practicing skills.

Figure 3.2

Group	Total Group	Alone	Partner	Small Group
When	☐ Topic introductions ☐ Procedures modeling ☐ Skill demonstrations ☐ Focus activities ☐ Background information ☐ Drill and practice ☐ Directions and procedures ☐ Wrap-up session ☐ Lecturettes ☐ Guided practice ☐ Media clips ☐ Computer ☐ Performances ☐ Reports ☐ Celebrations of learning ☐ Reflections	☐ Contracts ☐ Agendas ☐ Menus ☐ Choice boards ☐ Journals ☐ Diaries ☐ Logs ☐ Practice/drill ☐ Information processing ☐ Question responses ☐ Manipulative use ☐ Note taking ☐ Reviews ☐ Reflections ☐ Computer work ☐ Research ☐ Performances ☐ Assessments	☐ Manipulatives ☐ Reviews ☐ Practice/drill ☐ Cooperative learning ☐ Performances ☐ Listening and speaking activities ☐ Sharing information ☐ Answering questions ☐ Checking work ☐ Games ☐ Puzzles ☐ Computer activities ☐ Problem solving ☐ Research ☐ Study buddies ☐ Revising/editing ☐ Double-entry journaling ☐ Reflect	☐ Text talk ☐ Conversation circles ☐ Literary circles ☐ Cooperative learning ☐ Consensus building ☐ Applying information ☐ Practice/drill ☐ Brainstorming ☐ Performing ☐ Discussing and explaining a process ☐ Reflecting on learning ☐ Reviewing information ☐ Problem solving ☐ Research ☐ Presenting ☐ Previewing books or materials ☐ Publishing ☐ Using manipulatives
Where	☐ Desks ☐ Rugs ☐ Labs ☐ Media center ☐ Gymnasium ☐ Tables ☐ Outside ☐ Standing cluster ☐ Commons areas ☐ Bleachers	☐ Learning zones ☐ Center ☐ Station ☐ Lab ☐ Desk ☐ Floor ☐ Rug ☐ Chair ☐ Glider ☐ Rocking chair ☐ Study carrel ☐ Loft	☐ Learning zones ☐ Centers ☐ Stations ☐ Labs ☐ Chosen space ☐ Floor ☐ Chairs ☐ Desks ☐ Table ☐ Sitting side by side ☐ Standing ☐ Sitting back to back to work. Facing each other to share and discuss.	☐ Learning zones ☐ Centers ☐ Stations ☐ Labs ☐ Grouped tables and/or chairs ☐ Clustered desks ☐ Floor ☐ Standing cluster ☐ Outside

MANAGING KNOWLEDGE BASE GROUPS

What Are Knowledge Base Groups?

Knowledge base groups are formed according to the student's level of understanding on the topic, skill, or standard that is being assessed. Like a coach practicing specific skills at different levels, a teacher must take into consideration where students' skills currently are, including everything the learner knows prior to introduction of the information. This knowledge is acquired over a lifetime through personal and academic experiences. We recommend using no more than three knowledge levels by analyzing the formal or informal preassessment data in a differentiated classroom.

> **Curriculum Rewinding:** Students on this level need an introduction to the basic information. They have little or no knowledge of the new topic or skill.

> **Grade Level.** These learners are ready for the new grade-level information. They possess the proper background experiences and understanding.

> **Curriculum Fast-Forwarding.** Students on this level know and understand the information. They are ready to extend their knowledge and explore related areas.

The adjustable assignment model is designed as a planning tool to use in selecting and customizing instructional strategies and activities for these knowledge base groups. See more about this planning tool in Chapter 2.

What Are the Instructional Benefits of Using Knowledge Base Groups?

- Each student can relate prior experiences to the new standard, skill, or topic because instruction begins with the learner's current knowledge.
- Lessons are customized for individuals and groups, so they instruct and challenge students on their success levels.
- Students are more eager to learn because they are not bored and frustrated.
- The groups are fluid. By responding to analyzed assessment data and observations, the teacher can move a student to a more appropriate group that is working on a higher or lower knowledge level.
- A student may work on a fast-forwarding level on one topic and on the rewinding level on another topic. This establishes an accepting tone and addresses the cognitive needs based on the learner's strengths and needs.

Teacher's Role

- Select the best formal or informal preassessment tool to identify each learner's background and prior experiences. Analyze the data to form the knowledge base groups.
- Design and implement a plan of instructional activities to address the needs of each group or individual.

- Identify ongoing assessment tools for the unit, topic, skill, or standard to monitor the ever-changing needs and appropriate group placement for each learner.

- Schedule time to meet with each level of the knowledge base groups. Give feedback with specific instruction, support, and encouragement.

- Realize that each student's prior knowledge and experience is unique for each topic, skill, standard, and concept. Use your best judgment to select the most opportune time and place to use knowledge base grouping.

Demystifying Knowledge Base Groups

Students need to understand that they may be on different knowledge levels with each topic and skill. Introduce students to knowledge base groups using an explanation similar to the following:

> When you turn on a video game, you select the level of speed or accuracy. You consider previous scores to choose the best level for you. In the same way, our preassessments and your daily work determine your level for each assignment or activity.

Student's Role

- Recall your experiences and what you know about the upcoming topic. Link what you know to the new information.

- Accept this knowledge level knowing that you can grow in it and excel.

- Challenge yourself to add to what you know.

- Know what you know and what you don't know. If you discover that you have learning gaps, fill them in so you can move quickly to grade-level material. If you know the grade-level information, see how much more you can learn about it.

- Share what you know with others.

FIVE (STAR) TIPS FOR MANAGING KNOWLEDGE BASE GROUPS

1. Use an appropriate formal or informal preassessment tool. If an informal assessment will identify the information needed to form the groups, use it instead of the formal assessment. Gather the information one or two weeks before planning the unit, so you can tailor instruction for the diverse needs of your students.

2. Implement knowledge base grouping when the preassessment indicates that the class has a broad range of knowledge on a standard, skill, or topic. In other words, some students have a high level of understanding, some are on grade level, and others are at the beginning level.

3. Select tasks that generate buy-in from the learners and meet their specific needs.

4. Adjust groups continuously for effective instruction. When a learner demonstrates that instruction is needed on basic key elements, that student should receive the basic information and quickly move to a higher level once the learning gap is filled.

5. Remember that knowledge base groups are fluid, changing with the learner's needs.

Examples of Knowledge Base Grouping

The following examples illustrate four ways a teacher can divide a class into three groups according to the student's knowledge base of a standard, skill, or topic.

The number of sessions and time allotted is determined by the number of lessons needed to reach the objectives.

Example A: Grade-Level Instruction for the Majority of the Class

The teacher preassesses learners on new information. During the first two days of the unit study, the total class works together. This is the third day of the study.

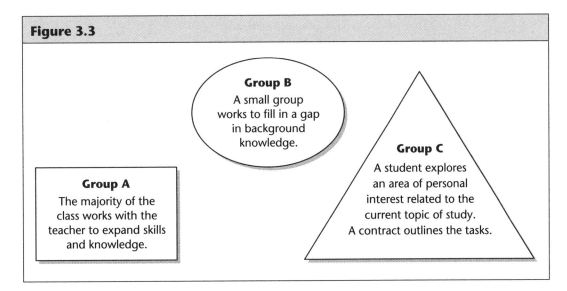

Figure 3.3

Group B
A small group works to fill in a gap in background knowledge.

Group C
A student explores an area of personal interest related to the current topic of study. A contract outlines the tasks.

Group A
The majority of the class works with the teacher to expand skills and knowledge.

Example B: Rewinding Instruction for a Small Group

A posttest reveals that most students have mastered the new skill. Three students had very low scores. Two students had perfect scores on the test.

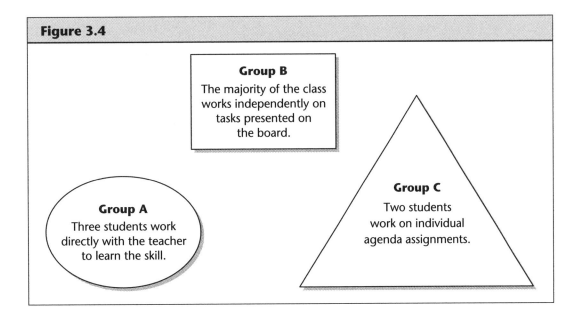

Figure 3.4

Group B
The majority of the class works independently on tasks presented on the board.

Group C
Two students work on individual agenda assignments.

Group A
Three students work directly with the teacher to learn the skill.

Example C: Curriculum Rewinding and Curriculum Fast-Forwarding

The teacher designs two different group assignments to target the students' needs revealed by the assessment data. The two group assignments are presented on the board.

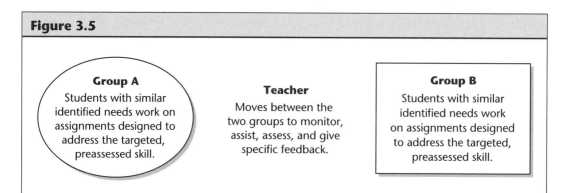

Figure 3.5

Group A
Students with similar identified needs work on assignments designed to address the targeted, preassessed skill.

Teacher
Moves between the two groups to monitor, assist, assess, and give specific feedback.

Group B
Students with similar identified needs work on assignments designed to address the targeted, preassessed skill.

Example D: Three Rotating Groups

In this example, students are engaged in three different group configurations that are occurring simultaneously. All groups rotate through the work session with the teacher, the independent work, and the center activities.

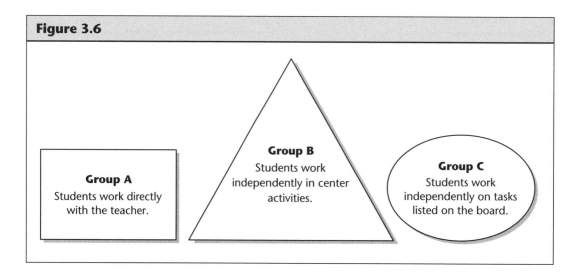

Figure 3.6

Group A
Students work directly with the teacher.

Group B
Students work independently in center activities.

Group C
Students work independently on tasks listed on the board.

MANAGING INTEREST GROUPS

What Is an Interest Group?

Interest groups are formed with learners who are eager to learn more about the upcoming topic or skill. These study teams are appropriate for all grade levels and curriculum areas. Students work with a topic-related area because they want to learn more about it.

What Are the Instructional Benefits of Using Interest Groups?

- Students gain an opportunity to investigate and explore an exciting topic in depth.

- Interest is a strong motivational tool that increases the desire to learn more.

- Learners are given the opportunity to delve into favorite topics using their most comfortable learning styles and favorite intelligences.

- Allowing students to work in their interest area gives them a sense of ownership in their education and develops self-directed, independent learners.

- Students learn information and take more responsibilities when engaging in assignments of interest.

Teacher's Role

- Assist the individual or group in selecting an interest area to be sure that the focus is on information or skills related to grade-level standards. Probe for ideas through discussion and brainstorming sessions or use surveys and inventories.

- Analyze the chosen interest area to plan activities that challenge and enrich the learner. These student-focused groups involve activities that can be accomplished with little adult supervision.

- Select a method to form interest groups such as the following:
  o Sign up for an area of choice.
  o Write a contract.
  o Use a survey and compile the data to identify interest.
  o Allow teams to select an interest topic related to the current study.

- Provide adequate time for the student or group to dig into the chosen topic.

- Set forth expectations that include the goals, guidelines, timelines, and assessment tools to use before, during, and after learning.

Demystifying Interest Groups

Explain interest grouping to your students as a great opportunity to explore a topic that appeals to them:

Your favorite pastime, hobby, or activity is something you enjoy; it is something that appeals to you and keeps your attention. You will have opportunities to choose a specific area of interest within our current topic and work with others who share your interest.

Discuss a few categories such as movies, songs, sports, and books. Ask students to name their specific areas of interest in each one. Wrap up the session by presenting a few upcoming unit topics. Challenge students to identify their areas of interest for each one.

Student's Role

- Ask yourself: What do I like best about this topic? What areas do I want to know more about?

- Use the teacher-compiled list of options to select an area that relates to the current topic to explore or investigate. Obtain teacher approval.

- Join the interest group to obtain the directions, procedures, role, and timeline for the assignment.

- Work through the tasks to learn more about your area of interest.

- Reflect on and celebrate everything you learned.

**FIVE (STAR) MANAGEMENT TIPS FOR
MANAGING INTEREST GROUPS**

1. Survey students to identify their areas of interest related to the current study. Use this information to provide appropriate choices so students can study and grow in an area of interest.

2. Strategically provide choices to broaden knowledge. Match standards with interest assignments.

3. Learn as much as you can about your students. The more you know about them, the easier it is to plan effective, meaningful learning opportunities.

4. Allow students who are working together on a subtopic to showcase their extended learning experiences.

5. Remember, when students have an affinity for a topic and have rewarding experiences in their study, they are more likely to remember the information for a lifetime.

Examples of Interest Grouping

Example A: Research Dig!

The class is beginning a study of the ocean. Five students select an area of interest to explore for more information.

- Each individual selects a role or task to accomplish during the investigation and research.

- The members compile the information.

- The group prepares a presentation to teach the information learned in the investigation.

- Each student uses a rubric as a self-assessment tool.

Example B: Jigsaw

Each learner selects an area of interest from a choice board and joins the designated team. Each group has a different assignment that it is responsible for exploring. The team works, discusses, and studies the information together. The results and findings are shared with the total class.

Example C: Contract

Students select a skill or topic of interest related to the current study. They design a contract or agreement that extends learning in this area. The contract outlines the tasks, time frame, the product, and assessment tool to use. The teacher makes additions or changes as needed. The teacher and students sign the agreement.

MANAGING ABILITY GROUPS

What Is an Ability Group?

Everyone has personal talents and weaknesses that they bring to the game. An ability group is formed with students who have similar capabilities for working with a standard, skill, or procedure. Each individual's achievement scores, IQ test results, academic perform-ance, and/or daily work are used as indicators of what a student is capable of learning. The experiences provide opportunities for a homogeneous group of students to work with materials and activities within their ability range, giving players with varying skills the opportunity to go into the game and show what they can do. When players or students are working to the best of their ability and there is no cap on their potential, they become proud, hardworking performers always working to improve their ability to be a better team member.

Ability groups often are composed of learners who are at risk, on grade level, or in the gifted and talented group. Some districts use these levels for homogeneous grouping or tracking within classrooms or schools.

What Are the Instructional Benefits of Using Ability Groups?

- When grouped according to ability, students are on the same instructional level, so the teacher can plan the appropriate pace with challenging strategies and activ-ities that focus on a skill needed by the group.

- Students usually receive direct instruction. It is often easier to plan for students who have a common weakness or need.

- The learners develop a bond as they work on the same skill or procedure.

- Learners who work at a slower pace are not threatened with frustration and fail-ure. High achievers are not bored or "checked out" during lessons.

- The activities are on the student's ability level, so they are more likely to grow in their learning and experience success.

Teacher's Role

- Analyze and compile the assessment data to identify specific, common needs to establish the groups.

- Strategically plan activities for the standard(s) on the group's ability level.

- Plan activities to target individual needs incorporating the learner's strengths.

- Provide opportunities for students using a variety of learning strategies.

- Use flexible grouping so students can move to the group that best meets their needs.

Demystifying Ability Groups

Explain to students that ability groups are used when they need to work on their level with a specific standard, skill, or topic. Compare ability groups to the levels in swimming classes: beginning, intermediate, and advanced.

When people take swimming classes, some are placed in beginning classes because they need to become accustomed to being in the water. They must learn the basics, such as breathing techniques and arm and leg stokes, needed to survive. Swimmers are placed in the intermediate level when they know and demonstrate that they can use the fundamental skills.

Some individuals may remain in the beginner's class for longer than others because it takes longer to learn the skills. Swimmers are placed in the advanced level because they have the physical and mental ability to use highly developed skills.

Individuals who did not advance in swimming may excel in other sports or hobbies. Engage students in a discussion of their experiences with working on varying levels of difficulty.

Student's Role

- Work to learn as much information as possible.
- Show what you know.
- Ask appropriate questions.
- Show respect for each team member.
- Complete your independent assignments and tasks.

**FIVE (STAR) MANAGEMENT TIPS
FOR MANAGING ABILITY GROUPS**

1. Assess! Assess! Use formal and informal assessment data to identify ability levels.

2. Address group and individual needs while using flexible grouping.

3. Teach the groups in varied ways, giving individuals numerous opportunities to learn information.

4. Provide practice, discussion, and processing time.

5. Place students in ability groups when you want to "zap gaps" for the student and challenge the high-end learner.

Examples of Ability Grouping

Example A: Skill Groups

Skill groups for an academic area are created according to the results of a preassessment. Students may need an introduction to the basic information, the grade-level lesson, or an extension of the skill. The specific needs of each group are addressed through direct instruction and specific assignments to advance learning on each level.

Example B: Reading Groups

A teacher and his or her students compile reading materials that reinforce a unit on the Revolutionary War. The teacher then divides the reading materials into four stacks (Red, Blue, Yellow, and Green) according to the level of difficulty. Before the lesson begins, the teacher assigns students to groups based on reading ability level and allows the Red Group to choose books from the Red stack, the Blue Group to choose books from the Blue stack, and so on. Each student learns because he or she is capable of reading the assigned material.

Example C: Academically Gifted Groups

A special class is designed to reach the students according to their ability level. For example, students who are identified as academically gifted and talented meet twice a week for problem solving, educational field trips, and challenging research activities.

MANAGING MULTIAGE INSTRUCTION

What Is Multiage Instruction?

Multiage instruction is designed for students of varying ages who are placed together for learning experiences. They are grouped by knowledge levels, interests, or skills. The productive learning atmosphere that develops is similar to the one-room schoolhouse or team of baseball or football players. For example, a dynamic freshman quarterback can sometimes lead a team of older players to victory and success. Mutual respect is formed, and age does not matter. They are proud to be members who get to wear the helmet that represents the team.

Multiage programs are most often found in self-contained classrooms. Teachers let go of their traditional thinking about learners' ages and grade levels.

What Are the Instructional Benefits of Multiage Instruction?

- Planning focuses on the standard and the learner's needs.
- Learners progress through content or skills at their individual pace.
- Students improve social skills as they interact.
- Students learn the value of working cooperatively to reach goals with classmates at different ages.
- The student's individual and group needs become the focus of all learning experiences.

Teacher's Role

- Select the instructional focus for the multiage groups: knowledge base, topic, skill, or standard.
- Use the most efficient assessment tool to obtain useful data.
- Monitor learners to assist and make placement changes as needed.
- Use intriguing instructional strategies to build a community of learners.
- Continually assess the multiage sessions. Include students in the assessment process by asking the following:
  o What did you learn?
  o What do you need to do next?
  o How did your group work together?
  o What problems did you experience? What solutions do you suggest?
  o What needs to be changed before our next lesson?

Demystifying Multiage Instruction

If students have never worked with others outside of their age range before, they may be initially uncomfortable with the idea. Dispel any fears by explaining the following:

> Just as adults of different ages work together in a job, in our class, you will work with students who are older or younger than you. One group may have several members of different ages. Multiage groups are formed so you can learn from each other.

Discuss multiage groups that are familiar to the students such as scouts and sports teams. Students often participate in events that have attendees of different ages.

Student's Role

- Realize that you can learn with and from classmates of different ages.
- Give and show respect to other team members.
- Share roles and power.
- Be a valuable contributor to learning experiences. Show what you learned.
- Grow in knowledge from the experience. Ask the right questions that lead to better understanding.

FIVE (STAR) MANAGEMENT TIPS FOR MULTIAGE GROUPING

1. Create teams with teachers who believe in the benefits of multiage groupings. Elect a team coordinator who will treat each adult as a valuable, instructional member and involve everyone in decision making. Use time wisely by sharing responsibilities. For example, if one teacher creates a manipulative activity, duplicates are made for the other teachers.

2. Begin multiage groupings by taking small steps. For example, use the approach on Fridays during one class period or on two days of the week. Gradually make adjustments and add to the strategies and activities that are working effectively.

3. Group students according to their academic and social needs, not age or grade.

4. Select flexible grouping strategies that fill in learning gaps and keep students moving smoothly on their learning journeys.

5. Explain multiage grouping to parents and other members of the learning community.

Examples of Multiage Grouping

Example A: Area of Difficulty

Students from several classes and grade levels are having difficulty with a targeted skill or standard. The students meet with a special teacher to have more hands-on opportunities to learn the information. Each session provides the group with active, engaging experiences. Each introduction, discussion, and assessment emphasizes the learning process.

Example B: Theme Project

Multiage groups are formed for a schoolwide theme project. Everyone in the school becomes a member of a team. Each participating teacher is assigned a group and a place to work with the group during the scheduled time. After completion of the project, the student body participates in a schoolwide learning celebration.

Example C: Self-Contained Classroom

Students are placed in a self-contained, multiage classroom for an academic school year with one teacher. The academic growth is emphasized rather than the age of the student.

MANAGING COOPERATIVE LEARNING GROUPS

What Is a Cooperative Learning Group?

A cooperative learning group is a heterogeneous group composed of two to four students who work together as a team. Each group member has a vital role to play. On a football team, each player has an assignment and must fulfill a part for success. When one member lets the team down, the play may not gain yardage or a score. In the same way, each member of the cooperative group must fulfill his or her tasks and participate fully. The teacher strategically assigns students to groups so that they are balanced in terms of ability level, learning styles, and/or intelligences.

What Are the Instructional Benefits of Cooperative Learning Groups?

- As a student engages in discussions and other interpersonal, cognitive tasks, the brain creates memory pathways that enhance long-term memory.
- Participants' social skills are enhanced as they contribute, compromise, and respect the ideas of other individuals in a group setting.
- Students learn to share ideas, problem solve, make decisions, and come to consensus.
- Members learn the value of using individual strengths to reach the group's goal.
- Students give and take to create win-win situations for the team.

Teacher's Role

- Identify the purpose(s) of using the cooperative learning strategy.
- Assign students to their cooperative teams based on diverse abilities, backgrounds, intelligences, and/or learning styles.
- Present the task with the guidelines, expectations, and assessment tools.
- Identify specific roles and responsibilities.

    Examples

o *Captain*	*Leader*	*Director*
o *Recorder*	*Secretary*	*Scribe*
o *Messenger*	*Supply person*	*Gopher*
o *Timekeeper*	*Pacer*	*Task master*
o *Illustrator*	*Designer*	*Design director*
o *Reporter*	*Newscaster*	*Narrator*
o *Monitor*	*Checker*	*Enforcer*

- Explain the assessment tools that will be used for the team and individual team members. Engage the group in discussing what they learned and the productive social skills used by the team.

Demystifying Cooperative Learning Groups

Introduce cooperative learning groups by discussing productive teams that are familiar to students.

Examples: Sport teams, dance troupes, play casts, astronaut crew

Lead a brainstorming session for responses to the following:

- What makes a team successful?
- What happens when a team member fails to complete his or her assigned responsibilities?
- Why are roles identified for cooperative work?

Student's Role

- Agree upon a name, symbol, slogan, and cheer for the team.
- Show respect for each team member.
- Complete your assigned roles with independent and group tasks.
- Assist and support everyone for team success.
- Review the facts and skills learned independently and from the group.

★ ★ ★ ★ ★
FIVE (STAR) MANAGEMENT TIPS FOR COOPERATIVE LEARNING

1. Create groups with two to four students who get along socially so they will be cognitively productive. Unless, of course, breaking a social barrier is one of your goals. Smaller groups make students more accountable for completing tasks.

2. Establish roles and responsibilities for tasks. Be sure the students understand their individual roles and are accountable for carrying out specific assignments.

3. Give clear, specific directions with individual and group expectations.

4. Make materials and supplies accessible.

5. Select an assessment tool that places more emphasis on individual learning than group evaluation.

★ ★ ★ ★ ★

Examples of Cooperative Learning Groups

Example A: Jigsaw

A class is ready for a new chapter in the text. A section or important passage is selected for each group. The team members select or are assigned specific roles to carry out the tasks. They read the assignment, brainstorm the findings, and compile the most important information. Each group prepares a presentation for the class to teach and showcase the most valuable details in the assignment.

Example B: Think, Pair, Share

Students individually list facts learned in a lesson. They meet with an energizing partner and decide who will be Partner A and Partner B in their cooperative team. They take turns sharing and compiling facts and then brainstorm together to add to their list. Their combined list is then posted to share with the class.

Example C: Unit Review

Students form cooperative learning groups to review content information received during a unit of study. Each individual shares important facts from the lessons and activities. The students assume individual tasks such as recording the information, designing a graphic organizer, and writing a summary to create a review exhibit, poster, or game.

MANAGING RANDOM GROUPS

What Is a Random Group?

A random group is a team formed arbitrarily using luck of the draw or chance. When the task can be accomplished without consideration for the learners' commonalities, use this approach.

It gives students opportunities to work in heterogeneous groups and complete tasks with classmates who are not usually in the same group. The emphasis is on the novelty and unique way the group is formed. This promotes sharing ideas, pulling on strengths of others, and cooperating.

What Are the Instructional Benefits of Random Grouping?

- Students practice skills and learn how to work cooperatively with other peers with whom they do not normally get a chance to work.

- Success in working with a variety of groups builds self-confidence, respect, and pride.

- Communication skills improve as students interact in different learning situations.

- The mystery and novelty of the unknown grouping arrangement generates curiosity and anticipation for the upcoming lesson.

- The teacher is able to assess learners as they participate in challenging assignments in unique grouping scenarios.

Teacher's Role

- Select the most effective random grouping scenario for students to work with the identified topic, standard, or skill.

- Use a variety of strategies and techniques to form random groups. Continue to use the same approach until students become accustomed to using it. Introduce a new random grouping technique and add it to the mastered list. Some common random grouping strategies:

  Counting Off: Students number themselves by counting off to form the number of groups needed. Example: If six groups are needed, ask participants to number themselves by counting off from 1 to 6. Ask the 1s to form a group, the 2s to form a group, and so on.

  Alphabetical: Use the class roll to call names sequentially. Ask students to line up alphabetically by first or last names. The first three students form the first group. The next three students form the second group, and so on.

Birth Date: Line up according the birth month or day. The first four students form one group. The next four students form the second group. Continue until all students are in a group.

Draw Names: Write each student's name on a strip of paper, Popsicle stick, shape from the unit, or a blank card. Place the names in a hat, basket, can, envelope, box, bag, mug, or holiday container. The teacher or designated student draws names for each group from the container.

Matching Categories: Students form groups by finding matching pairs. Distribute a matched set from categories similar to the following:

Animals/habitat	Words/definition
States/capitals	Problem/solution
Pictures/captions	Chemical elements/symbols
Characters/book	Historical figure/quote
City/country	Question/answer

- Explicitly state and model the purposes, guidelines, roles, and expectations for the activity.
- Ask students to quickly and quietly form their groups.
- Identify a reflection tool for the groups to summarize everything learned in the activity.
- Be actively involved as a facilitator: monitor and assist while students engage in the activity.

Demystifying Random Grouping

Gain your students' interest in random grouping by telling them the following:

In our classroom, we will form groups in many different ways to study and learn. When we form random groups, no one will know who the group members will be. This includes the teacher because the teams will be formed by chance or luck of the draw.

Student's Role

- Greet your team members with a smile or "high five."
- Follow the rules and guidelines to create a winning team.
- Do your part as a productive group member throughout the assignment.
- Give words of encouragement when a team member fails or struggles with a task. Use praise statements when a member is successful.
- Identify the highlights learned.

FIVE (STAR) MANAGEMENT TIPS FOR RANDOM GROUPING

1. Prior to the assignment, prepare group directions and procedural steps, group formation and movement, and materials needed.

2. Vary the ways random groups are formed. Use the same scenario until students are familiar with the strategy's rules and guidelines.

3. Select a strategy that involves little movement if students have had few experiences with transitions into group work.

   Examples:

   Form a group with four other students who sit near you.

   Create a group with two other students who sit at your table.

4. Use random groups often to allow students the opportunity to work with different classmates. If a group is not productive, disperse the team and move individuals randomly to other groups.

5. Reflect on the cognitive and social lessons learned by each group member as well as the team as a whole. Provide opportunities for teams to present information in novel ways and give cheers to celebrate learning.

★ ★ ★ ★ ★

Examples of Random Grouping

Example A: Vocabulary Sort

As students enter the classroom, the teacher hands each individual a word from the unit of study. When it is time for group work, each student finds three other students who have words in the same category.

Example B: Sound Off With Numbers

Seven groups are needed to work on different sections of content information. Students count off from 1 to 7. Students with the same number form a group and select the best place to work.

Example C: Team Challenge

The class is divided into two equal teams for a review challenge using a game such as hangman or jeopardy.

MANAGING PEER TUTORING

What Is Peer Tutoring?

Often a coach assigns a player to teach, demonstrate, or give pointers to another team member on a particular skill or play. A peer can often help more than a coach, especially if there is mutual respect between the two players. Peer tutoring works in the same way, engaging one student in teaching one or more classmates. Assign students as tutors when they have the "aha" experience. This is when you hear statements that indicate understanding, such as "Yes! Now I know how to do it." When this occurs, students are excited about learning and sharing their new skill or information.

Peer tutoring needs to be a valuable experience for all students who participate. The strategy should not be used to keep students busy.

What Are the Instructional Benefits of Peer Tutoring?

- A peer tutoring session provides extra practice for the tutor and the student needing the extra help.
- Immediate, special assistance can be given to a student when the teacher is busy with another student or group.
- Both participants develop a sense of responsibility for learning.
- Tutors gain a feeling of accomplishment and confidence.
- The tutor is presented with an opportunity to take the information or skill to a deeper processing level.

Teacher's Role

- Carefully select the tutor using criteria similar to the following:
  - o The student will benefit by processing information while sharing with a peer.
  - o The student needs to build confidence through the teaching experience.
  - o The student is able to share the information in a beneficial way.
- Explain the directions and guidelines.
- Designate a place and time frame for the tutoring experience.
- Provide the tutor with appropriate teaching materials, including visuals and manipulatives.
- Check with the tutored student to find out what was learned in the experience. Express appreciation to the teaching peer for sharing.

Demystifying Peer Tutoring

Define and discuss "peer" as an equal. Emphasize the value of learners helping learners.

When an individual is working on a computer, assistance is often needed from others who have a better understanding of a program or techniques. Help is provided with step-by-step instructions to troubleshoot and solve the problem.

In the same way, a peer tutor serves as the assistant to help a classmate in need.

Student's Role (Tutor)

- Review the information or skill you will teach.

- Identify the most important term, steps, or phrases and choose the best way to teach it.

- Prepare the supplies and work area.

- Teach the skill or information in small steps or small chunks using your own explanations and examples.

- Assist, encourage, and praise the student you are tutoring.

Student's Role (Tutored)

- Learn all you can from the tutor.

- Take advantage of the opportunity to learn more about an area of weakness or a trouble spot.

- Show respect toward your tutor. Realize that this is a way to get the assistance you need.

- Stay focused on the explanation! Ask questions to get clarification when you need it.

- Rehearse and review the newly learned information with your tutor.

- Thank the tutor for helping you.

FIVE (STAR) MANAGEMENT TIPS FOR MANAGING PEER TUTORING

1. Choose a tutor who can explain the information in a way that the student will understand. Take time to give the tutor teaching guidelines and tips.

2. Provide the needed teaching supplies such as chart paper, markers, notepads, and pens.

3. Use a student who has had a "light bulb" cognitive moment as the tutor. Avoid overuse of high-end learners as peer tutors. They need opportunities to expand their knowledge base, too.

4. Give specific directions, such as the following:

   - Collect the materials and supplies you need.

   - Find a comfortable place to work.

   - Sit side by side when you work together, check work, or read from the same page or article.

   - Work quietly for _____ minutes.

   - Explain the information so the learner can understand it.

   - Move to the computer and use the _____ game for practice.

   - Follow the steps on the poster, paper, or book.

   - Work with the information on pages _____.

5. Require a product, explanation, or another form of accountability.

Examples:

- Meet with me during _____ to report on your session.
- Place your work in the "IN" basket.
- Complete the rubric and place it in your portfolio.
- Display completed work in your exhibit space.

Examples of Peer Tutoring

Example A: Catch Up

A student was absent when a new skill was introduced in a center. A peer guides the learner through each step in the activity.

Example B: Sharing an "Aha" Moment

A student reveals a "light bulb moment" in a math class saying, "Oh! I know how to work these problems now. I answered five correctly." This student is placed with a learner who is struggling with the problems.

Example C: Using an Expert

Two students need to complete an assignment using a word-processing program on their computers. A student who completed the assignment successfully is assigned as a tutor for the two learners.

CONCLUSION

The effective blending of total group, alone, partner, and small group activities is a great way to meet the needs of interpersonal learners and independent thinkers in your classroom. Put on your baseball caps to "coach" each student with the rules and guidelines for moving in and out of the grouping scenarios quickly and quietly to maximize learning time. Model the rules and guidelines. Use a variety of grouping designs such as knowledge base, ability, or interests. This gives students opportunities to work with information in different ways to meet their diverse intellectual, social, and emotional needs—and gives you a cohesive, winning team in your classroom.

IN THIS CHAPTER, WE PRESENT SOME OF THE MOST PRACTICAL and effective strategies for differentiating instruction and show how to get the most out of each approach in your classroom. Each teacher is encouraged to build a treasure trove of strategies. This is a challenging but rewarding task.

Choosing the right hat for the right occasion is valuable for making the outfit a hit! Likewise, choosing the right strategy is necessary for making the activity a hit. It is necessary to have a wide variety of hats from which to make the best selection. Teachers need a variety of instructional strategies and activities to use at the appropriate time and occasion.

STRATEGY SELECTION

In the past, a teacher gave one assignment to the total group. This general approach did not work well because often some students were frustrated by the assignment's level of difficulty and some were bored. Thankfully, there has been a paradigm shift from "one assignment fits all" to designing activities that fit each student's needs.

Like the magician, a teacher always needs a "bag of tricks" from which to pull. He or she can pull things out of the bag to stimulate, challenge, and intrigue minds. Each act is carefully planned with a beginning, a middle, and an end. Suspense builds throughout the performance. A magician turns the attention into curiosity and anticipation. The audience hangs onto every piece wondering, "How did that happen?"

> A goal of differentiated instruction is providing opportunity and support for the success of far more students than is possible in one-size-fits-all approaches to teaching and learning.
>
> —Tomlinson and McTighe (2006)

Each performance is tailored for the age and type of group in the audience. Each trick is strategically placed in the show plan. The format flow must meet the audience's needs. The trickster must assess before, during, and after the performance for quality, adjusting and revamping. Like the magician, a teacher needs to constantly reassess the timing of activities, deciding which activities use time the best.

Strategy selection is based on the assessment data gathered before, during, and after learning. Once the assessment results are analyzed and the students' strengths and weaknesses identified, the teacher determines the best strategy to present, practice, reinforce, or enhance the content standard for each learner.

Managing the differentiated classroom is easier when the teacher maintains a repertoire of instructional strategies to use in planning for individual and group needs.

The magician has some favorite tricks to place in the lineup of the program but is constantly finding new ones to ham up his or her act. Constantly, audience members try to figure out the mystery. They are challenged by the wonderment. Usually there is that most challenging trick, and the audience leaves still trying to unlock the mystery of the trick played on the mind.

Analyzing the Instructional Strategy

Strategy selection is a tactical process. When considering a new differentiated instructional strategy, ask questions similar to the following:

Is this instructional strategy . . .

- The most effective way to teach this material to this student?
- Teaching the content for the learner's understanding?
- Using accessible materials and resources?
- Appropriate for the learner's age and characteristics?
- Developing a successful, self-directed learner?

Remember, if the strategy is boring or frustrating for you, it will be 10 times more boring or frustrating for students! Be sure they understand the purpose of the strategy, have clear directions, and are able to complete the tasks independently.

Assessing the Instructional Strategy

Avoid using a strategy simply because it is in your collection. If you do not know if a strategy is effective, consider this well-known saying, "When in doubt, throw it out." In other words, if you do not recognize the benefits of a strategy, the student does not need to waste time using it.

After using a strategy, consider the following questions:

- Was the strategy effective for the learner?
- What part of the strategy was most effective? Why?
- How can I improve this strategy?
- What materials or resources do I need to make it more useful?
- Where and when can I use this again?

Evaluating the overall success of the strategy's use is a vital step in improving and planning curriculum.

Warning for Instructional Strategies

The most effective strategy becomes ineffective with an unconscious action. Use the following list to become consciously aware of these pitfalls.

Figure 4.1			
Warning	*Pitfalls*	*Examples*	*Suggested Prescriptions for Prevention*
Overkilling	Giving too many directions or too much information at one time.	All facts are presented in one teacher-directed lesson.	Present appropriate chunks of information for students to process before presenting the next chunk.
Suspending in midair	Leaving learning fragments with no links. No bridging from one lesson to another.	There is no wrap-up for the lesson on Friday. A new skill or topic is started in the next class session.	Link the current lesson with the previous lesson.
Staying in a rut	Spending too much time on one aspect of the lesson.	This often occurs when the teacher or students are carried away with their interest in a topic.	Maintain the pace of the lesson by following the instructional plans.
Flip-flopping	Moving to a new standard or skill before the first one is mastered and flip-flopping between them.	The term *latitude* is introduced, but not mastered. The term *longitude* is introduced. The discussion refers to latitude.	Complete a segment of learning and develop it before moving to the next one.
In a holding pattern	Pausing the lesson until one or two students understand a skill or procedure.	Everyone slows down or stops their work while one student receives special instruction or assistance from the teacher.	Maintain thrust or momentum during instruction. Give the student having difficulty appropriate instruction or an alternative assignment during the total group's practice session.

Giving Effective Directions

Observe your students closely when it is time to focus. Emphasize the importance of concentrating and understanding directions. Paying attention is a skill that varies. Be aware of each student's focus or listening ability so you can give individual special directions or simple reminders such as a "heads-up" signal.

A student cannot complete an assignment independently without clear and concise directions that are easy to follow. Treat each direction as a commercial to build excitement for completing the task. Begin and end each set on a high note.

- Give an established signal so everyone knows it is time for a direction.

- Explain, demonstrate, or model each step separately using terms the student understands.

- Post directions in writing. Use color coding, symbols, or pictures to emphasize each step.

- Make each direction clear, simple, and specific. Provide enough information to keep the students' attention, but not too much to confuse them.

- Provide time for students to repeat the directions before work begins. Partners may take turns going over the directions by restating them or role-playing the procedures.

Creating Buy-In to Instruction

The student has to buy into new learning for the brain to receive and retain information. In other words, in order to benefit from instruction, the learner must first open the gate to the processing center. The student's desire to learn opens and closes the gate. The individual must see a personal need for the information and want to learn it for himself or herself.

Use the following suggestions to generate buy-in:

- Build in discussion and reflection time to lead an individual to realize a need for the current or upcoming information. Give students opportunities to create meaningful connections from prior knowledge and experiences.

- Give choices to students so that they can demonstrate what they know and their thinking processes.

- Actively engage students in authentic tasks related to the learning. This creates vested, personal interest in making the new information work for their own needs.

- Plan activities that target the learner's intelligences so the student can work with the information in zones of strength. Label the intelligences in the activities to analyze the learning opportunities and methods you are using.

- Set high expectations. Show your passion and enthusiasm for the topic or skill. It's catching! Teach students to answer the following questions to create "buy-in."

  o Why do I need to learn this?

  o How will I benefit by investing my time in this activity?

  o What is the purpose of this information?

  o What is in this for me?

  o What are some ways I can link my experiences to this new information?

Don't forget to use the student's interests, sense of humor, and curiosity to create buy-in. Adding mystery and suspense to build a sense of anticipation are other effective means of generating buy-in.

After teaching the information, the question is, "Did the student learn?" If the student did not learn, ask, "Did I generate buy-in and select the most effective strategy for the unique needs of the learner?" It is important to constantly assess the learners, their needs, and the level of engagement and learning that took place during the use of a particular strategy to make sure it is a "hat" to keep.

MANAGING FOCUS ACTIVITIES

What Is a Focus Activity?

A focus activity directs the learner's attention to the current topic or skill. Carefully design it to draw the student's mind to the content information.

Though they seem similar, focus and sponge activities serve separate purposes. A sponge activity is selected for the learner's needs but does not relate to content. A focus activity is used more often because it directs attention to the current study.

What Are the Instructional Benefits of Focus Activities?

A focus activity prepares the learner's mind for the upcoming information. It leads the student to mentally engage with the task at hand.

Use these activities to spark a discussion, to bridge to new information, or to create a brainstorming list. The activity introduces content, reviews, and practices or extends learning.

Effective Focus Activities . . .

- Prepare the students' minds for learning.
- Provide more time on task for teaching and learning.
- Establish an expected daily routine.
- Demonstrate the value of time on task.
- Intrigue students so they are eager to explore the topic or skill.

Teacher's Role

- Plan a focus activity to mentally engage the learners ASAP!
- Remove distractions and post the assignment in a creative way.
- Present a purpose and compelling reason for the learner to engage in the activity.
- Provide meaningful links from the lesson to the learner's world.
- Give learners opportunities to identify their knowledge base and prior experiences with the topic or skill.

Figure 4.2

Outside the Classroom	In the Classroom	Beyond the School Doors
• Classes changing • Custodians working • Bells • Hallway noise • Traffic • Talking • Weather • School events	• On the wrong page • Unrelated thoughts • Intercom messages • People coming in and going out • Movement of students • Talking • Social interests • Special guests	• Dispute with someone • New pet • Family addition • Family conflict • Illness • Upcoming event • Disaster • Performance • Holiday or birthday

Demystifying Focus Activities

Introduce focus activities by discussing the purpose of the focus devices on cameras, binoculars, microscopes, and video recorders. Explain that it eliminates the people or objects outside of the important view and makes what is critical to the shot clearer or easier to see. In the same way, the brain has the ability to focus. Each student can train the brain to cut out thoughts, feelings, and visual images to tune in to important information. When the mind needs to receive and work with the vital information without interference, focus control is used.

Challenge students to list the distractions they often experience during instruction or at home. See Figure 4.2.

Discuss how students can use their focus control to deal with these distractions. Teach them techniques to manage a focused mind.

Examples:

- **Practice active listening:** Focus all of your attention on the person talking.
- **Probe with questions and restate response:** Ask for more details and clarification, if needed.
- **Be aware of the need to focus:** When the brain begins to wander off task, clear your mind and refocus.
- **Take notes:** Some people think and focus best when they make eye, hand, and mind connections.
- **Take a break:** When confused or stressed, take a deep breath or mini mental break to reduce tension, and then come back to the task. For example: remember your favorite joke or a funny movie bit.

Student's Role

- Gather and organize the materials and supplies you need.
- Unclutter your mind and prepare your brain to think about the task at hand.
- Be sure you understand the directions or guidelines.
- Do your best on the activity.
- Be prepared to share your work.

FIVE (STAR) MANAGEMENT TIPS FOR FOCUS ACTIVITIES

1. Establish general guidelines for focus activities. Choose a signal or identify a specific time for the focus activities to begin.

2. Select or design activities that challenge students to think about the upcoming lesson segment.

3. Determine the best way to give the directions to the students: They may be written or oral, displayed, or distributed.

4. Engage the learner using higher level thinking skills, including problem solving, questioning techniques, organizing thoughts, and gathering information.

5. Use a variety of grouping strategies that engage students in exciting and novel focus tasks. Include mystery activities, scavenger hunts, puzzles, or games.

★ ★ ★ ★ ★

Examples of the Effective Use of Focus Activities
Example A: Entering the Class

An artifact related to the topic or skill is displayed on a table in the center of the room. The teacher hands each student an index card with the following directions:

1. Record three words that describe the _____.

2. Predict three ways _____ will be important in our study of _____.

3. Share and compile your words and predictions with a partner.

Example B: Moving From One Group to Another Group

The following directions are posted, handed to, or stated to students:

1. On your way to our group, think of a story you have read or heard that relates to the topic we started yesterday.

2. Jot your ideas on a sticky note.

3. When you join the group, take turns giving the highlights of your story and tell how it relates to the information we learned yesterday.

Example C: Ending Class

The lesson ends 10 minutes earlier than expected. Students use their books for a review scavenger hunt. The teacher names important facts, words, places, characters, or events for students to quickly locate in the text.

MANAGING SPONGE ACTIVITIES

What Is a Sponge Activity?

A sponge activity fills gaps in instructional time caused by interruptions, early completions, or emergencies and allows the teacher to use time wisely before, between, or after learning segments. It addresses student needs, such as reenergizing the brain, but does not necessarily address content. Sponge activities are designed to benefit learners. They can be challenging, exciting, or humorous and may be presented as games, mind teasers, competitions, puzzles, or songs.

What Are the Instructional Benefits of Sponge Activities?

- A sponge activity is planned as a time filler to relax and recharge the brain. It gives the mind a time break from the stress of learning curriculum information. This relaxes the body and mind.
- These activities use time wisely when
  - An administrator, teacher, or parent needs to talk to you for a few minutes during a lesson.
  - The class is waiting to be called to an assembly or program.
  - The lesson ends before it is time for the classes to change.
  - A scheduled speaker is late.
  - An emergency occurs that engages the teacher.
- Smooth transitions occur with activities such as games or songs.
- Specific skills are enhanced using fun and stimulating activities.
- Students can use the time to socialize and enjoy being with classmates.

Teacher's Role

- Decide when to use a sponge activity instead of a brief assignment or a focus activity.
- Build a repertoire of sponge activities to fill various lengths of time and retain novelty.
- Create activities based on students' interests, favorite songs, or current fads.
- Select sponge activities to suit specific purposes and student needs.

Examples:

  - The students have worked on a mind-draining task. They need to relax the mind, so provide free time.
  - Students have been in one position too long. They need to stand, stretch, exercise in place, or move to another place.
  - A segment of a test or a special assignment is completed. Take a relaxing break by going to the restroom, get a drink of water, or visit with a neighbor.
  - Students need a different environment. Oxygen feeds the brain, so take them on a brisk walk.
  - The learners need a reward. Allow them to play a game.
- Beware of overusing sponge activities. They can absorb valuable instructional time.

Demystifying Sponge Activities

Give students the description of a sponge activity. It is used when there is extra time or a break is needed. Sponge activities use time wisely to relax, to exercise the brain and the body, or to have fun. You may be given time to take a walk, play a game, stretch, or have free-choice activities.

Student's Role

- Listen to the directions and complete the activity following the rules or guidelines.
- Assist classmates.
- Suggest sponge activities the class can use. Prepare to showcase the activity or skill.
- Take advantage of the time to clear cobwebs from your mind.
- Enjoy!

FIVE (STAR) MANAGEMENT TIPS FOR SPONGE ACTIVITIES

1. Identify skills or activities the students need that are unrelated to the lesson. Present sponge activities to enhance skills or citizenship such as the following:

Relaxation	Movement	Following directions
Taking turns	Listening	Courtesy

2. Prepare a toolkit of sponge activities to use before and after lessons:

   Physical exercises   Songs   Brain games   Competitions

3. Limit the time and use sponges wisely. Keep activities handy to match the amount of time and tone needed for quiet and still activities or active and noisy activities.

4. Allow students to lead their favorite sponge activities.

5. Socializing counts! Give students opportunities to interact. This is relaxing. It also gives students time to share and clear their thoughts before they need to concentrate on the lesson.

Examples of Effective Use of Sponge Activities

Example A: Completion of a Difficult Assignment

Ask students to stand and do some teacher-directed stretching exercises.

Example B: An Emergency Occurs That Engages the Teacher

Appoint a student as the sponge activity leader for a familiar game or song.

Example C: Students Are Entering the Room

Let students engage in a quiet activity of their choice for a brief period of time. Set a timer.

Managing Anchor Activities

What Is an Anchor Activity?

An anchor activity is a privileged task provided to engage the student when all teacher-directed assignments are complete. The task is linked to the current topic of study. For example, when a student completes the customized assignment, an anchor activity is available. Carol Ann Tomlinson refers to this as "ragged time." The activity supports the information in the current study. Each one is designed to engage students in meaningful experiences after they complete assignments.

In a differentiated classroom, individuals and small groups usually finish their tasks at different times. Often, when students complete class assignments, the time is filled with busywork or downtime. An anchor activity keeps learners from drifting too far from the study topic and engages them in an intriguing task connected to the current content area.

What Are the Instructional Benefits of Anchor Activities?

An anchor activity is designed to reinforce, practice, or extend concepts and skills related to the current study.

- They engage learners in meaningful activities.
- The choices develop self-directed, independent learners.
- Each one is presented as a privilege for completing tasks thoroughly and correctly.
- They give the teacher uninterrupted time to work with individuals and small groups.
- Students do not have to ask, "What do I do when I finish?"

Teacher's Role

- Plan an anchor activity that is appealing and enjoyable so students will be eager to do the additional work.
- Analyze the learning standards, skills, and concepts to make sure you design worthwhile tasks when creating an anchor activity. The tasks should focus on standards or skills that didn't receive as much coverage during the primary assignment as planned. The activities may be designed for review or reinforcement of needed skills identified on ongoing assessments.
- List the activities in a highly visible space such as the board, a large chart, or a choice design.
- Explain directions before students begin an anchor activity.
- Teach and remind students that an anchor activity is a privilege for learners who complete the assigned work to the best of their ability.

Demystifying Anchor Activities

Discuss the common definitions of the term *anchor,* including "to hold in place and to keep a vessel from drifting." An anchor activity is tied to the current study. It is available to individuals, partners, and small groups to review, to practice skills, or to explore the major topic.

Student's Role

- Complete and review assigned class work before moving on to an anchor activity.
- If choices are provided, select the one that sounds the most interesting to you and carefully follow the directions.
- Work quietly.
- If you need assistance, ask other classmates who are also finished with the assigned class work when the teacher is working with other students.
- Clean the work space and organize the materials before you leave the area.

FIVE (STAR) MANAGEMENT TIPS FOR ANCHOR ACTIVITIES

1. Design the anchor activity based on student needs. Make each one appealing and rewarding.
2. Decide if the activity needs to be designed for one lesson, two to three days, the length of the unit, or the grading period.
3. Most anchor activities will not be designed for assessment. However, if an activity needs to be assessed, provide materials and supplies students can use to check or grade independently with a partner or in a small group.

Examples:

    Answer keys   Checklist rubrics   Likert scales   Journal entries

4. Teach students how to move to the anchor activity when work is completed without disturbing classmates. Give clear directions, answer questions, and have materials ready for smooth transitions from the assigned task to the anchor activity.
5. Identify a space for students to display their finished products.

Examples of Anchor Activities

Example A: Using Content Art

A space for a unit of study mural, collage, or poster is designated for an anchor activity in a special area of the room. Students make creative additions to the ongoing project.

Example B: Using a Brainteaser Game

Students create or play games to reinforce information in the study.

Example C: Using a Scene Reenactment

Students design and write parts to role-play the important passages or scenes in a studied event.

MANAGING CUBING ACTIVITIES

What Is a Cubing Activity?

Cubing is an intriguing organizational technique that uses a game format to challenge the student's mind. Six options are provided that allow students to work with information from a current category, standard, skill, or topic. One activity, word, or question is written on each facet of a cube or six-sided shape. The student rolls the cube and is assigned the activity that comes up on top.

The six options can also be numbered and presented on a flat surface such as a bulletin board, overhead, board, or chart. By rolling a die, using a spinner, or selecting a number at random, the student is assigned the activity that corresponds with his or her number.

Cubing activities are designed by the teacher or students for work in total groups, alone, with partners, or in small groups. Each selection is coordinated with the content and targets the learners' needs.

What Are the Instructional Benefits of Cubing Activities?

Cubing activities engage students in learning because the activities present a variety of challenges. The students enjoy the gaming aspect that comes with the luck of the roll, draw, or spin. This strategy is designed to meet individual and small group needs in all content areas and grade levels.

Cubing activities:

- Are planned with content standards, concepts, skills, or steps in procedures
- Review, teach, reinforce, or extend lessons
- May be used as assessment tools before, during, and after learning
- Promote discussion and information processing
- Challenge students within their level of success, so they will not be bored or frustrated

Cubing is a flexible, instructional tool. It can be used with individuals, partners, or groups in a focus activity, a learning zone task, an assessment, or a homework assignment.

Teacher's Role

- Design the cubing activity
    1. Identify the purpose(s) of the cubing activity.
    2. Select the cubing form.
         Examples: *cube, grid, list*
         Provide directions for planning and creating the selected cubing activity.
         Clarify directions and answer questions if necessary.
    3. Identify a noun or category from the current study such as an artifact, date, event, character, term, or setting as the focus for the cubing activity. Decide if the activity is going to revolve around one noun or several nouns in the same category. For example, ask, "Is the cubing activity going to focus on one president, such as Abraham Lincoln, or will each group be assigned a different president?"
    4. Choose six activities or questions and write them in or on the selected form.
- Decide if students need to work alone, with a partner or in a small group.
- Decide which method students will use to identify their cubing number.

Examples:

- ○ Roll the cube with an option written on each side of it.
- ○ Roll a die or numbered cube.
- ○ Use a spinner.
- ○ Write a secret number, 1, 2, 3, 4, 5, or 6, before the six options are revealed.
- ○ Number off the group members from 1 to 6.
- ○ Assign a number to each team member.

- • Give materials and directions for playing the game. See Student's Role below.
- • Use cubing activities often. They can enhance instruction across the curriculum, in student-centered or teacher-centered activities.

Demystifying Cubing

Show students a cube. Introduce or review the definition of a cube emphasizing the six facets. Explain that there will be six ways to approach the selected topic:

> When playing a board game that uses dice, the number rolled determines the number of spaces the player moves. In our cubing activities, the number may be identified by rolling the dice, by using a spinner, drawing a secret number, counting off, or it may be assigned.

Student's Role

- • Determine your cubing number by following the teacher's directions.
- • Read the directions for the activity that match your mystery number.
- • Complete the activity for your number.
- • Review the skills or facts you learned.
- • Be prepared to share with your group.

FIVE (STAR) MANAGEMENT TIPS FOR CUBING ACTIVITIES

1. Introduce cubing activities using a large numbered cube. Create a cube from foam, posterboard, or a box. Die cutters often include patterns for cubes.

2. Once students understand the cubing strategy, move to variations of the activity. Place the six options in a different form such as a grid, a list, or in a unique design.

3. Create the list of six activity options that match content noun(s). (See examples below.)

4. Use the cubing method to assign activities for centers, oral reports, projects, daily work, cooperative groups, or homework assignments.

5. Establish a second-chance rule. If the student does not want to keep the first activity number, a second roll or selection turn is an option. *The original number cannot be used, however, if the student chooses to use the second-chance option.*

Examples of Cubing Activities

Example A: Cubing as a Research Activity

During or after a study, select six important subtopics, terms, events, or procedures that are a valuable use of time for the learner. Place the numbers 1 through 6 on small cards in a basket. Make numbered sets to match the number of students in the class. The students form research teams according to the drawn number. This may be used for individual research activities.

Example for research of a city, state, providence, or country:

Figure 4.3		
1. Landmarks	2. Rivers	3. Major Cities
4. Famous People	5. Historical Sites	6. Products

Example B: Cubing With an Object or Artifact

At the close of a unit, place an object or artifact in the work area of each cooperative group. Give each group a spinner with the numbers 1 to 6. On the board, list directions using key words from different levels of Bloom's taxonomy. Each individual spins, reads the corresponding activity, records the answer, and responds to the group.

Sample cubing list:

1. Compare the object with another object.
2. Give a definition for it.
3. Ask someone a question about it.
4. Identify the object's attributes.
5. Predict what will happen to it.
6. Brainstorm uses of the object.

Example C: Cubing With Genres

List six genres on a poster in a center, such as the following:

1. Billboard	2. Editorial	3. Fictitious story
4. Newscast	5. Interview	6. Cartoon

Post the following instructions:

- Roll the number cube to identify the genre to use.
- Write about _____ using your genre selection.

Example D: Cubing With Homework

As students prepare to leave at the end of the day or class period, each one rolls a number cube to identify the homework assignment from the list of options.

Display a list of five to seven vocabulary words with six homework options:

1. Create a crossword puzzle using all of the words. Use the meaning of each word as the key.

2. Design a graffiti board writing the words and their definitions in various colors, fonts, shapes, and designs.

3. Write a mystery paragraph using at least three of the words and a synonym for each one.

4. Design an advertisement using at least four of the vocabulary words.

5. Create a silly story using all of the vocabulary words or their antonyms.

6. Draw a cartoon using at least three of the words in speech bubbles.

MANAGING CHOICE BOARDS

What Is a Choice Board?

A choice board provides a selected list of activities that target the specific needs of students. Each activity is directly linked to the standards, skills, or unit being taught and is student focused so it can be completed with little or no teacher assistance. The choices can be presented in a grid, or on a list. They may be placed creatively on or around a palm tree or rocket.

Choice boards or designs are flexible tools that may be used by the total class, individuals, partners, or small groups in all areas of the curriculum and all grade levels. They may be placed in a learning zone or assigned as part of an agenda, project, contract, or other student-directed task.

What Are the Instructional Benefits of Using Choice Boards?

Students who are given choices become more responsible for transferring the information. When students choose activities in their areas of strength and interest, they are more comfortable with the learning process. They are more likely to show what they know when working in their favorite styles or modalities.

Choice boards:

- Are designed to meet the needs of individuals and small groups
- Teach, reinforce, practice, or enhance learning
- Give learners opportunities to select the ways they want to show what they know
- Enrich homework assignments, independent activities, or center work
- Give students ownership in their learning

Teacher's Role

- Identify the purpose of the choice board.

  Examples:

  To teach, practice, or review a standard, skill, or topic

  To debut a character

  To work with vocabulary words

- Determine the most suitable choice activity design to fit the learning situation and match the content information. For example, use an outline of a symbol from the unit or a seasonal design.

- Brainstorm a list of activities that will meet the learner's needs. Write each activity on a sticky note.

Figure 4.4

Identifying Keepers and Losers
Ask yourself the following questions to see if the activity you are assessing
"measures up" and should be a keeper.

☐ *Does the activity address the content standard and meet the student's needs?* The item must provide a learning experience in which the student practices, reinforces, enhances, or assesses the content focus. If it does not, eliminate it from the list of possibilities.

☐ *Is the activity a valuable learning experience?* If it is busywork and a time waster, omit it from the list of possibilities.

☐ *Will it take the "right amount of time" to complete the activity?* Analyze the time it will take most students to complete each activity. For example, if an item takes five minutes and other activities take 20 minutes, you probably need to eliminate the five-minute activity. Be sure the activity can be completed in the allotted time frame.

☐ *Are materials and resources available for the activities?* If you must purchase materials or spend valuable time finding items for an activity, remove it from the list.

☐ *Can students work on the activities with little or no adult supervision?* Is each activity (a) student focused, (b) age appropriate, and (c) within the learner's range of success? If not, it is a loser.

☐ *Is it easy to assess?* If you have to design a separate assessment tool, eliminate the item.

- Use the "Keeper and Loser" criteria checklist to identify the best activities from the brainstormed list. These are the "keepers." Eliminate the "losers."
- Place the keepers on the choice board or design.

Demystifying Choice Boards

Introduce the term *choice* by discussing the value of knowing how to make decisions. Ask students how and when they make choices in their daily activities outside of school, such as their selection of a video game, snacks, clothes to wear, or programs to watch. Emphasize that a special assignment with choices is a privilege. Talk to the class about the value of making wise activity selections.

Student's Role
- Read or listen to the directions for the choice board or design.
- Make a selection that's best for you—don't allow others to influence your decision!
- Follow directions to complete the selected activities.
- Ask two classmates before going to the teacher if you need help with the activity.
- Follow the directions to display, turn in, or store your work.

FIVE (STAR) MANAGEMENT TIPS FOR MANAGING CHOICE BOARDS

1. Create choice boards that use the information related to the standard or objectives of the study.

2. Provide activity choices that use a variety of intelligences or learning styles to ensure that the individual needs of your students are met.

3. When some students are on the readiness level and some are on the advanced/mastery level, try this activity arrangement: use odd numbers for practice activities designed for students on the readiness level and use even-numbered items for activities designed for students on the advanced mastery level.

4. Create choice boards designed to
   • Assess before, during, or after learning
   • Respond to a text
   • Solve a problem
   • Debut a character
   • Teach, review, or enrich

5. Present choices in novel, inviting ways so students are eager to work with the activities. Use intriguing graphics, colors, and fonts. Use designs or symbols from the content to present choices. Add interest-grabbing titles such as *Quick Pick*.

★ ★ ★ ★ ★

Examples of Choice Board Activities

Example A: Choice Boards for Adjustable Assignments

Find your level. Select three activities under your level to complete.

Figure 4.5		
Level 1	*Level 2*	*Level 3*
1.	1.	1.
2.	2.	2.
3.	3.	3.
4.	4.	4.
5.	5.	5.
Rewinding	**Grade Level**	**Fast-Forwarding**

Example B: Choice Boards for Presentations

Choose an activity from the list to support your research project.

Oral report	Mini-posters display	PowerPoint presentation
Simulation	Diorama demonstration	Make a notebook

Example C: Choice Activities as Test Bonus Points

Place five facts learned on a graphic organizer.
Make a list of _____.
Select a vocabulary word that was not on the test. Define it.
Draw pictures to illustrate _____.

Choice Board Themes

Figure 4.6

August	September	October	November	December
Stars School items Summer items	Fall things Leaves Trees	Leaves Pumpkin patch Apples	Thanksgiving items Election items	Holiday items D-Day
January	**February**	**March**	**April**	**May**
Fireworks Snowman Snowflakes	Valentines Winter items Lincoln hats	Spring symbols Wind Shamrocks Lamb/lion	Hats Flowers Butterflies Rain	Summer objects Maypole Memorial Day

General Choice Activity Shapes/Designs

The following list of shapes may be used with content themes as choice designs:

Wheel	Book	Hand	Octopus	Pyramid	Star
Scroll	Tic-tac-toe board	Bingo board	Flower	Tree	Steps

Figure 4.7

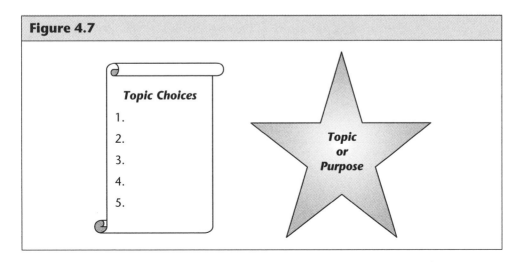

Book Report Choices

Figure 4.8

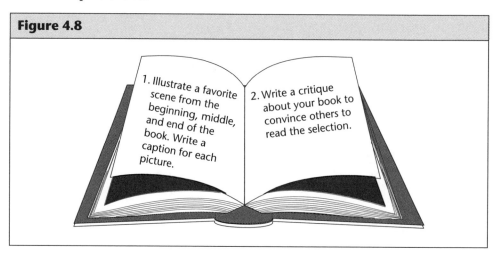

1. Illustrate a favorite scene from the beginning, middle, and end of the book. Write a caption for each picture.

2. Write a critique about your book to convince others to read the selection.

Figure 4.9

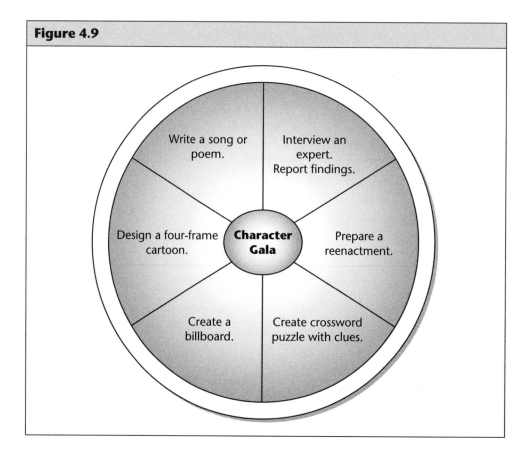

Write a song or poem.

Interview an expert. Report findings.

Design a four-frame cartoon.

Character Gala

Prepare a reenactment.

Create a billboard.

Create crossword puzzle with clues.

MANAGING GRAPHIC ORGANIZERS

What Is a Graphic Organizer?

A graphic organizer is a design, drawing, or shape used to categorize or organize data related to a certain topic. It is a visual/spatial and logical/mathematical means of arranging thoughts and plotting key information.

A variety of graphics can be used as organizers, from basic grids and boxes connected by lines to more elaborate shapes for holidays and unit themes. The form chosen for the organizer depends on the intended use: to categorize information, to retain information associated with a shape, or to plot data.

What Are the Instructional Benefits of Using Graphic Organizers?

A graphic organizer is a picture for the mind to associate with the words placed on it. This mental image assists the brain as it stores and retrieves the associated information.

A graphic organizer provides a place to plot thoughts around an idea. Often this is more exciting than writing sentences and paragraphs. Since organizers can be any shape or design, these graphics offer a variety of choices to fit the topic. They work for many students. Some learners can use graphics easier than writing the information in paragraph form.

A workable organizer that fits the information is an invaluable start for brainstorming ideas and plotting information. This is a way to sort, classify, and identify relationships between thoughts and ideas. It can stand alone as a writing activity or be used as an excellent prewriting activity.

Organizers present information in a design that gives the learners the freedom to plot the needed facts or data in their own creative way. These experiences teach students how to arrange information in a personal logical format. Graphic organizers are beneficial note-taking tools for independent or group brainstorming. They can be used to present assignments for plotting the key points of a partner or group discussion, a reading passage, a homework assignment, or a test question.

Teacher's Role

- Introduce and model each graphic organizer. To effectively model an organizer, use it several times during direct instruction and while leading group discussions. Use it in several different subject areas to show that the same graphic organizer can be used across the curriculum.

- Have students work with a new graphic organizer in partner, small group, or independent assignments. Have students share their products and explain the placement of the information.

- Allow students to choose their own graphic organizer from the designs that have been used and modeled in the classroom. This gives each learner the opportunity to plot information in a manner that is most effective and memorable.

- Add to your list of organizers so learners expand their toolbox.

- Provide adequate time for a student to add more information and place it in a personal way when assessing use of an organizer.

Demystifying Graphic Organizers

When you draw a picture to depict a thought or plot information on a graphic organizer, you remember the information because of the design. You use the organizer because it is easier to remember than sentences or paragraphs.

Show students familiar graphic organizers such as family trees and television schedules. Discuss the information and where it is plotted. Discuss why each piece of information is on the graphic.

Student's Role

- Learn the purpose(s) of each graphic organizer. Watch your teacher carefully when a new organizer is modeled to understand where and each piece of information is plotted and why it is placed there.

- Contribute to the discussion when working with a partner or group. Give your input on where each piece of data belongs in the organizer.

- Choose and use the graphic organizer that best suits the information to be plotted.

- Learn and become comfortable with as many organizers as possible so you have a wide selection of study tools.

★ ★ ★ ★ ★

FIVE (STAR) MANAGEMENT TIPS FOR USING GRAPHIC ORGANIZERS

1. Explain, model, and provide guided practice with each graphic organizer before using it as an independent assignment.

2. Watch for ruts! Familiarize yourself with a broad assortment of graphic organizers and challenge yourself to use as many as possible during the year to present your students with many options.

3. Graphic organizers are great tools for planning and assessing a lesson. Choose the organizer that suits the topic and situation when teaching content information.

4. Don't be afraid to create a new graphic organizer! Try it out before presenting it.

5. Remember that picture organizers appeal to the visual/spatial part of the brain, while matrix and sequence organizers appeal to the logical/mathematical part of the mind. To address the individual learning styles of your students, it is important to allow them opportunities to select their own graphic organizers from a choice board.

★ ★ ★ ★ ★

Examples of Graphic Organizers

Example A: T Chart

Introduce the T chart using two vocabulary words by drawing the letters in large, bold colors. Select two nouns from the content information to explore, and write them on each

Figure 4.10	
Noun A	*Noun B*

side of the "T" as category titles. From discussions or text reading, guide students to select information that gives more detail about each noun. At another time, assign a T chart organizer and have partner groups to plot the attributes of two different nouns from the study.

Example B: Picture Vocabulary—Word and Meaning

1. Each student folds a piece of paper into six equal sections.

2. The teacher assigns six new words that have meanings that can be illustrated.

3. The students write one word in each box. After reading the meaning of the word in the text, each student draws a picture with the definition under the word in the box.

4. The completed pages are shared with a partner and used later as a study sheet for a test.

Example C: Weekly Journaling Hand

1. Have students draw a hand shape in their personal journals on Monday.

2. Instruct them to write the days of the week on each finger.

3. Above the finger tip for Monday, each student writes the most important fact learned that day.

4. Tell students to add a new entry each week day. At the end of the week, they will have five reflective facts for review.

MANAGING CENTERS, STATIONS, AND LEARNING ZONES

What Are Centers, Stations, and Learning Zones?

Centers, stations, and learning zones are synonymous terms for designated areas where students can find hands-on, learner-focused, problem-solving activities. Each one is designed to provide students with opportunities to explore, practice, and work with content information. The activities may reteach, extend, and enrich current learning areas or lead students to discover new subject matter. After third grade, consider using the age-appropriate term *stations* or *learning zones* for centers.

What Are the Instructional Benefits of Using Centers, Stations, and Learning Zones?

Centers, stations, and learning zones are designed to accomplish several objectives simultaneously to meet the diverse needs of individuals or groups. Structured and exploratory activities can be presented. Each area is customized for students to work with specific skills and creative or critical thinking.

Other instructional benefits are listed below:

- A structured center is established for students to work with specific standards, skills, or procedures within their ability and knowledge level. The activity rules and guidelines are established.

- In an exploratory center, the rules are established and materials are provided. Learners create or problem solve in their own way.

- The teacher is able to assess the learner's knowledge base and understanding as the student explains the thinking process.

- Choices are offered that address individual learning styles and intelligences to challenge minds.

- Students learn to take responsibility for staying on task, furthering their own learning, and using time wisely.

Teacher's Role

- Plan, develop, and name each center or station. Label it with a title that coordinates with the subject area and/or grade level.

- While designing a center, use questions similar to the following to create a quality work area:
  - Is it student centered?
  - After receiving directions and rules, can the student be a productive worker at the center with little or no adult supervision?
  - Are multileveled activities included to fill learning gaps and present challenges for the students?
  - Does the work area provide practice and enrichment?
  - Is it designed to promote critical and creative thinking?

- Decide how many students can work productively at each center. Post the number.
- Introduce each center. Provide clear directions for the activities and explain the rules. Topics to address include the following:
  - Acceptable noise levels
  - Proper use and care of materials
  - Directions for moving in and out of centers
  - Setup and cleanup procedures
  - Directions for the activity with expectations and adventures a student explores in each center
- Model! Model! Model! Illustrate the correct use of centers via role-playing and demonstrations.
- Adopt one of the following procedures for students to move to and from each work area:

  Rotation: Each student works in a center for a set amount of time. Everyone moves to the next center at the sound of a signal.

  Choice: The first group of students chooses a center. The next group selects an available center.

  Assigned: The teacher assigns groups or individuals to centers with activities designed for their specific learning needs.

Demystifying Centers, Stations, and Zones

Explain to students that centers, stations, and learning zones are work areas set up to help them learn more about a topic or skill. Discuss the fact that they may be assigned to work there alone, with a partner, or with a small group. Emphasize that the materials and supplies are shared with other classmates, so they need to be used with care and stored properly. Also stress the importance of cleaning and organizing the area before leaving it. Point out that the learning zones are created for explorations, discoveries, and inventions. Use an explanation similar to the following:

> When inventors or artists work, they explore and work in a specific area where the materials and basic supplies are used. They rely on their knowledge and creative minds often without assistance from experts in their field. They analyze the task to learn and improve their product, skills, or process. The tasks are completed in one or several sessions. The materials are stored properly so they are ready to use the next time.

Student's Role

- Learn the rules and procedures for center time.
- Receive your assigned center from the teacher or select a place to work.
- Move quickly and quietly into and out of a center.

Figure 4.11	*Learning Zone Materials List*	
Brain Booster Center	*Writing Center*	*Reading Center*

Games
Board games
Card games
Television games
Computer games
Handheld games
Mind games
 	
Puzzles
Board puzzles
Floor puzzles
Crossword puzzles
Sudoku
Logic
Jigsaw
Anagram
	Writing Implements
	Pencils
	Pens
	Crayons
	Chalk
	Markers
	Colored pencils
	
	Materials
	Paper in varied colors,
	    shapes, sizes
	Paper with and without
	    lines
	Gel bags
	Salt trays
	Wipe-off boards
	
	Reference Tools
	Pictionaries
	Word walls
	Boxed word files
	Unit dictionaries and facts
	Thesaurus
	
	Computers
	Topic References
	Research References
		Reference Tools
		Class-made books
		Dictionaries
		Thesaurus
		Word lists
		Students' writing
		
		Factual Materials
		Trivia books Fact books
		Unit reading materials
		Newspapers
		Brochures
		Magazines
		Computer Web access
		Leveled materials
		Facts about interests
		
		Fiction Materials
		Favorite books and stories
		Poetry
		Songs
		Comic books

Skills Center	*Art Center*	*Listening Center*

Manipulatives
Visuals
Examples
  Leveled activity folders:
    Levels 1, 2, 3
  Self-checking keys
  Computers
	Variety of Art Media
	Scissors
	Glue
	Paste
	Tape
	Easel and paints
	Markers
	Colored pencils
	Paper in different colors,
	    shapes, sizes, and textures
	
	Display Areas
	Clothesline
	Table
	Doors
	Walls
	Bulletin board
		Headphones
		Listening stations
		CDs/CD Player
		DVD players/DVDs
		Computers
		Tape recorder
		Class-written books
		Factual and nonfiction
		    books
		Music pieces

★ ★ ★ ★ ★

**FIVE (STAR) MANAGEMENT TIPS FOR USING
CENTERS, STATIONS, AND LEARNING ZONES**

1. Begin slowly.
   • Refer to these activities with age-appropriate titles. For example, use *centers* for the younger students and *stations* or *learning zones* for older students. When the age-appropriate name is used, more students buy into using the activities.
   • Establish one or two centers to acclimate students to center use. Increase requirements and the number of centers as your students become comfortable with the strategy.

2. Prepare more center and station selections than the number of students in the room. Make choice activities available when assigned activities are complete. This provides more options on free-choice center days.

3. Make needed resources and materials accessible. If there is no space to store materials in or near the center, designate a shelf, crate, or half of a supply cabinet as "student accessible." And let your students know where they can find their materials.

4. Provide a place where students can proudly display their completed projects and products.

5. Design "Open" and "Closed" signs.
   • When a center or station is not working because you observe a disturbance or a rule being broken, post the "Closed" sign at the center. Do not give students second chances. "Nip it in the bud" when the disruption is observed. Reopen the center after you conduct a class meeting, discuss the problem, and review your expectations. Reopen the center with a celebration.
   • If students dread going to a center, close it. Negative feelings are evident by deep sighs and avoidance. Keep the center closed until you add some pizzazz to it. Students often have ideas to improve the work area. Make necessary changes and reopen the center with a big advertisement that reflects the changes or additions.

   ★ ★ ★ ★ ★

• Follow the written or oral directions in each center and complete the tasks to the best of your ability.

• Clean and organize the center when you are finished working, preparing it for the next learner.

Examples of Effective Centers, Stations, and Learning Zones at Work

Example A: Guiding Students From a Structured Activity to an Exploratory Option in One Work Area

Once a structured assignment is completed, add exploratory options to engage the student longer in a productive activity at one center.

Structured Center Assignment

During a lesson in a social studies unit, the students enter a "Create a _____ Center." They invent the new object using posted step-by-step procedures such as the following:

1. Invent a new _____ using the materials in an assigned box.

2. Draw a picture to scale of the new invention.

3. List the attributes.

4. Draw the background using the related information.

5. Display _____ (the product) in your assigned space.

6. Return unused materials to the box.

Exploratory Option

Now it is the student's turn to use the available materials in the box to design and create anything. This moves the learner from using a structured center to an exploratory option. This keeps students engaged in productive activities for a longer time period in one location.

Example B: Presenting Multiple Options

Create a choice board that supports the center's objective.

The students at the station complete the assigned reading selection. Each student selects an activity related to the reading from the "After Reading Choice Board" posted in the station. The student gathers any materials the activity requires from the designated shelf or cabinet before beginning the chosen assignment.

Example C: Transitioning From Center to Center

Give specific directions for the student to follow when tasks are completed and the area is clean so the student knows to automatically move to a specific center or area.

After completing an experiment in the center, the group tidies up and returns any unused materials and equipment to their proper storage spaces. Students move their desks together or go to a designated space to draw and/or write the steps used in the experiment experience.

Remember, quality is more important than quantity.

MANAGING AGENDAS OR MENUS

What Is an Agenda or Menu?

An agenda or menu is a purposefully planned list of ongoing activities that personalize independent work assignments. These terms are used as synonyms in this resource. An agenda or menu is a list of assignments for independent or group work. They are tailored for specific needs that are identified in the assessment results. They may be assigned to a student or group who is not ready for the class assignment, or they may be assigned as more challenging tasks. They may be presented on paper, a dry-erase board, in a folder, or on a chart.

An agenda is usually given for a designated period of time. Tasks are selected by the teacher. These activities are designed specifically for the learner's needs: to fill in the learning gaps, to work with grade-level skills and materials, or to fast-forward the curriculum.

What Are the Instructional Benefits of Agendas?

An agenda can be adapted to the needs of individual students at all grade levels in all curriculum areas. Design it for the student to use during one class period, a day, a week, or a grading period.

- Agenda items presented as a list of activities are customized to meet the student's particular needs on his or her level of readiness.
- The student selects the order of the activities.
- The student works independently learning how to take responsibility for completing tasks with little adult supervision.
- The learner works at the appropriate pace.
- The student learns to manage personal time.

Teacher's Role

- Identify the students who need an agenda assignment using assessment data.
- Create a form with the list of teacher-selected activities based on the unit of study. The standards and skills are customized for individual learners.
- Include a timeline for checkpoints with the completion date.
- Talk to the student about agenda work. Explain the agenda's guidelines for each activity on the list, the assessment tool, and your expectations.
- Vary assignment using the learner's learning styles, intelligences, and modalities. A student working with an agenda needs to work with activities and materials that are appropriate to challenge the mind.

Examples of agenda items:

Complete your activity from the cube.

Choose two items from the choice board.

Write a journal entry related to _____.

Use the _____ to create a replica of _____.

(Continued)

(Continued)

Read the selection and take notes.

Complete a computer assignment.

Complete three activities in the _____ station.

Plot the information on the graphic organizer.

Create a collage.

Record your step-by-step thinking as you complete_____.

Solve the following problem and explain how you solved it.

Create a song, rap, or poem using fact about _____.

Demystifying Agendas and Menus

Introduce the various uses of the words *agenda* and *menu* in terms students understand such as the following:

> An agenda or menu is a list of items. When you attend a program, there is often a list of events that occur. When you plan your after-school activities for an afternoon, this becomes your list or agenda. Lists are often taken to the grocery store so items can be checked off as they are placed in the basket. Recipes consist of a list of ingredients with directions to complete.

In a few schools, students refer to their assignment notebooks as agendas. While most students have likely heard the question, "What is on your agenda today?" some may be more familiar with other uses of the term. Explain that an agenda or menu assignment is a list of activities that are to be completed within a specific time period.

Teach students to honor each other's differences. Help them understand the fact that because everyone has had different learning experiences, they enter each topic with varying knowledge levels and learning needs. To accommodate these unique needs, different assignments are given. This explains the purpose of agendas or menus with different tasks in each folder.

Student's Role

- Listen carefully to receive the directions and guidelines for the agenda.
- Ask any questions or state concerns you have about the agenda assignments before beginning.
- Carry through the task assignments on the agenda.
- Pace yourself so you are able to do a thorough job on each task and finish on time.
- Turn in finished products on the designated completion date.

FIVE (STAR) MANAGEMENT TIPS
FOR USING AGENDAS OR MENUS

1. Use preassessment data to identify the student(s) who needs an alternate, differentiated assignment.

2. Select student-focused activities that address the learner's assessed needs.

3. List the activities that are easy for the student to read and follow. Thoroughly explain each one so the learner can work independently to complete them.

4. Specify the places, times, and materials for the agenda work.

5. Give students an opportunity to showcase the products created during their agenda assignments. This builds self-esteem and encourages them to do their very best work.

Examples of Agendas or Menus

Example A: An Agenda for All Grades and Curriculum Areas

During this agenda assignment, students select activities from a teacher-made choice board or agenda list.

NAME _____ Due Date _____

I will complete the following activities: Completed

Activity 1. _____

I learned. . . . _____

_____

Activity 2. _____

I learned. . . . _____

_____

Activity 3. _____

I learned. . . . _____

_____

Activity 4. _____

I learned. . . . _____

_____

Checkpoint Date #1 _____ Checkpoint Date #2 _____

(Continued)

(Continued)

Signatures:

Student _____

Parent _____

Peer _____

Teacher _____

Example B: Agenda for Integrating Subjects in a Self-Contained Classroom

The teacher gives the following assignment to integrate subjects across content areas for all class members to complete during the week. Note that the activities are differentiated within this total group assignment because students may be on different pages, working with different skills, and making choices.

Student's Name _____ Due Date _____

☐ Read pages _____ in the social studies book and take notes.

☐ Complete the math manipulative sheet and check it from the key. Make corrections with the green pen and place it in the teacher basket.

☐ Choose two activities from the science choice board to complete. Place the completed activities in your science folder.

☐ Make a journal entry listing five things you learned this week.

Student Signature   _____

Reflective Comments _____

Example C: Agenda for One Subject Area

Student's Name_____ Due Date _____

☐ Complete the computer program _____ and the response sheet.

☐ Make a puzzle with all of the vocabulary words. When it is completed, place it on the bulletin board.

☐ Observe the _____ and predict what will happen next. Draw or write your prediction.

☐ Practice _____ with a partner using the _____.

☐ Write ____ journal entries during the week to describe facts you are learning about _____.

MANAGING ACADEMIC CONTRACTS

What Is an Academic Contract?

An academic contract is a form outlining an alternative to the current study and related assignments that the student presents to the teacher for approval. Specifically tailored to suit an individual's needs, a contract is usually granted to a student who demonstrates mastery of upcoming skills or topics and needs more challenging work, though it may also be granted to a student who has an idea for an alternate grade-level assignment. The teacher and the student must agree upon the contract. Once the teacher gives final approval, the alternate research project, study, or tasks are outlined on a form with a time frame for completion.

The grade is determined by the content, process, and/or product. Grades can be assigned for the individual tasks and/or the total contract.

What Are the Instructional Benefits of Academic Contracts?

The heart of an academic contract is the focus on the student's interest area that extends learning in topics or skills related to the current study. Contracts can be used to serve two major instructional purposes in the differentiated classroom. (1) A contract avoids wasting a student's time and prevents boredom because the learner is not required to repeat previously learned information. Remember, the student is assigned the academic contract as an alternative assignment because of the strong knowledge base related to the information planned for class instruction. (2) Another way an academic contract can be used is to replace the regular assignments when a student, who may or may not be performing at an advanced level, has an idea for an alternative. The student outlines and submits the proposal to the teacher for approval. When a contract is approved, the learner is not expected to complete assignments given to the rest of the class.

Each academic contract is designed to intrigue and challenge the student. This differentiated assignment gives learners opportunities to move on within a unit to expand specific interests.

Teacher's Role

Before the Assignment Begins: The Designing Stage

- Preassess the class to gather data on the learners' knowledge base, attitudes, and interests related to the planned topic. Use the results to identify the students who need an academic contract.

- Conduct a preconference with the student.
  - Explain the purpose and value of the special assignment.
  - Present the guidelines and procedures for an academic contract assignment.

Examples:

You'll need to work in _____ or _____ areas.

Do your work when _____.

You have permission to go to _____ or _____ to obtain more information.

      ○ Discuss the learner's interest areas related to the current topic that would be worthwhile for in-depth study. Once you both settle on a subtopic, ask the student the following:

What tasks would you like to complete to learn more about it?

What resources or materials do you need?

How much time will it take to complete your tasks?

How will you present your final product?

How would you like to be graded on your work?

      ○ Tell the student to develop a proposal for approval by doing the following:

Identify the standards, skills, and concepts you plan to include and address.

Develop challenging but doable tasks that address content information.

Outline necessary materials and resources.

Set a timeline for conferences, checkpoints, and due dates.

- Allow the student time to gather ideas and outline the tasks.
- Conference with the student about the contract proposal and give your approval if appropriate. Approve it only if the plan is student focused, uses time wisely, and teaches the student more about the current study.
- Create or select appropriate forms to use as monitoring and assessment tools.
- Come to consensus on the nature of the assignment, assessment tools, grading system, and timeline. Sign the agreement and ask the student to sign it, too.
- Assign a personal place for concentration with adequate workspace for assignment completion. Be sure this space is not distracting or disruptive to the work of other students. Consider using a remote desk, table, computer station or lab, reference area, media center, or the floor for personal spaces.
- Designate a space for artifacts that is out of the way of normal classroom traffic. Place printed computer findings and products in a personalized folder. Keep completed paper assignments in a separate portfolio folder designated for the project along with the signed contract agreement, the timeline, and any activity logs. Include all self and/or teacher assessment pieces as integral parts of the portfolio.

During the Academic Contract Work: The Work Stage

- Follow progress checkpoints as designated on the timeline. Hold a midpoint conference to discuss solutions to any problems or concerns. Adjust the assignment or timeline, if necessary.
- Keep tabs on supplies to be sure needed materials and resources are available during work time.
- Support, encourage, and praise the student.
- Remember to provide uninterrupted time for the student to work on the assignment. Independent contract work usually occurs when the rest of the students are

working on the known information. If extra time is needed, consider time before or after class, study periods, or using it for homework assignments.

- Periodically ask questions from the following list:

  What have you done so far?

  What have you learned?

  How can I help you?

  Do you need more or different materials?

  Have you made any new discoveries?

  Do we need to revamp or change anything in your assignment?

  Show me some examples of your work.

After the Completion of the Academic Contract: The Feedback Stage

- Schedule a conference for the student to present the completed academic contract.
  - Obtain the student's evaluation of the contract as soon as the tasks are completed.
  - Use the list of questions during the conference that are not addressed in the evaluation.

    What did you learn?

    What were your favorite tasks?

    What did you find most challenging?

    If assigned another contract, which segment would you want to keep?

    What needs to be changed the next time?

    Did you understand each assignment, task, and procedure? If not, identify and explain the problem(s).

    Did you need more assistance? If yes, when?

    Were you given enough time? If you answered no, explain.

    Would you like to complete another assignment like this? Why or why not?

- Assess the final product and give specific feedback to the student.
  - Identify new information or skills the student learned.
  - Did the student miss anything that was needed?
  - Did it meet the specified goals and objectives?
  - Identify the effective tasks and segments.
  - What aspects of the contract need improvement? Why and how?
  - Was it worth the time in your professional opinion? Why or why not?
  - What will you change before you make a similar assignment?

- Provide time for the student to respond to your feedback and revise or revamp as needed.

- Decide if it is beneficial for the student to present the contract activities to the class or special guests. If so, provide time for the student to prepare the presentation.

Demystifying Academic Contracts

Introduce the term *contract* by discussing formal agreements such as those used in hiring employees or the agreement that performers have for movies or concert performances. Emphasize the importance of the agreement and the significance of the signatures.

Explain that a contract is used for a different assignment that may be selected by the teacher or presented as an option with some class assignments.

Student's Role
Before the Assignment Begins

- Select an area or subtopic that will add to your knowledge in the unit of study.

- Develop a way to organize, display, or present the new information or product.

- Design a timeline for the contract activities.

- Conference with the teacher to share ideas; outline expectations, rules, and guidelines; select the assessment tools; and obtain approval.

- Familiarize yourself with the grading system.

During the Academic Contract Work

- Focus on the assignment and maintain progress by following the timeline.

- Generate a question and concern list for a mid-contract conference. If you are stalled and cannot "work around" a part of the assignment that troubles you, do not wait until the mid-contract conference to ask for explanations or assistance.

- Use a variety of materials and resources to gather and learn the new information.

- Keep yourself on task by enjoying and challenging yourself with new discoveries.

- Label and date each contract task and record your progress in a log.

- Store completed papers and products in the designated area(s).

After the Completion of the Academic Contract

- Assess the final product.

- Review the guidelines and requirements to be sure the contract is complete.

- Check the timeline to be sure each step was followed.

- Write an evaluation of the assignment using the teacher's list of questions as a guide.

- Plan a final conference presentation.

FIVE (STAR) MANAGEMENT TIPS FOR USING ACADEMIC CONTRACTS

1. Analyze the student's contract proposal to see that it addresses the learner's needs, enhances content information, and is a valuable use of the student's time. Make additions and deletions as needed.

2. After approval, organize tasks cooperatively and strategically with the learner.

3. Schedule conferences to monitor and discuss progress, new discoveries, and needs during the completion of the work according to the timeline. Praise accomplishments.

4. Select the monitoring and assessment tools.

5. Keep notes during each stage of the contract. Record the things that work and areas that need improvement for future contract assignments.

Examples of Academic Contracts

Example A: An Expert on the Unit of Study

A preassessment reveals that a student is an expert on the information planned for instruction. It is obvious that this individual will be bored with the lessons.

With the teacher's invitation, the student submits a written proposal with alternative assignments to work on during the independent work time of the study. The teacher approves or disapproves and works with the student to come up with more acceptable or topic-specific activities.

Example B: An Expert With a Skill or Concept

A new student joins the class. You are planning an upcoming unit to teach specific math skills and concepts. A preassessment indicates that this student has mastered the skills and concepts. The student designs a contract to illustrate how the information is applied in everyday situations. The findings are presented in a creative way to the class to enrich their understanding of the skill.

Example C: Expert Beyond the Grade Level

- A student enters the class knowing how to read the grade-level material. This student is provided with challenging reading assignments during independent work time. The contract may include an assignment on a computer program, illustrating a favorite story or preparing a read-aloud session for a special time or class.

- A class in the upper grades is learning to design Web pages in a computer class. One of the students has been designing Web pages for local businesses. The teacher asks this student to submit an academic contract proposal to further his Web page knowledge in an independent study while other students are learning basic information.

Example D: A Sample Academic Contract

Name _____   Date _____

Student Explanation of Proposal for Teacher

My Plan

Resources and Materials Needed

I need _____ amount of time.

My Due Date will be _____.

Conference Date _____

Teacher Approval _____ **Teacher Denial** _____

Teacher Suggestions, Comments, and Additions

Signatures

Student _____   Date _____

Teacher _____   Date _____

MANAGING PRODUCTS

What Is a Product?

A product is an object or *artifact* created by the student. It is visible evidence of student work and learning. Products are often in the fom of an exhibit, diorama, PowerPoint presentation, computer printout, booklet, or report.

What Are the Instructional Benefits of Products?

The most valuable components of a product activity are the thinking processes that take place. Products are designed to be teacher directed, student centered, or a combination of these approaches. Each one is customized to meet the unique needs of learners. Products can also serve as effective instructional tools when they are shared with other students.

Creating a product:

- Actively engages the student's mind
- Takes the learner through a thinking process
- Provides a purpose and goal for tasks
- Teaches the student to follow directions, steps, and timelines
- Allows the student to showcase accomplishments

Teacher's Role

- Identify the students who would most benefit from creating products. Identify their strengths by asking yourself questions such as, "Are these students the visual or kinesthetic learners?"
- Determine which product assignment provides the most effective way for the student to learn the content information.
- Designate specific checkpoints and assessment tools.
- Provide materials and establish the time for the student to complete the product.
- Present the product. Identify a time and place for the student to present the product.

Demystifying Products

A product is anything created or completed by the student. It is evidence of a learning experience. Emphasize that each student has different strengths, talents, and interests so each product will be unique. Use the following artist analogy to introduce products to students:

> Some sculptors are experts in working with marble, others work best with steel, and others are specialists with glass designs. Each artist is strong in different areas and approaches the work in different ways.

Explain that product assignments may be given to individuals, a small group, or the total group.

Student's Role

- Review the directions your teacher provides.
- Give your best effort to create a quality product.
- Check the guidelines to be sure you followed the directions correctly. If you discover you've missed something, make necessary revisions or adjustments.
- Review the procedure and what you learned from the process with a partner.
- Showcase or store the product according to the directions.

FIVE (STAR) MANAGEMENT TIPS FOR PRODUCTS

1. Emphasize the processes used in creating the product more than the product. Provide time for the students to develop their game plan. Assign a processing partner so they can discuss their procedures, progress, and needs.

2. Establish checkpoints for teacher-learner conferences so the students can explain their thinking process. This keeps the students progressing on the right track. At the completion of the product, give feedback on the process the students used as well as the product created.

3. Plan various ways to use student products to teach, reinforce, review, and enhance learning.

4. Let students know that their efforts and work are valued. Products engage the learners' creative skills as well as their organizational skills. Avoid using only A+ work for display. All learners need encouragement and praise for their best work.

Ways to display the product:

Hang It

| Ribbon | Rope | Yarn | Clothesline |
| Wire rings | Coat hanger | Hooks | String |

Glue, Tack, or Staple It

| Poster board | Butcher paper | Wallpaper | Cardboard box |
| Construction paper | Bags | Boxes | Bulletin board |

Tape It

| Doors | Shelves | Windows | Shades | Blinds | Easel | Floor |
| Posts | Desks | Chairs | Ladder | Wall | Ceiling | Chart stand |

Exhibit It

| Table | Shelf | Desk | Floor | | Windowsill |
| Box | Rug | Bulletin board | Computer overhead | | |

Create special audiences for product presentations!

| Parents | Community leaders | Guest classes |
| Grandparents | Review team | Administrators |

5. Because the value of a product is not completely objective, use a variety of assessment tools and strategies to determine a student's grade.

Examples:

Peer evaluations	Self-assessment	Rubrics	Likert scales
Journals	Ticket out the door	Presentation	

Examples of Products

Example A: Math Visual

Each group creates a visual to show the steps in a math problem. Students solve their problem. They discuss the steps used to solve it and create a visual to display the step-by-step procedure.

Give each group a math problem that requires different steps to solve. Provide the following directions:

1. Place each step on a separate, large strip of paper.

2. Color-code the steps. For example, number 1 is purple, number 2 is green, and so on.

3. Challenge students to display the steps in a unique way. Example: Use a shoebox. Place the steps on each side of the box.

Example B: Showcase Display

Use a growing product display to showcase important details in a study. The products reflect information learned. Students add their products to the display on a covered refrigerator box, a timeline, a wall, or a table.

Example C: Create Sack Products for Presentation Displays

Students decorate the outside of sacks to reflect information learned in a unit using symbols, drawings, written facts, captions, graphic organizers, and pictures. Place artifacts and/or props in the bag.

Adapt the following independent product assignments on agendas, choice boards, academic contracts, or anchor activities (see Figure 4.13):

Figure 4.13

Visual	Auditory	Tactile	Written	Mathematical
Draw a graph, symbol, or design to represent. . .	Listen to a tape and . . .	Use the yarn to outline or make_____	Write a song using ten that you learned	Place the fractions in sequential order from the lowest to the highest number
Color-code	Learn from a discussion group	Draw small, individual boards	Write the important information in the genre of your choice	Develop a matrix
Make an editorial cartoon	Create a forum and debate . . .	Select a folder game	Research and write a report	Plot the information on a Venn diagram
Design a graphic organizer	Tell a partner the highlights	Write in . . . Salt JELL-O Sand Pudding Shaving cream	Respond to the questions: Who What When Where How Why	Create a graph and interpret it
Illustrate it	Create and interpret sounds for the setting	Show and explain using a manipulative	Create a word game or puzzle	Design a timeline that depicts . . .
Make a collage	Create a rap and share it with your group	Demonstrate a simulation	Write and perform a reenactment	Choose a formula and prove it
Create a diorama	Interpret a passage or song	Mix the ingredients	Design and write a mini-book	Write the sequential steps
Design a shoebox float	Create the background music for the topic	Feel it and examine attributes	Brainstorm in a group and plot ideas on a graphic organizer	Design a number game
Create a mini poster display	Write the lyrics	Collect artifacts	Come to consensus and write an editorial or point of view	Interpret appropriate data
Create a mural	Listen to . . .	Use a prop	Write step-by-step process thinking	Conduct a Web search
Make a book	Create a riddle	Develop a display	Interpret a graph	Categorize and sort
Decorate the sides of a paper bag	Write a poem	Work in a learning zone	Identify and label an example	Solve a problem and draw the procedure

MANAGING CONTENT

Teachers usually select content to teach one or more standards. Some districts require teachers to follow a timeline to teach specific content. For example, a math teacher may be required to teach Chapters 3, 4, and 5 during the second six-week period.

Know your content thoroughly so it will be easier to decide where and when to plug in the standards. When the content is familiar, it is easier to place it in sequence and create links and connections.

Required skills are presented to teachers as mandated standards. District administrators usually give teachers freedom to select the content from approved textbooks and auxiliary materials.

Selecting Content

Use questions similar to the following to guide the content selection process:

- Is this content segment essential for the learner?
- Is it the most valuable way for students to learn the concept or skill?
- Which segments of the information does the learner need? Do I need to use selective abandonment and eliminate irrelevant content?
- Are the content segments organized to make learning flow sequentially?
- When do I use this content information?

  Do I teach it next?

  Do I save it until later?

Always remember that it is not necessary to teach content information just because it is in the teacher's guide and supporting materials. Use the textbook and supplementary materials as resources. Select relevant information and the sequence for teaching it.

Selecting Appropriate Materials and Resources

Select resources to meet student needs, coordinate with the content, and enhance learning:

Examples

- Books that teach the standard on the learners' various reading levels
- Supplementary materials provided by the textbook company, such as books, posters, computer programs, workbooks, videos, and CDs
- Internet sources
- Local resources available from civic organizations and businesses
- Books on tape, stories, poems, and songs

Use High-Tech Tools to Enhance Instruction

Figure 4.12

Calculators	Computer Programs	Recorders and Discs
Handheld	Learning games	CD or tape burners
Calculators with printout	Puzzles	Prerecorded audios
Talking calculators	Word processors	Tape recorder
	Spell check	MP3 players
	E-mail homework	Stereo/jam box
	PowerPoint	Camcorders

CONCLUSION

Choosing the Correct Instructional Strategy

Remember, like the magician who chooses the tricks in his or her act with the audience in mind, it is important to purposefully select instructional strategies to meet the learner's unique needs. Keep your students hooked by pulling out many different hats from your strategy repertoire and using a variety of strategies and techniques, constantly exploring novel ways to intrigue and engage learners. Don't be afraid to try on a new hat to reach a learner.

Refer to each strategy with its title or special name, and be sure students understand related terms and phrases. Use each strategy until students "own it" so well they use it in other subjects.

Develop a broad repertoire of tricks or instructional strategies to meet the unique needs of learners, so that every time you pull out your "magician's hat," you are reminded to take all student needs into account. In a differentiated classroom, each strategy must be accessible and ready to use as soon as a need is recognized. While planning, keep a strategy list in sight for quality selection. Continuously add to the list as you implement new strategies and delete those that are not effective in your classroom. This avoids both overuse and nonproductive instructional time.

Use the students' interests and areas of strength whenever and wherever possible. It must be meaningful and meet the needs of the learner at that particular occasion! Like a magician's trick, the perfect strategy will make your unit, lesson, or activity a hit!

Differentiated Assignments

The following list of follow-up activities may be used as differentiated assignments after students learn information by reading a passage or listening to a lecturette. Use these ideas to develop agendas, choice boards, homework, anchor activities, centers, or projects. Use differentiated assignments to intensify the learners' knowledge of a standard, skill, concept, or unit.

Record findings	Discuss with a partner
Hold a small group text talk	Develop questions
Write a song	Create a rap
Develop a chant	Write a limerick
Write a poem	Create a commercial
Develop a collage	Role-play
Create background music	Create a reenactment
Make a caricature	Draw a picture
Develop an editorial cartoon	Make a diorama
Write a cartoon strip with speech bubbles	Color-code
Illustrate the _____	List the attributes
Write adjectives or phrases to describe _____	Create a timeline
Develop a mural	Design a new game to review _____
Play a game	Design a poster
Design a puppet	Draw the setting
Find the missing piece(s)	Draw a map
Write an editorial with your point of view	Use a manipulative
Make a bar graph and interpret the data	Design a brochure
Create a pie chart and explain the results	Scavenge for information
Develop a key	Prepare a point of view
Act out the vocabulary words	Name the causes
Create a vocabulary game	List the reasons
List the synonyms or antonyms	Write the main idea
Write a summary	Write the directions
Develop a critique	Draw a conclusion
Write your opinion	Write the fact(s)
Discover how it works	Name examples
Develop the sequence	Debate the issue
Invent a new way to _____	Identify the sounds
Conduct an interview	Write an ad
Teach someone how to _____	Make a mobile

ASSESSMENT IS AN ESSENTIAL, ONGOING PROCESS IN A differentiated classroom. It is a chance for you to put on your detective hat and compile evidence of student needs in given situations. Sometimes an observation will give a teacher what he or she needs, just like simple observations aid in solving cases. A blending of informal and formal assessment tools are used to gather data before, during, and after learning to identify individual strengths and needs. Like the investigator of a case, the teacher compiles all of the information for the report. Some cases require deeper investigations, such as fingerprinting and DNA analysis, to gather the necessary data. Teachers assess by going deep in the mind to find out what the student knows and what each learner needs next. The results are analyzed and used to customize instructional plans.

Preassessment is a prerequisite for differentiation. The teacher needs to know how to select and administer the most appropriate assessment tools. Managing the tools is a complex task, but remember that each learner benefits with personalized instruction.

Managing Preassessment

What Is Preassessment?

Preassessment is a formal or informal test administered to pinpoint what the learner knows about an upcoming standard, skill, topic, or concept. The teacher analyzes the data to identify the student's background knowledge, prior experiences, abilities, interests, and attitudes in relation to the new learning.

The most useful preassessment data is gathered one to two weeks before planning. This gives the teacher time to analyze the learner's strengths and needs for the upcoming study. This close examination is crucial because the results are used to strategically plan each lesson for individuals in a differentiated classroom. When students' strengths and weaknesses are addressed in a plan, the teacher is working smarter, not harder.

What Are the Instructional Benefits of Using Preassessment?

- An effective preassessment reveals the student's knowledge base related to the upcoming topic or skill and identifies the entry point for instruction.
- Preassessment data pinpoints the learner's knowledge on standards concepts, and objectives.
- It reveals specific needs for reteaching, grade-level instruction, or enrichment.
- The teacher can make informed grouping decisions when a preassessment reveals a wide range of understanding in the classroom.
- Preassessment results guide the teacher in selecting or designing the most appropriate instructional strategies to accommodate identified individual and group needs.

Teacher's Role

- Preassess students one or two weeks before the new unit or study begins.
- Use the data to identify the entry points for instruction and to make grouping decisions accordingly.
- Plan lessons and activities for individuals and small groups based on their current knowledge levels.
- Use the preassessment session as a promo for the upcoming topic or skill.
- Develop a repertoire of formal and informal preassessment tools, and let the data needed determine which tool to use in a given situation. For example, if an informal assessment unveils needed information, use it instead of a time-consuming, formal assessment.

Demystifying Preassessment

Introduce the term *preassessment* by discussing lessons needed to learn a sport. Here is a metaphor you can adapt for the word's debut:

> The coach preassesses each person's skills so that he or she can set up the practice session. Individuals who routinely play the game begin with more advanced skills and information. People who are playing for the first time begin with the basics.

Explain that you use preassessments in the same way to identify each student's knowledge of an upcoming topic or skill. Remind students to honor the strengths of others and to respect their weaknesses or needs. Emphasize the importance of students doing their best and being honest on each preassessment because the information helps you plan and organize lessons that "make strengths stronger" or "zap the gaps."

Student's Role

- Show what you know and what you do not know so you can learn more.

- Search your memory bank to reveal any experiences you have had to link to the lesson.

- Share your personal knowledge and experiences related to the topic on the assessment. Express any concerns and questions you have.

- Realize that a negative experience you had with a topic or skill in the past can be replaced with a positive experience. Always remember that it is never too late to learn.

- Identify areas of interest you would like to explore during the upcoming study.

FIVE (STAR) MANAGEMENT TIPS FOR PREASSESSMENTS

1. Explain to students how preassessment data guide planning for their unique needs. Emphasize the value of the results, so they will use their best responses for the questions. Use upbeat, positive comments so students do not become stressed out about the "test." Negative thoughts interfere with thinking.

2. Preassess for an upcoming topic at least one or two weeks before the unit begins so the gathered data can be used to plan for the specific needs of this group of students.

3. Introduce and demonstrate a preassessment tool the first two to three times it is used or until students know how to use it.

4. Use a variety of formal and informal preassessment tools. Add each completed assessment to the class assessment toolkit to use in later sessions to gather data for planning a future unit.

5. Engage the students in the data analysis and planning.

Examples of Preassessments

Example A: Using a Teacher-Made Pretest

Develop a pretest similar to the following to discover what students know about an upcoming topic.

- List five things you know about _____.
- What experiences have you had with _____?
- Illustrate _____ on the back of your paper.
- Write one or two paragraphs that describe _____ to a friend.
- Tell me what you would like to learn about _____.

Administer the test one or two weeks prior to the beginning of the introduction to the material. Gather the data and analyze it to plan differentiated instruction for the upcoming unit. Use the same test as a posttest.

Example B: Color-Coding the Facts

Provide a list of key content facts such as the major characters, events, dates, and places from the upcoming unit or topic. Ask students to color-code each entry based on their level of understanding.

Green dot: *I know it!*

Black dot: *I know a little about it.*

Blue dot: *I don't know anything about it.*

Example C: Getting in Shape

Announce the next unit using an exciting advertisement such as a jingle or ad.

Explain to students that this preassessment activity is designed to actively engage them in a self-assessment and lets them help you plan instruction for the upcoming topic or skill by "Getting in Shape."

- Display three large outlines of the following shapes with a descriptor key. Example:

  circle = I know a lot about it.

  square = I know a little about it.

  triangle = I don't know anything about it.
- Make a list of the most important facts in the upcoming unit.
- State a fact from the list.
- Tell students to stand in front of the shape that represents their knowledge of each fact as it is read.
- Gather data to plan the new study by using a chart similar to the following to record where students stand. Students may number each fact on a card and record a response for each one by drawing the selected shape.

Figure 5.1

Fact	Circle *I know a lot about it!*	Square *I know a little about it!*	Triangle *I don't know anything about it.*
1.			
2.			
3.			

MANAGING ONGOING ASSESSMENT

What Is Ongoing Assessment?

Ongoing or continuous assessment is essential in the differentiated classroom. The teacher observes and monitors individuals as they engage in activities and class work in order to adjust or customize instruction as needed. Students also monitor themselves during learning with self-assessment tools designed to help them examine their own work. Students know how and when to obtain assistance when a problem or gap in learning occurs. They also learn to recognize their own progress and use praise statements as self-affirmations.

What Are the Instructional Benefits of Ongoing Assessments?

- Constant assessment keeps the teacher abreast of progress, misunderstandings, and aha moments.

- Students receive assistance as soon as a need is identified. This immediate response for intervention keeps them from falling behind, getting frustrated with a task, or losing valuable learning time.

- By gathering the appropriate data and recording findings, you can see patterns and customize future assignments accordingly.

- Analyzing the data to find out where students are in understanding assists in diagnosing flexible groupings, as well as adjusting assignments and tasks to best serve individual needs.

- When you assess during learning, students do not become bored with information or skills they know. Neither you nor the student has to wait for the summative assessment results to find out what has been learned and what needs have yet to be met.

Teacher's Role

- Assess using an array of teacher- and student-focused tools to obtain thorough data in an efficient manner.

- Act on your findings promptly—adjust assignments for individuals as soon as a need reveals itself.

- Move the learner to the most effective grouping design to zap gaps or enrich learning using TAPS (Total group, Alone, Partner, or Small group).

- Establish ways for students to self-assess, make corrections, and set new goals as they work.

- Examine the assessment data to create and tailor the individualized plans so each student is adequately challenged and not bored or frustrated.

Demystifying Ongoing Assessment

Explain the importance of the teacher and each student using assessment during learning to "zap the gaps" or extend learning. Be sure they know the importance of asking for assistance when they do not understand a step or a part of the assignment while they are working. Let them know how and when to ask for assistance to keep on track in the learning journey.

Compare ongoing assessment to the work of an artist. As work progresses on the painting, the artist pauses to study the texture, color, and design. Adjustments are made as needed.

Student's Role

- Let the teacher or a study buddy know when you do or do not understand directions or a task.
- Remember that the assessment results guide the teacher's plans for your lessons and activities.
- Show what you know.
- Use self-assessment as you work to identify what you need next.
- Consider each mistake or misunderstanding as an opportunity to learn.

**FIVE (STAR) MANAGEMENT TIPS FOR
USING ONGOING ASSESSMENT**

1. Explain ongoing assessment and the teacher and student roles for "zapping gaps" during learning. This keeps planning on track in the learning journey.

2. Introduce and model each assessment tool used during learning. For example, if an observation checklist is an observation tool, show the form to the student and explain its use. This removes apprehension the learner may have during an assessment. For example, when a teacher is observing and using a checklist, the student often thinks, "Why is the teacher watching me and taking notes?" "Will the notes be sent to my parents?" A simple explanation makes the learner feel like a partner in the learning process as it removes the negative messages. Remember that the brain functions best in a positive state.

3. Use the brain jamming activity (Example A) to introduce metacognitive strategies for students to use during learning. Verbalize the inside thinking that accompanies each assessment tool.

4. Give corrective feedback or praise.

5. Be prepared to adjust plans, assignments, activities, or group placement to meet individual and group needs.

Examples of Ongoing Assessment

Example A: Brain Jamming

During a reading of a text, the student ponders specific questions to conduct a personal probe of the brain. The responses may be used as an internal check of comprehension, to identify needs, to connect to new learning, and to prompt self-praise.

Examples:

What was the author saying?

How can I remember this?

Do I need this part?

What do I think will happen next?

Example B: Project Partners

The teacher assigns long-term individual projects to several students. Each student receives a project packet at the beginning of the assignment, which includes a timeline with designated dates for certain parts of the project to be completed. Periodically, each student meets with the project partner to discuss the parts completed, the problems encountered, and the light bulb happenings during the project process. During each conference, the students share information and strategies. They fill out an individual or partner checklist and comment page to record findings from each conference session. The partner interaction emphasizes the project *process*.

Example C: Card Responses

Students are in the middle of a unit of study, and the teacher needs feedback to see if the students understand the information presented in four categories. A class set of response cards are created with the four categories listed on the left-hand side of each card.

The teacher asks a question or makes a statement related to one of the categories. After a thinking period of approximately 10 seconds, the students pinch the appropriate category to answer the question or correspond to the statement. The teacher says, "1 . . . 2 . . . 3 . . . Show me!" Each student holds the card for the teacher to see. This informal, game-like assessment shows what has been learned by each individual and which parts require review or reteaching.

For example:

- Prime number   Composite number

- Invertebrate animal   Vertebrate animal

- Fiction   Nonfiction

- United States   Canada

MANAGING ASSESSMENT AFTER LEARNING

What Is Assessment After Learning?

Assessment after learning identifies the skills and concepts mastered by each student following a segment or unit of study. Informal assessments are typically used to identify standards, skills, or concepts for review or for reteaching. Formal assessments are typically used when a grade is needed. In each assessment approach, the results are analyzed to see if each learner reached the goals or objectives. New plans are tailored to provide more experiences.

What Are the Instructional Benefits of Using Assessment After Learning?

- Assessments administered after learning reveal specific, individual needs.
- The results determine the learner's knowledge level and guide planning for the upcoming study.
- The data becomes a direct guide for the student to identify problem areas and to recognize progress.
- When the assessment reveals that more than one student had similar errors, the teacher can correct the flaw in that part of the lesson and revise the instructional strategy or materials.
- The results can be compared to previous assessment performances in order to monitor progress over time. The teacher can use the information to discuss the learner's strengths and needs in parent and student conferences.

Teacher's Role

- Design or select summative evaluations that make it easy to identify what a student learned and did not learn during the study.
- Compile and examine the data from formative assessments to pinpoint individual and group strengths and weaknesses.
- Use the analyzed data to make informed instructional plans. For example, a student who fails to master a skill is assigned customized activities for review and practice.
- Administer questions and evaluations in different forms to give students opportunities to show what they learned. When more than one kind of test is administered, different views are produced of the learner's knowledge, strengths and needs.
- Whenever possible, involve students in the data analysis so they can learn to set new goals for learning.

Demystifying Assessment After Learning

Explain the importance of using assessment after learning to uncover needs that can be addressed in the new plans. Use a mini-lecturette such as the following to compare the summative assessment to a championship skating event:

> The trainer and the skater analyze each aspect of the performance to identify skills that need improvement before the next competition. The low marks from the judges indicate areas that need more instruction and/or practice before the next competition.

Student's Role

- Review your notes and the text for the test. Identify the most important facts or skills to remember.

- Self-assess before a test to find out what you know and what you need to practice or review before the test.

- Show what you know on the test!

- When you receive the assessment results, use the information to identify the things you learned and pat yourself on the back. Highlight or mark the things you did not learn so you can "zap the gaps." Correct them and improve with more instruction, review, or practice.

- List what you would like to learn when an assignment option on this topic or skill is presented to you.

FIVE (STAR) MANAGEMENT TIPS FOR USING ASSESSMENT AFTER LEARNING

1. Choose the summative evaluation that will most clearly reveal what students learned during the study.

2. Use a combination of assessment formats such as teacher-made tests, portfolio conferences, presentations, multiple-choice tests, open-ended questions, manipulative tasks, games, and graphic organizers. A broader picture of the student's strengths and needs is obtained when the work is viewed from different angles.

3. Provide students with self-assessment tools, including questioning techniques to use in assignments and activities to develop self-directed, independent learners.

4. Engage students in peer and small group assessments after learning. During this time, they identify correct answers, fix their errors, and set new goals.

5. Analyze the assessment results to adapt instruction to immediate needs or to design plans.

Examples of Assessment After Learning

Example A: Draw What You Know!

Draw the life cycle of the butterfly on the chart paper provided. Write the name of each stage next to its picture with two to three descriptive sentences.

Example B: Create What You Know!

Use the manipulatives to create a model of an atom. Use scrap paper to label each component. Ask your study buddy or a classmate to use the diagram provided to check your work.

Example C: Explain What You Know! Portfolio Partners

Partners find a comfortable meeting area to sit with their portfolios and a checklist of the activities and assignments they completed. As they examine each portfolio, they discuss what they learned, including their thinking processes, areas of growth, and needs. Each partner takes a turn sharing and listening. After both students share, they mark the checklist and record comments in their own portfolios as evidence of this meaningful, learning event.

Assess Your Use of Formal and Informal Assessment Tools

List the assessment tools you currently use before, during, and after learning. Label each one as informal or formal.

Assessment Tools That Make the Difference

Figure 5.2		
Tools Used Label as Follows:		
I = Informal		F = Formal
Before	During	After

Figure 5.3		
Time	Examples of Tools	Examples of Verbal Responses
Preassessment tools	☐ Squaring off: Four corners Body signals ☐ Stand up, sit down ☐ Thumb it Response cards ☐ Know/Do not know ☐ Like/Dislike ☐ Pretest ☐ Journal ☐ KWL Chart	I know … I want to learn … I do not know … I know some about … To improve I need to … I need … I like … I do not like … I am afraid of … I look forward to … I hope I get to learn …
During assessment tools	Body Signals ☐ Fist of 5 ☐ Reach for the top ☐ Arm gauge ☐ Speedometer arm	I am learning … I am confused about … I want to learn … This activity is easy for me because … This is hard because … I need … I have learned …

(Continued)

Figure 5.3 (Continued)

Time	Examples of Tools	Examples of Verbal Responses
	☐ Checkpoint tests ☐ Word or fact wall ☐ Check and correct ☐ Observation ☐ Anecdotal records ☐ Portfolio gathering ☐ Write it to show it ☐ Wipe-off boards, write and show answer ☐ Talk the thinking ☐ Show the process ☐ Show with a manipulative ☐ Link it to previous learning ☐ Notes ☐ Journal ☐ Learning log Response Cards ☐ + or − ☐ Yes or no ☐ A B C D ☐ Face the fact: happy, so-so, sad	I have a question about … I like … I do not like … I hope I … I need to change the way I am doing… It will help if I can … I understand … I will explain … I know … I do not know … My least favorite part is … My favorite part is … I need to tell you … I need to explain … Why am I doing this? How can I use this later?
Post assessment tools	☐ Portfolios ☐ Wraparound reflection ☐ Posttest ☐ Conversation circle ☐ Rotation reflections ☐ Paper pass ☐ Partner or small group sharing ☐ Carousel ☐ Teach it to someone ☐ Whip-around responses from each student ☐ Talking topic ☐ Grand finale celebration ☐ Blank page at the end of test: "Tell me what you know about this subject that was not examined in this test." ☐ Center response logs Graphic Organizers ☐ Donut ☐ Wheel ☐ Flowchart ☐ Ladder ☐ Hand ☐ Star	I was successful because … I can improve by … Now I know … I will use this to … Next I need to … I am still questioning … I learned … My favorite part was … This was my least favorite. I liked … I did not like … Next time I need … My biggest ahas were … I need to learn more about …

MANAGING SELF-ASSESSMENT

What Is Self-Assessment?

Self-assessment occurs when students analyze their own individual work. They analyze what they know, what they don't know, and what they need to learn next. Using self-assessment tools before, during, and after learning, students find and correct their own mistakes in daily work, projects, tests, activities, and homework.

What Are the Instructional Benefits of Using Self-Assessment?

- Students develop a sense of ownership and control over their personal progress when they know how to use assessment tools to analyze their own work and use results for self-improvement.

- Learners receive immediate feedback when they check their own work. When students identify their own mistakes and are able to make corrections right away, they are more likely to stay focused and motivated.

- Reward for a job well done is immediate during self-assessment. Learners gain a sense of pride as they confirm correct answers.

- Self-assessment frees the teacher from extra paperwork and provides more time for instruction. Students work harder and the teacher works smarter!

- Students learn to appreciate their strengths and accept their weaknesses, value progress, and learn from their mistakes.

Teacher's Role

- Introduce the term *self-assessment*. Explain the value of using self-assessment to improve in a subject or skill. Discuss the fact that adults are not always available to check work.

- Take the learners step-by-step through processing techniques they can use while discovering and correcting mistakes.

- Teach students how to use a variety of self-assessment tools. Guide students through a practice session using each tool and model, model, model the self-assessment cycle until the expectations are understood and established.

- Create a list of personal affirmations for students to use.

  o I am great and getting greater.

  o Over the top!

  o Wow! I learned a lot this time.

  o I am proud of this work.

  o I did my best.

- Teach students to recognize their correct responses and successes. Emphasize the value of always improving and setting new goals.

Demystifying Self-Assessment

Introduce the term *self-assessment* as a way for a person to look at his or her own needs in order to improve. Explain the value of using self-assessment for improvement by giving examples from the students' world outside the classroom.

Example:

> An individual who swims the 200-meter butterfly stroke in 2 minutes and 45 seconds assesses his ability during and after the session. The swimmer may decide to work on correct form, pacing, breathing techniques, or the turnaround speed at the end of each lap to improve the time. Specific goals are set for the next practice session.

Explain that each time students correct mistakes, they are growing and improving. Share facts and stories that focus on individuals who continually moved toward meeting their potentials. For example, as a boy, Benjamin Franklin analyzed his improvement every day and recorded his thoughts and goals in a journal.

Student's Role

- Learn how to use a variety of self-assessment tools.
- Check your work, correct it, and learn from your mistakes.
- Use self-talk to monitor your progress.

    Examples:

    Do I understand the directions?

    What questions do I need to ask?

    Do I need to recheck my work?

    How can I use this information?

    Is this my best work?

    Could I improve my responses?

    What else do I need to know?

    Do I know what to do next?

- Think about your thinking as you process information and explain it correctly.
- Monitor your progress by identifying your needs and setting new goals.

FIVE (STAR) MANAGEMENT TIPS FOR SELF-ASSESSMENT

1. Demonstrate strategies for students to check over their work before turning it in for a grade. For example, when students complete a math problem, show them step-by-step procedures to review the work.

2. Model each assessment tool until students have a full understanding of it. When students are familiar with it and can use it independently, assign the tool as a self-assessment activity.

3. Designate a specific area as a Self-Check Zone or Feedback Station where students can check their work. Provide an answer key and a colored pencil or pen for checking. Post directions so students know where to place checked, corrected work.

4. Encourage students to self-assess activities completed in learning zones, centers, and stations. Keep small pieces of paper available for students to assess their likes, dislikes, understandings, and misunderstandings.

5. Remember, at the beginning students need to check their own work as soon as possible after completing an assignment. When students know how to find errors and make corrections, each self-assessment becomes an instructional activity for the learners.

Examples of Self-Assessment Tools

Example A: Students Learning From Mistakes

It takes time for students to find and correct their mistakes, but it is one of the most beneficial experiences you can provide. Use self-assessment procedures similar to the following to give immediate feedback:

1. Provide time for students to check their papers after a written assignment.

2. Post rules for self-checking.

Example:

- Use the green pen to check your work. Each green mark represents an area of needed growth.
- Draw a green line through the incorrect answer or step.
- Mark correct answers with a checkmark or star, or don't do anything to them at all.
- If you cheat, you will lose your self-checking privilege!

3. Call on a student to announce correct answers when time permits.

4. Use the self-assessment score as a learning tool or as one part of the formal grade.

Example B: Self-Assessment Prompts

Teach students to monitor their own progress. Present prompts similar to the following to coordinate with lessons:

Before

- My current level is _____.
- To improve, I need to _____.
- I need the following tools and materials: _____, _____, _____.
- I need help with these new words: _____ _____ _____.
- I need more information about _____.

During

- This activity is (easy/difficult) for me because I _____.
- I need to change the way I am _____ .
- I need to learn more about _____.
- I need help with _____
- I am spending too much time on _____.

After

- I was successful because I _____.
- I can improve by _____.
- I completed _____ today. To improve tomorrow, I need to _____.
- I correctly answered _____ on this lesson. I can answer _____ in the next lesson. For example: *On the last timed test, I answered 15 problems correctly in 10 minutes. This time I will answer 20 problems correctly in 10 minutes.*
- I read _____ pages and I learned _____.

Example C: Self-Assessment Rubric

The following sample of a self-assessment rubric may be used by students in all activities and assignments.

Figure 5.4	
4 Star learner	• I always do my best. • I show that I care about my school and the community. • I use everything I know to learn more. • I can share what I know to teach others.
3 Polishing my learning skills	• I can work alone with little assistance. • I work without complaining. • I check my own work.
2 Ready to believe in me	• I am learning to think about how I learn. • I can work with others. • I know more than I thought I knew.
1 At the beginning	• The teacher reminds me to stay on task. • It is hard to get started on assignments. • Classmates tell me to listen and work. • I need to learn how to be a good team member.
My self-assessment level on this rubric is _____. I am at this point in my learning because _____.	

MANAGING INFORMAL ASSESSMENT

What Is Informal Assessment?

Informal assessment provides a quick but useful analysis of the learners' knowledge and skills for planning instruction and for self-improvement. The results are not used as a grade because the analysis is subjective. The informal tool is presented in an intriguing and challenging way that requires each student in the class or group to provide an individual, observable answer to a question, prompt, or quiz. The teacher observes the student responses. When a general need or learning gap is noted, an intervention with an immediate fix may be implemented to keep the learner on track. When the results reveal a specific need that cannot be met directly, it is recorded for future strategic planning.

What Are the Instructional Benefits of Using Informal Assessment?

- Informal assessment provides a quick view of group progress and individual needs.
- Informal assessments frequently gather the needed data in less time than formal assessments.
- There is minimal preparation and no recorded grades.
- Informal assessments are presented in novel and challenging ways, including game formats.
- Test-phobic students are engaged and show what they know without being hindered by fear.

Teacher's Role

- Develop a treasure trove of informal assessment tools, so the appropriate one can be selected as needed.
- Model each informal tool and technique until you are certain students can use it with little or no teacher guidance.
- Analyze the results and use them effectively in planning instruction for the diverse needs of learners.
- Create a nonthreatening environment and encourage students to be honest in their responses because their levels of understanding are used to plan their assignments and activities.
- Emphasize that it is important to "know what you know and what you do not know so you can learn more."

Demystifying Informal Assessment

Introduce informal assessments as quick, easy tools to obtain an overall view of what students have learned. Explain that these informal assessment tools are selected so the teacher can use the results to plan for individuals and groups. Compare formal and informal assessments. Help students understand that the results are not used to determine a grade. Most formal assessments take more time and are used for grades.

Explain the importance of being honest with responses on informal assessments so the "right" activities and assignments are made to meet the diverse needs of the students.

Student's Role

- Learn how and when to use each informal assessment tool.

- Answer truthfully without checking other classmates' responses so the teacher will have accurate information to plan the best activities and assignments for you.

- Enjoy the assessment activity but realize the importance of it.

- Use informal assessments to check your knowledge before, during, and after learning.

- Remember you can move from the lowest level to the top with knowledge and experience.

FIVE (STAR) MANAGEMENT TIPS FOR USING INFORMAL ASSESSMENTS

1. Use a variety of informal response tools to teach students how to analyze what they know.

2. Engage students in informal assessments using body movements to show what they know. Directions may be as simple as saying the following:
   - Stand up if you know a lot about _____.
   - Lean over on your desk, if you know some things about _____.
   - Sit if you do not know anything about _____.

3. Move forward with instruction when informal responses indicate that students know the information.

4. Observe reactions and facial expressions for valuable feedback. Pleasant expressions reflect understanding. Proud gestures indicate confidence.

5. Be alert and aware of student reactions to informal assessments such as hesitation and reluctance to respond to questions or prompts. When students look to classmates for answers, they need more instruction. When a few students require more instruction or practice, address their needs in a small group.

Figure 5.5

Informal Assessment Tools		
Bodily/Kinesthetic	*Visual/Spatial*	*Verbal/Linguistic*
Make a motion! • Create a signal • Use a hand signal • Use a nonverbal reaction • Wave a mini flag or sign	***Show it!*** • Use response cards • Respond on individual dry-erase boards • Use color-coded signals such as Popsicle sticks, signs, or disks • Create specific design • Design a model	***Respond orally*** • Use short answer • Give your point of view • Record your answer • Tell a friend • Brainstorm responses
Act it out! • Be a human replica • Simulate • Demonstrate • Use a manipulative • Use a prop	***Draw it!*** • A picture • A mural • A mini poster • Symbols • A caricature	***Report it!*** • To the teacher • To a peer • To a volunteer • In a video • On a blog
Show feelings/emotions • With a body signal • Likert arm • Thumb it • Using facial expressions • Role-play • Response cards • Miming	***Create it!*** • A replica • A display • A mini poster • A timeline • A diorama	***Write it*** • As a journal entry • On a chart • As notes • In a list • In a different genre

MANAGING RESPONSE CARDS

What Is a Response Card?

A response card is an informal assessment tool that allows teachers to check for understanding, knowledge, interests, and feelings before, during, or after a lesson. The cards may be used with an individual or with a group.

Each student receives identical cards with response options written on each side of the card in a multiple-choice format. When the teacher asks a question that requires a response, each learner holds up the card and indicates the correct answer by grasping or pinching the answer with a thumb on one side of the card and a forefinger on the opposite side of the card, pointing to the answer on both sides. For instance, when practicing multiple-choice responses, each student receives a card with ABCD written in the same place on the front and back of the cards. When a question is posed, students study the possible answers that are posted and draw their conclusions before answering. Each student selects the answer to the question by pointing to it or by pinching the selection and holding the card up for the teacher to view. The teacher observes the action of the fingers.

What Are the Instructional Benefits of Using Response Cards?

- Often, when a teacher asks a question or seeks a response, one student responds. Other students do not have to think or make an effort. This supports passive learning behaviors. When response cards are used, *all* students are actively engaged because each individual is accountable for answering each question.

- An individual learner's knowledge can be gauged with a glance.

- The teacher has an opportunity to call on a student who responds correctly and follow it with a brief discussion. It is easy to take advantage of the teaching moment when several wrong answers are evident on one item. Elaboration is unnecessary and boredom is avoided when everyone indicates the correct answer.

- A quick mental or written note identifies learners for reteaching or review later.

- Response cards are easy to design for all grade levels and subject areas.

Teacher's Role

- Decide where and when to use response cards for assessment. If the response card activity is the best way to assess a skill, ask the following:
  - What is the card design?
  - When will it be used?
  - Who will use it?
  - How will the results be recorded?
- Decide who will make the response cards:
  - The teacher makes the set.
  - Each student makes a card. Provide clear directions with a sample the first time students design the card.

○ Set up a response card production center. As students finish tasks, they enter the production center to design the assessment cards using facts learned in assignments or activities.

- Explain the purpose of the informal assessment with concise, clear directions for using the response card.

- Design response cards to use as needed before, during, or after learning with the total class, a small group, or partners.

- Collect data from the responses by making mental or written notes for future planning.

- Teach students how to create response cards from their assignments. Provide opportunities for students to use them as self-assessment tools in learning zones or review sessions.

Demystifying Response Cards

Tell students that response or answer cards are designed for them to show what they know in assessment activities and games.

FIVE (STAR) MANAGEMENT TIPS FOR MAKING RESPONSE CARDS

1. Use 3 × 5-inch or 5 × 8-inch index cards or tag board. Use cards that are big enough to write the answer choices in large print. It is time-consuming and expensive to laminate the cards, so make three or four extra cards as replacements for lost or damaged cards.

2. Use bold markers to make responses easy to see across the room. Colors that work best are black, purple, blue, brown, or green. Avoid yellow, red, orange, pink, or lighter shades. Use markers that will not bleed through the card.

3. Place items in a vertical list using big and bold print. Turn the card over and write the same entries in the same position as the entries on the front of the card. When the learner uses these duo response cards with the lists of possible answers on the front and back, the teacher and the student view the revealed response at the same time.

4. The first time students make a response card, show them how to hold it between them and a light or window to be sure they write each word on the back in exactly the same place as the same word on the front. This makes it easy for the student to grasp or pinch the selected response between the thumb and index finger.

5. If you plan to add entries to the same card later, leave adequate space. For example, if the group studies two countries, write them on the response card and leave enough space to add additional countries later. Collect the response cards in a plastic bag, folder, envelope, or recipe file box.

The response card has a list of several answers to a question or a multiple-choice statement. One answer is the best response. Select the correct answer and show it by pinching the answer.

Explain how their responses assist you in selecting activities and assignments.

Student's Role

- Be honest! Do not look at another student's card because the teacher uses your responses to plan activities and assignments for you.

- Consider all possible answers thoughtfully and choose the very best response.

- Pinch the answer by placing your thumb on the correct answer on one side of the card and your index finger on the correct answer on the opposite side of the card.

- Hold the card up when you hear the signal so you can see the answer on one side of the card and the teacher can see your answer on the other side.

FIVE (STAR) MANAGEMENT TIPS FOR USING RESPONSE CARDS

1. Identify options for storing, distributing, and collecting response cards that fit your classroom situation:
   - Hand each student a card for the lesson as they enter the door. Have them return the cards on their way out.
   - Place cards in a basket, so students can pick them up.
   - Place the cards in several locations around the room for easy accessibility: in the center of a cluster of desks or on a shelf, table, or cart.
   - If you decide that each student will keep a personal set of response cards, consider the following storage ideas:
     - Manila envelope
     - Baggie
     - Notebook—punch a hole in the upper left side of each card
     - Folder

2. State the lead-in question or statement. Direct students to hold the cards close in front of them to study the options. This is their thinking time. Give a signal when it is time for students to reveal their answers, such as "1, 2, 3 . . . Show Me!"

3. Observe how students approach their answers. If someone is not answering honestly, guessing, or looking on someone's card, record the insecure action as an assessment!

4. Look closely at the students' reactions because they reflect feelings about what they know. Call on a learner who answers correctly and quickly to explain it.

5. Use the following chart to guide observations as students select answers on their response cards.

(Continued)

(Continued)

Figure 5.6

Observation	Revelations and Reactions
The learner quickly indicates the correct answer without looking around for assistance.	This indicates confidence with the answer. Call on this student for the answer and an explanation.
The student points to an answer and then checks with classmates to see if the answer is correct.	This learner needs to use confidence builders such as: *Yes! I've got it!* *Give me a high five!* *I have the right answer!* *I am so proud of me!* Do not tell this student to keep his or her eyes on his or her own card. Use the student's action as part of the data to plan confidence-building instruction.
The student waits and then looks at the answers of classmates before responding.	This action implies that the student does not know the answer and needs to learn more about this piece of information. Reteaching may be required. Remember to avoid saying, "Turn around!" because the action is a valuable part of the assessment.

★ ★ ★ ★ ★

Examples of Response Cards in Action

Example A: Ready Response to Reinforce a Concept or Skill

The teacher greets students at the door with premade response cards. Each student receives a card for use at a point in the lesson. When it is time for group responses, the card is ready and accessible; no time is wasted in distribution. After using the cards, students drop them in a basket on their way out of the classroom. The teacher stores the cards for the next lesson.

Example B: Turning Confusion Into a Light Bulb Moment

The class is confused about the difference between two or three categories presented during instruction. Students quickly form four-member teams. One person in each group tears a piece of paper into four equal parts. One section is dealt to each member. The teacher gives directions for making a response card using the confusing terms. Once all cards are completed, the teacher provides a question. Each group discusses the question and comes to consensus on the correct response before pinching the correct answer on the cards. When a signal is given, they raise the cards for the teacher to view and praise each light bulb moment. The teacher continues to give questions and discussion time. Students drop their response cards in the trash can as they leave the room.

Example C: Partner Response Cards

Place response cards in a center for partners to use as a game for review or reinforcement. Partners face each other. The teaching partner reads each fill-in-the-blank statement or question while the other student responds. Answers are checked using a key. If an answer is wrong, they are encouraged to talk about the confusion. Students swap roles so each one has an opportunity to be the teacher as they play the game.

MANAGING SIGNAL RESPONSES

What Is a Signal Response?

Students use a signal such as a raised hand or an action sign to respond to a question. It is a quick, informal way to assess knowledge, feelings, attitudes, and interests.

What Are the Instructional Benefits of Signal Responses?

- A signal is a quick, nonthreatening assessment tool for the differentiated classroom.
- The teacher gathers needed data in a brief period of time.
- No student materials are required.
- Students actively engage in the assessment and have fun with the game-like format.
- The assessment strategy can be used before, during, and after learning.

Teacher's Role

- Select a signal that reveals the information needed for planning. Be sure it is easy for students to learn.
- Demonstrate use of the signal.
- Use the same signal often so it becomes a routine response for the group. Avoid using one signal as the "only" response. When one signal is used too often, it may become a mundane procedure. The learner thinks "Here we go again!" and stops taking the response seriously. When the student is comfortable using a signal response, introduce a new one. Introduce new signals to add novelty to the informal assessment strategies.
- Remember to use signals to check attitudes, feelings, interests, understanding, and knowledge.
- Use signals to assess understanding before, during, and after the lesson:

    Before: Use a signal response a week or two before the information is taught to reveal the students' attitudes, interests, and knowledge base related to an upcoming standard, skill, concept, or fact.

    During: Present questions during learning to identify students who need to have specific segments adjusted or revamped. The responses also uncover the student's comfort level, confusion, understanding, or a need for more explanation.

    After: Use signals after learning to identify the learner's immediate needs and information to address in plans for the next learning experience. Use the responses to reveal the student's strengths, interests, and overall understanding.

Demystifying Signal Responses

Tell students they have used signal responses throughout their lives. Give them some examples, such as the peace sign, raising their hands, and nodding or shaking their heads to indicate yes or no. Explain that the sender and the receiver must understand the meaning attached to the signal.

Explain that signals will be used to give you information for planning lessons and activities. Introduce signal responses by asking to use the "Thumb It" signal to indicate their knowledge of a sport, historical event, or vacation site.

Thumbs up = I know a lot!

Thumbs to the side = I know something.

Thumbs down = I don't know anything about it.

Student's Role

- Understand how to perform the signal response for questions.

- Know the purpose and meaning of each signal.

- Be honest when using a signal because it expresses your personal feelings, interests, and knowledge. Each signal is important because it helps the teacher plan lessons.

- Use signals that are assigned for you to use individually or while learning in a group. Remember that the signal may not be understood by everyone in the class.

FIVE (STAR) MANAGEMENT TIPS FOR USING SIGNAL RESPONSES

1. Assess with a signal reponse a week or two before the information is taught so you can use the data to develop plans for individual students. Also use signal responses during and after learning.

2. Teach the signal, the purpose, and the meaning and explain how the information will be used.

3. Use the quickest, easiest signals to reveal what the student knows.

4. Build the learner's repertoire of signal responses. After a signal is learned, it may be used strategically for an individual student, a small group, or the total class.

5. Use signal responses as one part of the data when making curriculum decisions!

Examples of Effective Response Signals

Example A: Telling Hands

When you have five minutes before or after a lesson, preassess for an upcoming lesson. Use a list of vocabulary words, concepts, or facts for the study. After demonstrating how it works, ask students to use the following "Telling Hands" activity responses as a preassessment.

Hands reaching up forming a "Y" = *YES! I know it.*

Hands touching high over the head forming an "O"= *Oh, I know a little about it.*

Hands over the ears = *I have never heard this.*

Example B: Stand! Bend! Sit!

Use the following signal responses to assess vocabulary words, concepts, or facts:

Stand = I know it, use it, and can explain it.

Bend (at the waist) = I have heard of it.

Sit = I don't have a clue about this.

Continue the discussion by calling on students who are standing to tell what they know.

Option:

Announce that it is "Stand and Deliver" time! Each student who is standing becomes a Stand and Deliver captain. Divide other students into small groups. Assign one captain to each group to share his or her knowledge about the topic and to lead a discussion about it.

Example C: Signal and Shout (A Review for a Test)

At the end of a unit, the teacher and/or students develop fill-in-the-blank statements as a review for a test.

The teacher tells students to point to their brain when they know the answer. The teacher reads one statement, provides thinking time by waiting for individual signals, and then rings a bell. Students who know the answer shout the answer in unison. Students who do not know the answer or do not shout the correct response write the statement and correct response as a study note. The steps are repeated.

MANAGING STAND AND SHOW!

What Is Stand and Show?

Stand and show is an informal assessment tool designed for students to stand in order to indicate their knowledge level in relation to a standard, topic, or skill. Words or numbers are posted to indicate varying levels. The place the student chooses to stand identifies the learner's knowledge level. Stand and show may be used to identify the learners' interests or feeling about a topic or skill. It can be designed to use before, during, and after learning to identify progress with any topic or skill.

What Are the Instructional Benefits of Stand and Show?

When students stand and show their level of knowledge, the teacher has a clear view of where each individual stands and the overall positions taken by the whole group. The names of students on each level are recorded to plan strategies and activities.

The novelty added to assessment generates positive attitudes toward learning. Post novel signs such as the following to present the various levels.

Examples:

- I know a lot!   I know a little!   I don't have a clue!

- Expert   Amateur   Beginner

Movement is a major benefit of stand and show. Each student stands in a section of the room designated to the area of his or her choice. After a sedentary task or test, students usually are relieved to move out of their seats.

When the stand-and-show activity is used with several topics or skills, students can see and appreciate how knowledge levels are diverse and constantly changing.

Teacher's Role

When stand and show is identified as the best assessment tool to gather the needed information, consider the space, furniture arrangement, and the amount of time allotted.

- Decide how the learners in the sections will express themselves after they take their positions. Some options include the following:
    - Form small discussion groups. Each group member presents his or her opinions or reasons for taking this position or stand.
    - Conduct a brainstorming session to identify the important facts. Create a graffiti-style poster to display them. Share highlights in a creative way with the rest of the class.
    - Lead a class discussion of the information by calling on volunteers in each position.
    - Make a list of students in their selected positions so you can design the instructional plan to meet their diverse needs.
    - Use the same informal tool until the class understands how it works. Add a different format for novelty.

Demystifying Stand and Show

Tell students they will stand in specific places to show the level of what they know, believe in, or find interesting in relation to a topic, skill, or standard. Emphasize that some students will stand in different areas because the place chosen is determined by each person's current knowledge base and experiences. Explain how each student's position helps you plan each lesson to teach whatever each person needs to learn in the upcoming study.

Student's Role

- Be sure you understand the directions for the stand-and-show activity.
- Choose your position because it shows what *you* know or like. Do not be influenced by your classmates' selections.
- Respect everyone's choice.
- Share the reasons you chose the position.
- Realize that your position helps the teacher plan assignments and activities that are specifically designed for your needs.

FIVE (STAR) MANAGEMENT TIPS FOR STAND AND SHOW

1. Identify the purpose of the stand-and-show assessment activity.

   Examples:

   To assess the learner's knowledge base   To express feelings

   To state a belief   To give an opinion

2. Establish areas with enough space to avoid overcrowding. Students may need to stand among desks or other furniture.

3. Give explicit directions before learners move to their positions.

4. Ask students to select and write their stand-and-show position before actually moving to that designated area. Tell students to discuss the reasons they selected the position after everyone is in place..

5. Establish a system for student movement that fits the activity and the arrangement of your classroom.

Examples of Movement Systems

Everyone moves to his chosen spot on the count of three. Label sections of the classroom. Call each section to move.

- 123 Go!
- Section Call!
- Gender Call!
- Position Call!
- Alphabet Call!

Examples of Stand and Show

Figure 5.7		
Activity	*How does it look?*	*How does it work?*
Four corners or squaring off!	Label four classroom corners or areas to indicate levels of understanding and knowledge. Example | I do not know.	I know a little.
I know a lot!	I am an expert!		• The teacher names the topic, standard, skill, or concept. • Students go to the area that matches their knowledge or topic understanding. • Lead a discussion that emphasizes how they can move from the lower levels to the expert level.
Human bar graph	Post signs on the wall to indicate levels of understanding. Students move in front of the sign that reflects their individual level, forming a straight line at each one. Compare the lines to the bars on a bar graph. Each student represents one section of a bar on the graph. Ask students to stand in place so the lines are straight both horizontally and vertically to create the bar graph.	• Each student in a line becomes a segment of the bar on the bar graph. • Compare and contrast the number of students in front of each sign. • Discuss their differences.
Show your number	The teacher asks, "Where do you stand on the line?" Students stand in front of a number chosen on a Likert scale of 1 to 5.	• Post the numbers 1 to 5 to form a Likert scale. Be sure the numbers are spaced. • Name the topic, skill, concept, or standard. Give students time to identify their knowledge levels. Students take their positions. • Groups discuss their reasons for choosing the positions.
Circle gab	Conversation circles are formed with students who have common beliefs, opinions, experiences, or backgrounds.	• Each student joins other learners on the same knowledge level. • They discuss and brainstorm to defend their view, opinion, thinking process, or background.
Energizing partner	Students choose partners and share the information learned. They meet in designated areas.	• Partners meet to discuss, share, review, brainstorm, read, or check an assignment. • The same partner teams meet for a period of time. • This gives them the opportunities to bond and develop mutual respect, trust, and friendship.

Managing Formal Assessment

What Is Formal Assessment?

Formal assessment is administered to gather specific, documented data for analysis. Patterns of strength, weakness, or needs are analyzed to identify the student's status in the mastery of the standards. End of the unit tests, rubrics, portfolios, and anecdotal records are examples of formal assessments.

What Are the Instructional Benefits of Formal Assessment?

- The level of mastery can be identified and recorded.
- The data gathered at the end of a learning segment is used to develop plans for students' identified strengths and needs.
- The results provide information that is analyzed to make changes in the student's instructional program or placement in special classes.
- Students can be instructed in the use of test-taking skills to use throughout their academic careers.
- Formal assessment results are used for reporting purposes because they are more objective and reliable than informal assessment.

Teacher's Role

- Collect formal assessment tools such as rubrics and checklists to use before, during, and after learning. Add new tools to your repertoire. Make a list of the assessments and place a checkmark beside the tool each time you use it. This adds novelty and identifies the assessments that require an introduction before they are used.
- Select the most effective and efficient assessment tool that will yield the results you need for planning.
- Administer formal preassessments one to two weeks before the unit of study begins. Analyze the data to identify the learner's entry point or readiness level for instruction.
- Report formal assessment results to other teachers and to parents as needed.
- Use formal assessents to determine mastery of standards, facts, or skills for a segment of learning.

Demystifying Formal Assessment

Use a lecturette similar to the following to introduce formal assessment:

> A formal assessment is a test to find out what you know about a topic or skill. It also reveals what you don't know or understand. A formal assessment gives the teacher specific information to plan your lessons and activities. You may receive a grade, points, or a score on a formal assessment. The results often become a part of a grade and may be reported to other teachers and to your parents.

Student's Role

- Remember to show what you know on the test because the teacher uses the information to plan your activities and assignments.

- Ask questions if you do not understand the directions.

- If you complete the assessment early, check each response for accuracy.

- Always learn from your mistakes. When you get a test back and the results show that you do not know or understand something, ask someone for help or find the correct answers in your book or other sources.

- Remember, always, always, always, give your best to each test. Celebrate learning!

FIVE (STAR) MANAGEMENT TIPS FOR FORMAL ASSESSMENT

1. Use a formal assessment tool when an informal one will not provide enough information. Select the most appropriate formal tool to obtain the data needed to shows the learner's needs, progress, and mastery. Use a variety of formal assessment tools.

   Examples of Formal Assessment Tools

Fill in the blank	Academic journals	Open-book tests
Open-ended responses	Products	Portfolios
Quizzes	Reports	Rubrics
Standardized tests	Teacher-made tests	True/false tests

2. If directions and guidelines accompany the assessment, become familiar with them before administering it.

3. Teach the students how to use the selected formal assessment tool. Introduce the terminology and model the specific guidelines or procedures while explaining your thought process.

4. Use more than one formal assessment to make informed curriculum planning decisions that address the specific needs of each student.

5. Analyze the data from formative and summative assessments to obtain the formal grade.

Examples of Formal Assessments

Example A: Combining Formal Assessments

Students work in groups on an assignment and present the learned information as a team. The group, peers, and the teacher score the presentation using a rubric that addresses the cognitive and social aspects of the process and the presentation. After the completion of the presentation and the unit, each student is given an independent test to show what he or she has learned.

Example B: Develop and Administer a Pretest/Posttest

A teacher-designed pretest is administered to assess the identified standards one to two weeks before the unit of study begins. The data is gathered from the results to pinpoint the knowledge base of each learner. The standards are taught according to the identified individual and group needs. At the end of the unit, the pretest is administered again as the posttest to measure growth and mastery.

Example C: Teacher-Assigned Portfolio

Each student is given a folder at the beginning of a unit of study. During the study, the teacher instructs the students to place assigned artifacts into their portfolio. A list of ongoing entries is the front page of the portfolio. During and upon completion of the gathering, students conference with a portfolio partner, the teacher, or their parents to discuss accomplishments, insights, growth, and needs. Individual entries can be graded, and a portfolio grade assigned upon completion.

MANAGING PRETEST/POSTTEST

What Is a Pretest/Posttest?

A pretest is given to find out what the learner knows before the unit is taught. The test can be administered one to two weeks before the unit is introduced. This provides time to analyze the data gathered from the pretest results and to tailor plans for each student.

The same instrument can be used as the posttest at the end of the study to analyze areas of growth and identify parts that need further development.

What Are the Instructional Benefits of Pretests/Posttests?

- Teaching is more efficient when pretests and posttests are administered. The evidence shows what individuals, as well as the total class, need during and after instruction. A teacher can share the results and identify gaps and strengths.

- The teacher can use the data to design the flexible grouping strategies for the activities.

- Students know what is important in the study when they see the pretest information.

- Materials and resources can be gathered to match the student's strengths, learning styles, intelligences, and needs.

Teacher's Role

- Design the most efficient, effective test to show what the students know.
- Be sure the test covers the needed components being taught.
- Vary the questioning formats.
- Explain to students that they are not supposed to know everything on the pretest.
- Give the pretest as a posttest to analyze growth.

Student's Role

- Understand that the reason for taking the pretest is to show your background and knowledge base.
- Realize that the items you don't know will be learned during the study.
- Take it seriously! Do your best on the test.
- Learn everything during the study so you will know the answers on the posttest.
- Check your growth by comparing your pretest and posttest answers.

FIVE (STAR) MANAGEMENT TIPS FOR PRETESTS/POSTTESTS

1. The best tests are designed by the teacher. Remember, you know what you are teaching more than the people who designed the company tests!

2. Select questions from areas in the study. Check to see that the test covers the identified standards, skills, content, and objectives for the study.

3. Disperse the easy items among the difficult answers so students can search for the easy ones. This teaches students to be detectives! This way, no one should make a zero, and it is possible that no one will have 100% of the answers correct on the pretest.

4. Tell the students that their answers help you plan each activity and strategy for individuals and small groups.

5. Compare the pretest and posttest results. Share needs and growth with students.

★ ★ ★ ★ ★

Examples of Pretests/Posttests

Example A: A Formal Pretest/Posttest Grid

A teacher prepares a grid sheet with six subtopics and tells the learners to write anything they know about each category. At the end of the study, the students fill out another grid with the same categories and write what they know. It is exciting to see how much the learners know now. Lead a celebration cheer. YES! YES! YES!

Example B: Manipulative Pretest/Posttest

A teacher prepares a checklist for a skill being taught with each student's name on the grid. During the week, the teacher asks individuals to show different tasks and concepts with the manipulatives. When each example is performed correctly, the students place a checkmark or star beside their name on the checklist.

This revealing information is used to group the students for the upcoming unit small group assignments. The manipulatives are placed in a station during the unit of study. By the end of the unit, the teacher observes that most students have mastered the skills. This warrants giving the assessment posttest to the few students who did not master the skill to identify specific needs.

Example C: Using a Company Pretest/Posttest

The teacher reads over the company-made test carefully. Questions are identified to be addressed during the unit of study. Questions not addressed are announced to the group by saying, "You do not need to answer the following questions or items: ___, ___, ___." Any student would like to hear that statement!

MANAGING EFFECTIVE QUESTIONING

What Is an Effective Question?

An effective question is a mental probe that guides a learner's thinking toward an appropriate response. Questions are designed to review, process information, predict, or check memory skills. The student responses provide data for immediate instruction and planning. Questions are used in the appropriate format at the right time.

What Are the Instructional Benefits of Effective Questioning?

- Questioning is a quick way to check for understanding and to assess students' needs and strengths before, during, and after learning.
- Effective questions allow the teacher to guide a student's thinking. While helping a student process information, the teacher gets a sense of the student's problem-solving capabilities. The student gains a feeling of achievement for finding the answers by himself or herself.
- Questions can lead students to connect old and new learning.
- A question can be used to focus students' attention, stimulate curiosity, and challenge minds.

Teacher's Role

- Differentiate questions based on the learner's abilities, knowledge level, learning styles, preferences, and interests.
- Develop a variety of questioning techniques to use as assessments. This keeps students intrigued and challenged.

Figure 5.8	
Questioning Technique	**Directions for the Technique**
Random call	Ask a question and pause to provide "think" time before calling on a student to respond. This keeps students in suspense as to who will be chosen to respond, so everyone prepares a mental response. Randomly call on someone for an answer.
Unison call	Ask a question and provide "think" time. Call for an oral group response.
Quick call pass	Ask a question. Call on a student to quickly call on a classmate for the response. If the student hesitates, call on someone for the answer.
Cluster call	Distribute question(s) to groups. Each team selects a recorder and reporter. Students form a brainstorming cluster around the recorder. Each group comes to consensus on the best answer to the question. The reporter announces the team's best response to the class.
Partner call	Identify two students as A and B partners. The teacher asks a question, gives wait time, and calls on A or B partner to respond. The designated partner answers the question. The other partner verifies or corrects the response and adds information to it. This leads to a class discussion.

- Strategically ask questions as checkpoints for understanding before, during, and after learning segments so you can adjust your instructional pace if necessary.

- Use Bloom's taxonomy as a question guide to develop critical thinking and problem-solving skills.

- Ask effective questions to promote thinking that links new information to a student's personal world. For example, ask the learner how the information or skill can be used in daily activities at home.

Demystifying Effective Questioning

You can introduce effective questions by describing them as brain probes. Use dialogue similar to the following to discuss the purpose of questions:

> Questions are asked to learn what you know and don't know. They give you opportunities to give your opinions and thoughts about the things you are learning. They help you think in different ways. Often they lead you into more detail about what you know. All answers are accepted, honored, and valued in this classroom.

Use this coaching metaphor to help students understand the value of questions in their world:

A coach asks the players questions before, during, and after the game.

Examples:

What do you need to do to help us win this game?

What are the best moves to make against this team?

What will be the other team's game plan?

Questions are asked to provide assistance and guidance when the going gets tough.

Examples:

What happened out there?

Why didn't you _____?

What do you need to do the next time you are in that situation?

Student's Role

- Listen carefully to the entire question.

- Think before you answer. Get your thoughts in order and mentally prepare to respond.

- Follow the teacher's directions for responding.

- Don't be afraid to show what you know! Express yourself.

- If you write the response, pretend you are talking to someone and write down every word.

FIVE (STAR) MANAGEMENT TIPS FOR EFFECTIVE QUESTIONING

1. Present questions in novel ways.

Figure 5.9

Container Questions	Action Questions	Written Questions	Oral Questions
• Basket • Box • Bucket • Can • Compartment • Cup • Drawer • Envelope • Folder • Glass • Hat • Jar • Pan • Pouch • Sack • Sock • Suitcase • Tub • Tube	• Roll a cube with a question on each side. • Use a spinner. • Sing to favorite tunes. • Use game board formats. • Select easy or difficult questions from a container. • Toss a dice to identify the question choice. • Race with a classmate to the question. The winner selects the question for the opponent to answer.	• In a survey • On the board/overhead • In a PowerPoint presentation • In a journal • In a station • On a choice board • In a shaker or jar • In the book • On a test • Under desks or chairs • On ribbons • In a spotlight • In graffiti style • On the door • On a mobile	• Within the group • From partners • From individuals • From consensus • Read from written material • In a game format such as "21 Questions" • In a computer program • Recorded • In a rap

2. Occasionally give students unexpected ways to respond to questions. Use each response strategy until they master or take ownership of it. When you use it again, the learners will know how to use it without extensive directions.

Examples:

- Give partners time to whisper the answer to each other, agree on the best answer, and write it down.
- Engage students in physical actions for responses such as standing, sitting, or using hand signals.
- Ask each student to respond by writing a response in a shape related to the study.
- Use response cards with the possible answers written in unique fonts or neon colors.
- Ask students to record responses on a sticky note or small piece of paper. They wait for a signal and show the answer to a neighbor before the teacher gives the correct answer.

(Continued)

(Continued)

3. Use Bloom's taxonomy:

- Make a checklist of the key terms on each level of Bloom's taxonomy to monitor use.
- Introduce questions strategically throughout the plans to develop better thinkers and problem solvers.
- To differentiate, allow students to choose questions from a list designed for their level.
- Create questions from independent assignments or group work that require written or oral responses.
- All students need to know the definitions of words used in questions to be able to answer them. Post a chart of frequently used terms in the classroom. Allow students to brainstorm the interpretations of each term, and then write it beside each word. Learners understand each term when they use their own terminology.

Examples:

Sequence: Place in order.

Contrast: Tell how _____ and _____ are different.

4. An effective questioner understands that quality is better than quantity and timing is important. Knowing when to ask the right question is a talent that develops over a period of time.

It is crucial to consider the student's feelings and emotions for differentiated instruction. A lead-in question may be the key to opening conversations. Use open-ended questions such as "Tell me about . . ." or "What did you learn?" Questions such as these lead the learner to important self-discoveries, provide opportunities to express feelings, and allow the teacher to find out what the student knows about a specific topic or skill. They are excellent assessment tools.

5. Vary the types of questions. Remember to ask both explicit and open-ended questions. Be aware that most students have to be taught how to answer questions that require implicit responses.

Literal: The answer is in the writing. You can identify the information you need by pointing to it. Remember, the answer to a literal question is usually "right there."

| What | When | Where | Who | How |

Inferential: The answer is not stated outright—it is inferred—so you have to read between the lines to discover it. It is like seeing darkness behind a door. You use clues to guess what is on the other side of the door. Read the sentence and use the clues in the text to come up with an answer when you cannot point to it in the passage.

○ *How did the character feel?*
○ *What was the weather like?*

Evaluative: The answer explains the importance or value of the information. It gives the benefits of the facts or ideas.

○ *Why is this information (character or idea) important?*
○ *Will the characters become better citizens as a result of their experiences? If your answer is yes, tell how you think they will improve.*

Examples of Effective Questioning

Example A: Questioning Games for Novelty in a Small Group

Pull My String

1. Use one string for each student in the group.

2. Tie one end of each string to a ruler.

3. Ask each student to hold the other end of a string.

4. The teacher holds all of the rulers.

5. Ask a question. Give students time to think of the answer.

6. Pull a student's string for a response to a question.

On the Ball

1. Create a list of numbered questions.

2. Write a number on each ball.

3. Place the numbered balls in a large container.

4. Call on a student to pull a ball from the container and read the question that corresponds to the number.

5. Ask all students to prepare a mental response.

6. The student who selects the ball calls on someone to respond.

Mystery Question

1. The teacher or students prepare questions relevant to the current study.

2. The questions are hidden in a jar, sack, envelope, or can.

3. Each student selects a mystery question to answer.

Example B: Selecting the Right Question and Probing Statement for the Right Time

Differentiating Questions Across Content Areas

Intentionally select the best questions to uncover the information you need to probe the learner's thought and to guide the differentiated instruction. Figure 5.10 presents examples of different questions that may be used across content areas.

When the student is identified for an independent differentiated assignment, use questions similar to the those in Figure 5.11 before, during, and after the tasks for conversation starters and feedback. These interactions place the responsibility on the student to identify immediate needs and progress of the assignment. This provides the teacher with ongoing feedback related to what the student is learning.

Figure 5.10

Purpose of the Question	Sample Questions and/or Statements
To focus attention, stimulate curiosity, and challenge minds	What do you think about when you see _____ (a photo, object, word, etc.)? What are the important facts? What will happen next?
To find out what they know in order to identify needs before, during, and after learning	What do you know about this? What do you remember? Brainstorm a list of related facts and important details.
To check mental preparation to work	Do I need to explain a part of the directions for you? Do you have any questions about the steps you need to take? What do you need before you begin this activity?
To check for understanding	What steps did you use to get your answer? What were you thinking as you created the _____? How would you explain this in your own words?
To discover opinions or views	What do you think about this? What is your point of view or opinion? What do you think is the problem or solution?
To pinpoint the most valuable information	Can you tell me the most important part to remember? What was the main idea? What are the highlights?
To identify what the student wants to learn next	What would you like to learn next? If you had a choice, what would you choose to learn about _____? What was the hardest part for you? How can I help you?
To connect old and new learning	How do you know about _____? Where have you used this information? Does _____ remind you of an experience you have had? Tell me about it. How will your experiences help you learn this new information?
To organize ideas	What goes with this part? What are your thoughts about _____? Categorize them. What comes first? next? last? Can you name three highlights from the beginning, middle, and end of _____? List the highlights.
To address what the student needs to know	What would help you learn more about _____? What do you need to learn next? What was difficult for you?

Figure 5.10

Purpose of the Question	Sample Questions and/or Statements
To corral knowledge	How can you organize everything you know or remember about _____? Write your responses in your journal.
	Which memory tool can help you remember the important information?
	What do you know about _____? Design a graphic organizer for your answer.
To give personal ownership	How can you use this information in another class?
	How would you compare our new learning to an experience in your life?
	What is the best way for you to learn _____?

Figure 5.11

Before *The Designing Stage*	• What would you like to learn about this topic or study? • What tasks would you like to complete to learn more about it? • What resources or materials do you need? • How much time will it take to complete your tasks? • How will your final product be presented? • How would you like to be graded on your work?
During *The Assessing Progress Stage*	• What have you done so far? • What have you learned? • How can I help you? • Do you need more or different materials? • Have you made any new discoveries? • Is there anything that we need to revamp or change in your assignment? • Show me some examples of your work.
After *The Feedback Stage*	• What did you learn? • What were your favorite tasks? most challenging? most difficult? • If you are assigned another contract, which segment would you want to keep? • What needs to be changed the next time? • Did you need more assistance? ___ yes ___ no When? • Did you understand each assignment, task, and procedure? ___ yes ___ no If not, identify and explain the problem(s). • Were you given enough time? ___ yes ___ no If no, explain. • Would you like to complete another assignment like this? ___ yes ___no Why or why not?

MANAGING ANECDOTAL RECORDS

What Is an Anecdotal Record?

An anecdotal record is a note taken from the teacher's personal observations of a learner. The note is used to improve instruction for an individual or group. Consistent, well-kept notes and forms are the key to effective anecdotal records.

What Are the Instructional Benefits of Anecdotal Records?

- Because anecdotal records are the product of teacher observation, anecdotal records reveal information about a learner's strengths and needs.

- They provide individual data in academic areas and in social interactions and may include developmental characteristics.

- The teacher can observe a student before, during, and after learning and take notes on his or her apparent learning and social needs without disturbing his or her engagement in activities.

- Anecdotal notes supplement other forms of assessment data to ensure individual needs are adequately addressed in lesson plans.

- Strengths and needs are observed over a period of time, revealing growth or evidence of backsliding in a given area.

Teacher's Role

- Establish a record-keeping system that works best for you.

- Use specific, observable comments, such as the following:
  - The student does not know how to use context clues.
  - The standard has been mastered by the learner.
  - The student needs more instruction on _____.

- Avoid adjectives or subjective phrases, such as the following:
  - Good procedures
  - Working successfully
  - Poor work

- Observe and gather data regarding every aspect of the learner, including knowledge base, learning style, work habits, attitude, and interest level.

- Analyze the notes when developing plans so you can address significant patterns or target specific areas. Share your observations with students, parents, and colleagues during conferences.

Demystifying Anecdotal Records

Tell students that teachers keep anecdotal records or notes as they observe one student or a group. Notes are made before, during, and after lessons so a teacher can remember what he or she needs to do to help them. Let the students know that they may see you make notes as they work and that the information is used to plan their assignments and activities.

Student's Role

- Realize that some teacher notes are made to assist you in learning. Other notes identify your strengths.

- Tell the teacher when you do not understand directions, part of a lesson, or an assignment so it can be placed in the notes.

- Answer questions honestly as the teacher makes notes.

- Be aware that the teacher's notes may be used in conferences with you, your parents, and other teachers to help you improve.

- Remember that the teacher takes notes to plan the best lessons for you.

FIVE (STAR) MANAGEMENT TIPS FOR ANECDOTAL RECORDS

1. Establish a record-keeping system that works for you.

   Example:
   - Use a large 5 × 7-inch index card for each student.
   - Create a title or cover card to place on top of the note card to create privacy.
   - Write the student's name on the upper right-hand corner of the card.
   - Alphabetize the cards.
   - Punch a hole in the upper left-hand corner of each card.
   - Place a ring through the holes in the cards to form a class set.

2. When using observation as an assessment tool, make brief notes on the student's card.
   - Record the date and time of day for each entry and record your comments.
   - Write specific observable comments.
   - Beware of using adjectives and adverbs in your descriptions. Avoid subjective comments.
   - Focus observations on work patterns, growth, needs, and task behaviors that hinder or enhance learning.

3. When a student's card is filled on the front and back, create another card for the student and insert it on the ring. If you notice that a student only has one card containing a few brief comments while other students have multiple cards, this is a cue for you to observe this student more carefully.

4. Inform students about the purpose of taking anecdotal notes and show them some samples.

5. Refer to the accumulated data as documented evidence to support your perception of a student's needs in team meetings, teacher discussions, and parent conferences.

Examples of Anecdotal Notes

Example A: Observing Peer Tutoring

A teacher circulates during work time with a ring of large index cards to record findings. A student is working with a peer tutor on a skill he or she has not mastered. The teacher writes a note on the peer tutor's quality, easy-to-understand explanation of the skill. This shows that the tutor truly understands the concept. The teacher writes another note on the card of the student who is receiving instruction, outlining the problems and the accomplishments of the tutoring session. A note is made about gaps in learning or concepts the student grasps or is struggling to understand. This information helps the teacher remember what this student needs to practice and where to begin the next instructional activity.

Example B: Group Member Feedback

Students are working in groups on a cooperative learning activity. The teacher writes notes to each team and to some individual team members, sharing specific observations about the level of cooperation and social interactions within the group.

Providing specific observations helps students become more aware of their actions within a group setting and helps them make positive changes to be more considerate and effective members of a learning team. Watch for patterns of work in order to conference successfully with a student.

Example C: Noting Subtle Actions and Reactions

Be alert to a student's body language, including facial expressions and gestures.

While giving directions, observe and note signs of insecurity, misunderstanding, or concern. Make written or mental notes as reminders to praise students who listen, follow directions, work cooperatively, work independently, and engage eagerly in tasks.

Managing Surveys

What Is a Survey?

A survey is a questionnaire designed to identify personal information about the student's feelings, likes, dislikes, knowledge base, and other information. There are three types of surveys that need to be administered throughout the school year: (1) personal preferences, (2) study habits, or (3) knowledge base and experience regarding upcoming topics.

What Are the Instructional Benefits of Using Surveys?

By surveying for personal preferences, attitudes, and feelings, a teacher can get to know individual students. The more teachers learn about students, the more chances they have to set up opportunities for students to connect new learning to their worlds.

Teacher's Role

- Develop a questionnaire that fits the situation.
- Survey throughout the year because students are forever changing.
- Survey for different purposes at the appropriate time:
  - Strengths/weaknesses
  - Likes/dislikes
  - Habits/experiences
  - Attitudes/feelings/emotions
  - Content knowledge/background
- Tie results to instruction. Remember, the brain learns by making links and connections between the known and the unknown—or new—information.
- Use data to build rapport, especially with struggling learners.

Demystifying Surveys

Explain the basic meanings of the word *survey* using examples of their use from the learners' lives. Here is an example:

> Restaurants often use a form to ask their patrons what they enjoyed or need to eat, so they can use the information to plan their menus.
> In the same way, you may be asked to answer questions so specific lessons and activities can be planned for your needs and interests.

Student's Role

- The survey may tell the teacher about your previous experiences on a new topic.
- Be aware that a survey tells teachers how to plan for you.
- Answer all questions completely.
- Realize that your teacher can help you learn more about your interests.
- Let the teacher know when your interests change.

FIVE (STAR) MANAGEMENT TIPS FOR USING SURVEYS

1. Remember to use three different types of surveys as needed throughout the year to gain more knowledge about the learner.
   - Finding personal preferences
   - Examining study habits
   - Determining knowledge and experience about a topic

2. The most informative surveys are designed by the teacher.

3. Give parents surveys to find their view, reveal more detailed information about the student, or record the learner's answer.

4. Do not make the questionnaire too lengthy. It is better to divide up the questions so students or parents can zero in on quality answers.

5. Analyze the learned information and use the results to plan learning opportunities that appeal to students while addressing their individual personal and academic needs.

Examples of Surveys

Example A: Personal Preference Survey

What is your favorite subject? Why?

What is your favorite way to learn _____?

Example B: Study Habits

Where is your favorite place to study?

Who do you like to have help you with your homework problems? Why?

Example C: Unit Knowledge Base

What do you know about _____?

What does the word _____ mean?

What do you know about this person?

List the facts you know about _____.

MANAGING JOURNALS

What Is a Journal?

A journal is a place where thoughts are recorded so they can be organized, saved, and read at a later time. A journal entry is a writing activity that may have the details of an event, an experience, an observation, or a memory. The major purpose of a journal entry is to record the student's thoughts. Correct English usage and mechanics are not emphasized. The goal of journaling is for students to get their thoughts on paper and to generate creative thinking.

What Are the Instructional Benefits of Using Journals for Assessment?

- Individuals, partners, or small groups can use journals.
- A journal is an excellent learning tool for all subject areas and all grade levels. A journal assessment activity may be used for a daily lesson, weekly assignment, or unit.
- Journal assignments may ask the student to record important facts, steps, procedures, and other information during a study. These entries become resources for review and reference during independent study or test preparation.
- Writing new information helps a student process it.
- Journaling gives the teacher a clearer view of a learner's attitudes and beliefs about a topic.

Teacher's Role

- Identify the purpose for the journaling activity.

  To gather information about the student's comprehension of the lesson

  To explain step-by-step thinking

  To record interests and attitudes about _____

- Select a journaling strategy or genre. Use different forms because some students write better in one format than in another.
- Provide the necessary time, tools, and materials.
- Give lead-in statements to obtain specific information.
- Monitor journal entries and provide specific feedback.

Demystifying Journals

Some students may be confused the first time a journal activity is introduced outside of the English or language arts classroom. Explain that a journal is an effective learning and assessment tool for any subject:

A journal is a place to gather your thoughts. It is a special place for you to record important information, findings, facts, and ideas. It is a place to note what you are learning, what you don't understand, and what you would like to learn. A journal activity is an effective communication tool to use between a teacher and student.

Student's Role

- Follow the teacher's directions to decorate the cover of your journal.
- If allowed, add drawings, stories, and passing thoughts whenever you have extra time.
- Record the date, title, or purpose above each entry.
- Keep your journal neat, organized, and in a special place so it is easy to find.
- Use the journal as a study resource for reviews.

FIVE (STAR) MANAGEMENT TIPS FOR USING JOURNALS FOR ASSESSMENT

1. Give each student a sheet of colored paper for a journal cover. Tell students to personalize the cover by writing their name in large, colorful letters using a graffiti style. Instruct them to add symbols, words, and phrases that reflect the purpose of the journal. For example:

   Personal journal. Add symbols, words, and phrases that represent your family, hobbies, and interests to decorate the cover.

   Content journal. Decorate the cover with symbols and themes related to the study.

2. Use a variety of strategies for independent journal assessments. The following chart presents some ways to use journal activities for assessment purposes:

Figure 5.12

Graphics	Learn and Write
• Plot on an organizer	• Write about content information
• Draw the object and label it	• Answer a question
• Create a cartoon	• Brainstorm a list
• Design illustration frames for a sequence	• Free write
• Illustrate	• Draw a timeline and plot the information
• Create an advertisement	• Record a sequence
• Cut, paste, and write	• Write a recipe
• Create a graph and explain	• Write a sequence
• Draw a map	• Develop a fact sheet
• Diagram the parts	• Add a log or diary entry
• Design a caricature	• Develop an assigned lead-in

Graphics	Learn and Write
• Design a spreadsheet • Create a PowerPoint presentation • Create a brochure • Design a puzzle • Create a game and its rules • Make a shape book • Design a mobile • Decorate a shirt • Design a Web page	• Write an editorial or news flash • Write a letter • Create a song, poem, rap, cheer, or jingle • Write reflections • Write a summary • Write a critique • Write a report • Set goals • Explain your thinking process • Express feelings and attitudes • Write a progress report

3. Use flexible grouping during and after the journal assignment.
   • Brainstorm with a partner and write_____.
   • Discuss _____ in your group and record the best ideas.
   • Write your opinion about _____ and share it with your group.
   • Use a double-entry journal. You write on one side and your partner writes on the other side.

4. Add novelty to the writing experiences.
   • Use a variety of writing implements:

Gel pens	Colored pencils	Magic markers
Crayons	Chalk	Glitter glue

   • Use a variety of writing materials:

Construction paper	Poster board	Chart paper
Wrapping paper	Wallpaper scraps	Note pads

   • Use a variety of writing designs in assignments:

In a pyramid	Around the edges	On the outline an object/picture
In a spiral	In a different font	Using calligraphy

5. Identify various ways for students to share journals during the year. Periodically present choices for individuals and small groups to present or share journal work. Examples:

   • Display it on a table.
   • Share it with a partner, group, or another class.
   • Present it to family members on parent night.
   • Post a favorite page on the class Web site.

Examples of Journaling Activities

Students need time to write journal entries about their requests, comments, questions, and reflections.

Example A: Use Aha Boxes

Each student writes about an aha moment and draws a box around it.

Figure 5.13

MY AHA! Write the most important thing(s) you learned today here:

Example B: Using a Likert Scale

Our Likert scales begin with the number 2 because we believe students deserve a score above 1 for being at school and for participating. See the examples in Figure 5.14.

Figure 5.14

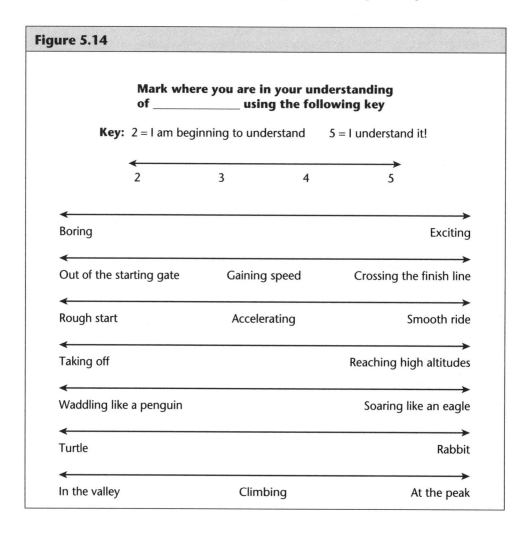

Example C: Draw It!

Draw a picture of an important _____ (place, character, or event in the lesson). Write a brief description of your drawing. Explain why it is important.

Example D: Color the Lesson Segment

Figure 5.15	
Select a color that suits today's lesson.	Tell why you chose this color.

Example E: Theme Song

Choose a song as a theme song for today's lesson. Explain why you selected this song.

MANAGING PORTFOLIOS

What Is a Portfolio?

A portfolio is a place where student work samples are gathered for a specific purpose. The collection reflects progress and growth, needs and strengths. It is an evolving showcase of the student's best work.

Portfolios are designed by the teacher or by the student according to specific criteria and guidelines set forth by the teacher. Portfolios can be binders, notebooks, folders, boxes, electronic disks, or CDs.

What Are the Instructional Benefits of Using Portfolios?

- Portfolios can be adapted to suit all grade levels and subject areas.
- When a student is given the responsibility to select his or her best work and determine which pieces need improvement or replacement, the student has a sense of ownership and control over the learning experience.
- Preparing a portfolio teaches self-assessment and reflection for improvement.
- A portfolio can be completed at the learner's individual pace.
- Progress points and a completion date for a portfolio teach the student how to set goals and generate a sense of pride and accomplishment.

Teacher's Role

- Explain the purpose and goals for using the portfolio.
- Establish the criteria for item selection.
- Engage the student in various aspects of the learning, such as the following:

  Planning the criteria   Selecting the samples

  Assessing the work   Designing the presentation

  Creating a display   Setting new goals

- Establish a timeline with checkpoints and a completion date.
- Identify and explain the assessment tools.

Demystifying Portfolios

Share the meaning of *port,* meaning to carry, and *folio,* meaning "leaves" of paper. Display several different kinds of portfolios, including a briefcase, a leather notebook, and a folder. Discuss portfolios that are required as part of many job applications. Show samples of portfolios the students will use.

Student's Role

- Personalize your portfolio with your name. Decorate it following the teacher's directions.
- Place the guidelines, assessment tools, and important dates inside the portfolio.
- Review the assessment tools and use them according to the timeline to assess your work and reflect on the ways you can improve future assignments.
- Add samples of your work throughout the study.
- Select your best work samples to showcase in the final conference.

FIVE (STAR) MANAGEMENT TIPS FOR USING PORTFOLIOS

1. Identify students who would benefit from creating a portfolio.

2. Determine the purpose, guidelines, and process of building and using the portfolio by
   a. Identifying the type of portfolio:
      ➢ **Teacher selected:** The teacher chooses the items for the portfolio.
      ➢ **Student selected:** The teacher provides the criteria and number of samples for the portfolio. The student chooses the items.
      ➢ **Teacher and student selected:** During a conference, the teacher and student come to consensus on the guidelines and criteria for the portfolio entries.
   b. Identifying the form of the portfolio:
      ➢ **Electronic portfolio:** Personal computer, organizer, travel drive, or CD
      ➢ **Folder portfolio:** X-ray folder, pocket folder, large Baggie, or homemade folder
      ➢ **Notebook or briefcase**
      ➢ **Box portfolio:** Pizza box, shoebox, or plastic storage box

3. Assign portfolio pals or teams so they can conference at scheduled times during the process to monitor progress and check over work. Teach students how to obtain quality results from a conference. Give learners opportunities to give progress reports to the class or a small group.

4. Give students the responsibility of selecting the portfolio work to be assessed. Examples:
   ➢ *Compile five pages that are the best samples of your work.*
   ➢ *Place a small tab on the pages that show your best work or progress.*
   ➢ *Draw a circle around the paragraphs that show your best work.*
   ➢ *Attach personal comments about the sample on the entry if you want to tell the teacher something about your work.*
   ➢ *Use a self-assessment or peer assessment form for the completed portfolio.*

5. Celebrate completion of the portfolio!
   ➢ *Invite parents for a special portfolio showcase/conference.*
   ➢ *Invite students from another class to view the completed works.*
   ➢ *Send electronic portfolios to family members, friends, or pals.*

Examples of Portfolio Assignments

Example A: A Second-Language Student Has (Very Little) Experience With English

Select portfolio activities the student can complete independently or with a partner. The following are the entry samples of the folder portfolio selected to show growth over a three-week period. The student shares and discusses each sample with a parent and/or teacher in a conference.

- Write common phrases needed in daily activities and illustrate each one.

- Draw the individual pieces of furniture in the classroom and label each one in your native language. Write the English word(s) on the other side.

- Read books that have English on one page and your native language on the opposite page. Record the important words, names of characters, or settings in English and in your native language.

- Draw a classroom map or seating chart and record the names of your classmates.

- Visit special areas of the school. Draw a picture of each area or space and label it in English and in your native language.

Use a form for the student to list completed portfolio assignments. Provide a space for the student to list each activity and date of completion. Include activities such as the above entries, the names of books read, story illustrations, poems, CDs, and completed center activities.

Example B: One Student Excels in the Upcoming Topic or Skill

1. Hold a conference with the student to identify interest areas related to the topic.

2. Work with the student to identify appropriate portfolio activities from a list of possibilities. Encourage the student to think of additional portfolio activities to add to the list. Decide how many entries the student must complete. The student checks the assigned activities in the first box. When the activity is completed, the second box is checked.
   Examples:

☐	☐	Essays
☐	☐	Discovered facts
☐	☐	Graphic organizers
☐	☐	Illustrations
☐	☐	Outlines
☐	☐	Poems
☐	☐	PowerPoint design
☐	☐	Procedure log
☐	☐	Research findings
☐	☐	Self-assessments
☐	☐	Study guides
☐	☐	Summaries of video clip
☐	☐	Web search findings
☐	☐	Writing samples

3. The student lays out a contract proposal and submits the action plan.

4. The teacher approves or rejects the proposal. Once the student and the teacher come to consensus, both sign it to signal acceptance of the contract terms.

5. Create a timeline noting checkpoints, conferences, and the deadline.

6. Identify the materials and resources the student needs.

7. Review the criteria and assessment tools with the student.

Example C: Three Students Need to Learn the Basic Multiplication Facts

Place a form in the front of the portfolio that outlines the activities and practice sessions. Include a place where you can note a self-assessment and the date of completion.

- Start the timer and use scrap paper to complete the 10 problems provided on the card. Record your time on the front of the card, and then correct your work using the answers on the back of the card. Record the number of problems you got right on the card next to your time. Work the same problem set two more times. Each time, check your responses and record your time and the number of correct answers. Place the card with your best score in your portfolio. Select three facts. Write a story problem for each one and illustrate it.

- Create a rap for one number (1s, 2s, 3s, etc.) on the multiplication table. Write it down and illustrate it.

- Say the facts aloud with a partner. Assess your work and write a summary.

- Complete worksheets #___ to # ___. Check them using the answer key. Place them in the "IN" basket.

MANAGING GRADES IN THE DIFFERENTIATED CLASSROOM

What Is Differentiated Grading?

Differentiated grading refers to the combination of assessment data gathered from two aspects of a student's learning world.

In a differentiated classroom, students receive alternative assignments to zap gaps or to work at a higher degree of mastery. Grades are gathered from the special assignments. When students work with activities and assignments that are tailored for their levels, they make high grades. If these scores are the only assessment results used in grading, a false picture of the learner is presented.

Only using assessment results from grade-level work is not an option either, however. Using these scores exclusively lessens the value of knowledge-level assignments. A student will put less effort into an assignment that will not help or harm his or her overall grade, and less effort results in fewer strides in learning.

This is why dual grading is necessary in the differentiated classroom. Some grades are gathered from the learner's work on knowledge-level assignments and activities. Other grades are recorded from data gathered on grade-level work performances and assignments. This blending of the grades rewards progress and provides a fairer and truer picture for a more accurate final grade.

What Are the Instructional Benefits of Differentiated Grading?

In traditional classrooms, the number and/or letter grade is often the focus of all assessments. They reflect the learner's standing in relation to the class. In a differentiated classroom, the assessment needs to reflect the student's knowledge level and progress. A number or letter grade is determined by combining the grade-level scores with the assessment scores on the customized tasks.

Differentiated grading:

- Is an integral part of customized instruction and guides planning
- Happens when grades are gathered from different measures and types of activities
- Presents a more complete view of the learner's progress and growth
- Honors students for effort and success
- Builds confidence

Teacher's Role

- Analyze your belief system in relation to assessment. Ask, "What message do I want to send to the student and parents?"
- Share your differentiated grading philosophy in discussions with the grade-level or subject area team and other faculty members so everyone is aware of your views on the differentiated grading system.
- Understand the dual grading process thoroughly before using it in your differentiated classroom.

- Explain this process to parents and students. Remember: Do not gloss over the fact that a student is not working at grade level. Be honest. This will ensure that everyone—parents, teachers, and students—is aware of whether or not a student is performing at grade level.

- Gather grades from all aspects of the learner's work, not just pencil-and-paper assignments. Use assessments from authentic tasks. Strategically select the grades that give the most complete report of the student's overall performance and growth. Remember, it is not about the quantity of the grades that you include in the grade book list, but the *quality*.

Demystifying Differentiated Grading

Explain to students that in a differentiated classroom, everyone is not graded in the same way, just as everyone is not taught in the same way. Grades are given on grade-level information and skills, but each person is also graded on his or her knowledge level, effort, and progress. Everyone encourages and assists classmates. Remind students that someone who is struggling with a topic now may become the best of the best with more knowledge and experience.

Student's Role

- Remember that grades are gathered from activities on your grade level and from work planned just for you.

- Don't just look at the grade on your work. Find the right answers to questions you may have missed and correct your mistakes.

- If you don't know how to make the corrections, ask the teacher or a classmate to assist you. Don't ask yourself, "Am I going to be graded on this?" Ask, "How much can I learn from this?" Realize that you earn a grade. The teacher does not give it to you.

- When you think your answer is right and it is marked as an error, ask for an explanation.

- Realize that a grade is simply a checkpoint. You can get better and better.

★ ★ ★ ★ ★

FIVE (STAR) MANAGEMENT TIPS FOR DIFFERENTIATED GRADING

1. Be selective in choosing grades to record. They need to represent the student's progress, growth, understanding, weaknesses, and strengths. Do not grade every page or record every score. Choose a few quality grades that reflect the same results as a multitude of grades.

2. Remember to use the appropriate assessment tools, such as rubrics and checklists, for authentic learning so students can show what they know. Ask yourself, "Which assessment tool will be the most effective in uncovering what the student knows?"

(Continued)

(Continued)

> 3. Let students grade their own papers so they receive instant feedback on correct answers and identify their own errors. Have students correct each mistake by drawing a line through the wrong answer and writing the correct response above it. The learner and the teacher use different-colored writing implements, so each one is able to target mistakes and zero in on corrections.
>
> 4. Remember, students are motivated when a grade is accompanied with a teacher note that explains how to improve.
>
> 5. Give two grades to present a more complete, blended picture of the student's abilities.
>   - Base the first grade on the student's progress within his or her knowledge or ability level. Measure the student's progress in filling in holes in learning or zapping the gaps to complete understanding.
>   - Use the second grade to reflect the student's ability in relation to grade-level expectations. This compares the learner to other students in the same grade or subject.
>
>

Examples of Differentiated Grading

Example A: Dual Grading

Two students excelled on the preassessment and are working on individual academic contracts. The teacher collects two individual grades from each student for the work they complete on their contract and another for the level of achievement they reached on their pretests.

A group of four students demonstrated a lack of understanding of the skill on the preassessment. They receive two special assignments to reteach the skill.

During independent work time, the remainder of the class is working on grade-level practice assignments.

A grade-level test is administered to all students except the two who had already demonstrated mastery. The grade is recorded.

In this scenario, each student receives two grades on the independent work and one grade from one of the class tests.

Example B: Grading and Analyzing Pretest/Posttest Results

A teacher-designed pretest is administered a week before the study begins. The results are analyzed to accommodate individual needs during the study. The preassessment itself is not used for a grade. The pretest is given at the end of the study as the graded posttest. The results are analyzed to identify the student's needs for future instructional planning. Students benefit when they can compare the pretest and posttest results and note progress.

Example C: Gathering Grades From Various Performance Evidence

Average grades from written work, oral presentations, daily activities, lab experiences, a portfolio, and the end-of-study test to create the final grade.

MANAGING TEACHER-MADE TESTS

What Is a Teacher-Made Test?

Teacher-made tests are assessments and evaluations created by the teacher to discover what the student knows before, during, and after instruction. The tests relate directly to the standards, skills, and concepts in a segment of learning. They are designed using various formats such as multiple choice, open-ended questioning, fill in the blank, matching, graphic organization, or a performance to show what the learners know.

The time involved in producing teacher-made tests is worthwhile because the tested items are customized for the group.

What Are the Instructional Benefits of Using Teacher-Made Tests?

- Each item on the test relates to the current lesson or skill and emphasizes the content information the teacher wants to emphasize.

- Because the items only focus on information that has been presented in the classroom, teacher-designed tests clearly reveal the parts of the lesson (or unit) the student learned and which need revisiting.

- A thorough pretest can be used as a posttest to determine individuals' growth and deficiencies.

- A teacher-made test compares individuals with other students in the class to develop appropriate learning plans.

- If many students incorrectly answer the same question(s), a teacher can revist his or her lesson plans to figure out other ways to make sure students learn the concept.

Teacher's Role

- Select the content information you want to assess. Consider each piece of information to determine which test format in your assessment toolbox will be most effective.

- Choose the most appropriate format to reveal the information students know.

- Design and develop the test. Thoughtfully plot the order of the questions. Do you want to format the test to progress from easier questions to more difficult ones? Would it be better to intersperse easy with hard questions?

- Give yourself a test rehearsal by taking the test as a learner. Check it to see that directions are clear. Eliminate questions that are not relevant and replace them with items that focus on the information learned. Create an answer key and revise as needed.

- Select the most appropriate time for the test. Explain the format, the grading scale, or weights that apply, and answer any student questions. Give words to encourage and build confidence before learners take the test.

Demystifying Teacher-Made Tests

Inform the students when a test is teacher made. Use a mini-lecturette similar to the following:

I made this test so we can see if you learned the most important information in our lessons. It will show you and me the things you know. It will also show us the items you still need to learn or practice. I made the test and answered the questions myself to be sure it would be the best test for you. Let's "Show What You Know"!

Student's Role

- Review and study for the test.
- Listen carefully to the test directions.
- State concerns or ask questions if you need clarification.
- Take the test. Read each question carefully. Answer each one thoughtfully to show what you know.
- Learn from your mistakes. After the test is checked and returned, correct the items that are wrong and study them to learn the right answers.

FIVE (STAR) MANAGEMENT TIPS FOR TEACHER-MADE TESTS

1. Remember, assessment drives curriculum. Preassess one to two weeks before the unit is introduced. Use an analysis of the data to develop lesson plans that work for the group. For example, when a student gets 100% on a test, this learner is exempted from the unit activities and assignments. The student engages in alternative tasks that extend thinking in areas related to the unit.

2. Use a teacher-made test as a pretest and as a posttest to address the most important information in the content study. Be sure each question addresses the most important information in the unit. Give the posttest when a majority of the group knows the material.

3. Place two or three easy questions at the beginning of the test. Disperse easy questions throughout the test. Tell students to search for the easy items.

4. Design the test so no one receives a zero, even on the pretest. This encourages the learner to search for other questions to answer.

5. If there is not enough time to develop the test, adapt a commercial test. Tell students to mark and skip the inappropriate questions. Learners should not be tested on parts that were not taught in the unit. Add questions needed from the unit of study.

Example A: Using a Pretest/Posttest

The teacher designs a preassessment on an upcoming topic to administer two weeks before introducing the unit. It also serves as the postassessment tool. The assessment is divided into three parts with different levels of difficulty. The teacher decides to give each section on a different day to avoid overwhelming students.

Example:

Part 1: Manipulatives

Show me, so I can develop hands-on experiences for you.

Part 2: Open-Ended Questions

Tell me what you know, so I can see how in depth I need to go to develop ideas.

Part 3: Multiple Choice

Find and mark the right answer, so I will know the information and facts I need to teach.

Example B: Using a Company-Made Pretest/Posttest

1. Examine the pretest/posttest provided by the textbook publisher. Use it only if it covers most of the material you plan to introduce in the upcoming unit of study.

2. Read each test item and decide if it is a keeper or loser.
   - Keep it if it will show what will be learned during the study.
   - Mark the items that will not be addressed or that are poorly stated.
   - Be sure every student will be able to answer some of the items.

3. At the end of class, take 15 minutes to distribute and administer the pretest.
   - Explain how the pretest assists in planning their lessons and activities. Tell students to answer the items they know. Explain that they are not expected to know everything on the test.
   - Pass out the test. Identify the items students do not answer. No one will mind omitting questions.
   - Give the same test as a posttest. Remember to add a blank page so they can write facts and details about something not addressed on the test. Give one point for each correct statement.

Example C: Using a Box Organizer for Assessment During Learning

Tell each student to fold a piece of copy paper to create six sections.

Provide a subtopic and/or vocabulary word from the current study for students to place in each box. The students fill in the boxes with the information they have learned.

MANAGING STANDARDIZED TEST PREPARATION

What Is Standardized Test Preparation?

A standardized test is an assessment that is administered with a set format. It has mandated guidelines, directions for administration, and time frames for each section. In most states, students in the public schools take the same test within their grade level. The classroom teacher follows the established guidelines to prepare students for the test.

Students must know how to follow oral and written directions, pace themselves, read statements, select the best response, and check work. Preparation begins the first day students enter the classroom and continues until the day of the test.

A few weeks prior to the test is not the time to teach test-taking strategies. When this occurs, the students often develop a negative attitude toward testing, especially when high performance expectations are overemphasized. When students know the test-taking skills and can apply them automatically, the weeks before the test become a celebration of learning.

What Are the Instructional Benefits of Standardized Test Preparation?

Practice test-taking skills using the content information throughout the year. This builds confidence in individual students and the class as a whole. Use the strategies throughout the curriculum and in a variety of activities. Play games highlighting vocabulary skills, practicing pulling information out of nonfiction passages in social studies, and have students take unit assessments in the same format from time to time. By giving the students different ways to practice these skills without isolating them as test preparation for the "big tests," they develop the skills without the test anxiety some students feel during standardized tests. Test preparation is built into the culture of the school.

Students who experience test preparation throughout the year:

- See tests as a time to show what they know
- Are familiar with words and phrases used in the directions
- Can apply test taking strategies automatically
- Know how to check their work
- Realize that results are used to help them improve

Teacher's Role

- Know your standards, your students, and the most effective ways to teach information so it is retained.
- Teach test-taking strategies and common standardized test formats throughout the year using the content information.
- Motivate and build confidence in students.
- Mold students so they are problem solvers and critical thinkers.
- Identify the test-taking needs of individual learners.

Materials: Pencils	Erasers	Scratchpad	Place marker
Personal: Water	Lighting	Movement	Desk position
Mental: A familiar environment		A familiar administering voice	

| Breaks: Fresh air | Cheers | Exercise |
| Emotional: Praise | Affirmations | Pats on the back |

Demystifying Standardized Test Preparation

Explain to students that each test gives opportunities for them to show what they know or what they have learned. The results show each student's strengths and weaknesses so you can plan the right kind of assignments and activities to prepare them for the state test in the spring. Use the following analogy to help explain the importance of test preparation to your students:

> When a music teacher begins practice sessions, the focus is on basic skills. Players work hard to learn those skills. Each time they practice, they get better and gain confidence in themselves. It becomes second nature, and the performers begin to look forward to the recital where they can perform these skills to "show what they know."

Student's Role

- Learn how to link, connect, compare, and retain important information in order to gain automaticity.
- Learn the inside secrets of taking a test:
  - Look for clues
  - Know how to eliminate the wrong answers
  - Pace yourself
- Apply the test-taking strategies you practiced throughout the year on the day of the standardized test.
- Practice completing work with a timer on different kinds of tests.
- Remember that the test is to show what you know. Do your best!

FIVE (STAR) MANAGEMENT TIPS FOR STANDARDIZED TEST PREPARATION

1. Teach test-taking strategies throughout the year using the content.
2. Use games or mystery adventures to help your students absorb information. Find out the ways students retain the most information.
3. Inform parents and students of the physical and psychological needs for top brain functioning.
   Examples:
   Rest   Eat nutritious snacks and meals   Be excited   Be confident
4. The testing environment needs to maintain the look and feel of the daily learning environment. Use the same room, the same voice, and the same desk arrangement, if at all possible.
5. Design activities the week before the test to celebrate what students know in order to raise their confidence levels and reduce pretest jitters. Then watch test scores soar!

Examples of Effective Standardized Test Preparation
Example A: Attacking a Passage

The students are reading a passage with new vocabulary words. They are looking for context clues such as antonyms, synonyms, or definitions. The teacher discusses the value of using context clues on a test. After the lesson, passages are placed in a learning station for extended practice.

Example B: Eliminating Incorrect Answers on Multiple-Choice Questions

While reviewing for a chapter test, students play a game based on the popular television game *Who Wants to Be a Millionaire*. The questions are based on important facts from previous lessons. By playing the game, students learn multiple-choice strategies such as how to eliminate incorrect choices.

Example C: Experiencing the Testing Environment

Introduce various aspects of the standardized testing environment during chapter and unit tests throughout the year.

Examples:

- ☐ Place and space desks in the standardized test arrangement.
- ☐ Provide each student with two pencils and scrap paper.
- ☐ Place a "Do Not Disturb, Brain Drain in Progress" sign on the door.
- ☐ Time the test.
- ☐ Maintain a quiet environment.

CONCLUSION

Assessment is an ongoing process in the differentiated classroom. Remember that detective hat and search for the most effective tools for assessment. Assessment is an invaluable step in planning a curriculum that will address the individual needs of every learner.

Effective differentiators first get to know their students, standards, and resources. Then, using formative and summative assessment results to diagnose learners' specific needs, interests, and abilities, they create individual-appropriate activities and ensure that students are continuously challenged but not overwhelmed. It takes time to learn about each aspect of the individuals in the class, but the investigative work will be rewarded as the "detective" discovers clues to students learning and achieving.

- Preassessing before planning curriculum for a given topic ensures that you will engage students at their current knowledge levels. Avoid basing lesson plans on previous groups of students or preconceived notions. Use a preassessment to hit your mark.

- Assessing during the learning prevents boredom and saves valuable instruction time. Once information has been mastered, no student is held back or forced to wait until a unit is over before he or she can move forward with more challenging activities.

- Evaluations after a unit of study show which parts of the learning have been mastered and which need to be continued or reinforced during the next unit of study.

Remember that clues give a detective information for solving a case. In a similar way, assessment tools give you data to plan instruction for each student. Using the right formal or informal tool, you can identify and confidently plan for the needs of each individual, small group, or the entire class.

PLANNING IS A COMPLEX, STRATEGIC PROCESS, ESPECIALLY IN the multidimensional features of differentiated instruction. The plan outlines steps for teaching the objectives or standards using the most effective strategies and activities for each learner's unique strengths and needs.

When a fire crew comes upon a blazing building, the captain of the fire department carefully charts the course he and his crew will follow. When the teacher puts on the fire captain's hat, plans are mapped out for students to follow as they learn and master content. Like the fire captain, who assesses each crew member's specific skills and talents, you must learn all there is to learn about the students.

Once the captain knows his crew's strengths, he assigns duties designed around their particular talents in order to ensure a safe plan of action. A teacher assigns tasks based on her students' strengths and talents, maximizing their learning capacities. It is crucial to design instructional plans with intentionality or purpose in order to avoid wasting the learner's time. Each strategy and activity is selected strategically to teach the objectives or standards in a way that leads each student to success.

Managing plans for differentiated instruction is a challenging but rewarding process. With this in mind, we designed and selected the following suggestions, techniques, and tips to assist with these multifaceted planning tasks so you can work smarter, not harder.

What Is Planning for a Differentiated Classroom?

Knowledgeable, successful teachers commit to making a difference in students' lives through planning. The plans are designed for a unit, a semester, or a year by teachers, grade-level colleagues, and/or administrators. Avoid becoming locked into a plan because it has to be adjustable and revamped to meet needs. Remember to keep it flexible to meet the ever-changing needs of individuals and groups.

1. Become familiar with the state's and district's mandated standards and objectives for your subject area and/or grade level.

2. Outline the standards or objectives in sequential order to fit the school's schedule.

3. Select meaningful content that presents the best medium for teaching the standard or objective. Keep in mind that this subject matter creates the mental links and connections for the learner as the standards and skills are woven into it.

4. Create a logical flow and timeline for introducing each standard with the strategies and activities.

5. List the materials and resources needed, noting items that must be acquired.

Preliminary Planning Tips

All teachers become more proficient as planners when they take the time to become familiar with all factors that need to be considered. It is necessary to know the following information to plan strategically for the diverse learners in today's classrooms:

Remember to:

1. **Know your students:** Focus on their individual strengths and needs. Be aware of their interests and the current fads so you can use them as attention-grabbing hooks or keys to learning.

2. **Know your strategies:** Maintain an array of tools and activities that continually challenge and motivate learners. Build on their sense of wonderment and anticipation about what will happen next.

3. **Know your standards:** Use the standards as a navigation guide to destinations in your instructional plans. Students must master the mandated standards to do well on the standardized tests.

4. **Know your content:** Become thoroughly familiar with the content so it will be easier to select the most relevant and beneficial information. Keep in mind that you do not have to teach or cover everything, unless it is mandated. Think of content as a conduit or channel for activities and strategies. The content is carefully selected to transmit or convey knowledge and skills to each learner. It gives students meaningful ways to make mental connections to the standards.

5. **Know your resources and materials:** Identify the most effective and appealing resources and materials to reach individual students. You will be able to select the most valuable resources when you know the needs and likes of the students.

Text Reference Self-Analysis

Where are you with implementing the categories of differentiated instruction? Try the following inventory for a self-analysis. Analyze your responses periodically to see growth. Refer to the page numbers in this book for reviews, additions, and management tips for using a new category.

Figure 6.1

Managing Categories	Page	Not Yet	Some	Often	Usually
Environment	9				
Affective	9				
Physical	23				
Differentiated models	35				
Adjustable assignment model	36				
Curriculum rewinding	38				
Curriculum fast-forwarding	41				
Curriculum compacting	43				
Problem-based model	45				
Project-based model	49				
Multiple intelligences model	52				
Triarchic teaming model	57				
Activity analysis model	60				
Student-directed model	64				
Teacher-directed model	67				
Nested model	70				
Threaded model	74				
Mastery learning model	78				
Managing grouping strategies	81				
Managing flexible grouping	83				
Total group	86				
Alone	89				
Partner	93				
Small groups	96				
Grouping designs					
Knowledge-based grouping	101				
Interest groups	105				
Ability grouping	108				
Multiage groups	111				
Cooperative groups	113				
Random grouping	116				
Peer tutoring	119				

(Continued)

Figure 6.1 (Continued)

Managing Categories	Page	Not Yet	Some	Often	Usually
Instructional strategies	123				
Focus activities	128				
Sponge activities	131				
Anchor activities	134				
Cubes	136				
Choice boards	140				
Graphic organizers	145				
Centers, stations, learning zones	148				
Agendas/menus	153				
Academic contracts	157				
Products	163				
Content activities	167				
Assessment tools					
Self-assessment	183				
Informal assessment	188				
Response cards	191				
Signals	196				
Stand and show	199				
Formal assessment	202				
Pretest/posttest	205				
Effective questioning	207				
Anecdotal records	214				
Surveys	217				
Journals	219				
Portfolios	224				
Grades	228				
Teacher-made tests	231				
Standardized test preparation	234				

A Planning Dialogue

In this section, a guide is provided for planning before, during, and after the unit. There are explanations of the steps and questions or statements to address as you plan at each stage. Use each management step for lesson preparation so you can thoroughly plan the curriculum for your differentiated classroom.

Planning Before Teaching the Unit

1. Choose the topic or unit and then select the standard, concepts, and objectives to address during the study.

The standards are the facts, concepts, and skills that students are expected to master in each grade level. These expectations are mandated by the state, district, or controlling entity. Textbook companies and local curriculum guides often provide the recommended scope and sequence for presenting the standards. Think of standards as the instructional destinations. Planning creates the best route to reach each learner. Students must master the mandated standards to create foundations for learning.

In a differentiated classroom, individual students' needs and strengths determine the order for the standards. The teacher relies on professional and personal judgment to select the standard and the most effective time and place to introduce it. Consider questions similar to the following when selecting each standard:

- ☐ Which standard will build on the learner's knowledge, experiences, and understanding?
- ☐ What skills need to be taught during this topic or unit of study?
- ☐ What important facts must be taught?
- ☐ How long will it take to teach the material so students on all levels will learn it?
- ☐ Does the student have the background knowledge and skills needed to understand the new standard?

2. Preassess the student to identify the knowledge base and interests, then analyze the data.

A formal or informal preassessment tool reveals the learner's level of experience and knowledge related to the standard. The preassessment is administered one or two weeks prior to the lesson to provide time to analyze the results and customize instructional plans.

This vital planning step leads to selection of the most appropriate strategies and activities for each student to learn the standard. During this phase, use questions similar to the following as a guide:

- Will an informal preassessment reveal the learner's prior knowledge and experiences with the standard or skill?
- What is the most efficient, informative way to preassess the student or students?
- What does the data tell me?

- Am I asking the right questions or test items in the most appropriate way to find each learner's knowledge base and needs?

- Do students understand how the assessment results will be used in planning?

- What is the most efficient way to give the learner constructive, specific feedback from the results?

- What are the entry points for instruction for each level? The learner's strengths and needs are recorded on a grid or chart.

  o What are the student's learning gaps or needs?

  o Which gaps do I need to zap to best help the student learn the required material?

  o Which students have common needs?

  o How can the learner's strengths be engaged to overcome the weaknesses?

- What is the learner's level of mastery?

___Beginning   ___Approaching mastery   ___High degree of mastery

"Rewinding"   "Grade level"   "Fast-forwarding"

3. Select the content, materials, and resources that most effectively teach the standards.

Content is the subject matter or information that is selected to teach the standards, skills, and concepts. The majority of content material is presented from textbooks. States usually approve two or more textbook companies for districts to use. Local educators adopt one publisher as the source of their texts and supplementary materials. Remember, just because it is in the adopted textbook does not mean that it is necessarily the best material to use to teach a skill or topic. If it is boring, confusing, or frustrating to you, it will be even worse for the learners.

In this planning step, rely on your professional expertise and reasoning to select the content to use in presenting the standards and skills.

Consider resources that are not included in the supplementary materials. Students, parents, and community members often have materials that enhance specific lessons. Tell students that you need their assistance to make the study more meaningful. Whenever it is appropriate, encourage the learners to teach the class or a small group using their materials.

Use the following questions to guide your selection of content, materials, and resources.

- Which segment of information will be used to teach the standard or skill?

- What part of the content should be emphasized to assist the learner in making links and connections to the standard or skill?

- What other resources do I have available that would teach more effectively?

- What parts of the content can be deleted for the learner?

- Does the content information present the standard or skill in a way that develops understanding for the learner?

4. Identify the flexible grouping designs.

Crucial decisions are involved in creating the instructional grouping designs. The recorded results of the preassessment data are analyzed to design the most effective grouping scenarios for instruction. The acronym TAPS (T = <u>T</u>otal group, A = <u>A</u>lone, P = <u>P</u>artner, and S = <u>S</u>mall group) is recommended as a guide to making grouping decisions in a differentiated classroom.

- What information is needed by the total group?
  - ___ Introductions
  - ___ Lecturettes and discussions
  - ___ Directions and guidelines
  - ___ Review of rules, ritual, or routines
  - ___ Reminders for independent and group work
  - ___ Wrap-up and summative evaluations

- How many students need independent instruction or assignments?
  - ___ Reteaching/rewinding
  - ___ Review
  - ___ Practice or reinforcement
  - ___ Enrichment/ fast-forwarding
  - ___ Compacting

- How will students be grouped to learn the standard or skill?
  - ___ Knowledge level
  - ___ Interest
  - ___ Ability
  - ___ Peer to peer
  - ___ Random
  - ___ Cooperative learning
  - ___ Project teams

- What groups do I need for the assignment?
  - ___ Total
  - ___ Alone
  - ___ Partners
  - ___ Small groups

- What criteria will I use to effectively move a student to another group?

5. Brainstorm a quantity of activities for each individual or group to produce quality plans.

The next step involves identifying and listing the best activities to teach the standard for individuals and/or groups. Consider all possibilities. This is a reference list for future ideas that can grow and grow. Choose quality activities from the list to meet the differentiated needs of groups and individual students.

- Will the activities and strategies teach the standard and the content information?
- Do I have challenging activities that will motivate learners at the different levels of entry points?
- Does the content information present the standard or skill in a way that develops understanding for the learner?
- Do the activities address varied styles, modalities, and intelligences?
- Do I have the most effective strategies and activities to make my plan?

Lay Out the Plan

1. Strategically select instructional strategies and activities for a quality plan.

Strategies and activities are selected to activate or set the learner's mental wheels in motion. This occurs when a student connects the new standard or skill to prior knowledge and experiences. Activation is maintained with interesting and intriguing activities.

The teacher strategically selects the strategies and activities to transfer the learning. In this fundamental step, instruction is designed for the student to take ownership of the new standard or skill so it can be used independently.

Become familiar with an array of instructional strategies to teach each standard on the student's level of need. Maintain a collection of techniques and approaches that continually challenge and motivate learners. Consider questions similar to the following when selecting the strategies and activities.

- How will I debut the new standard or skill in a way that will capture and focus the learner's attention?
- Which activity will create a connection from the new standard or skill to prior knowledge or experiences?
- What is the best way to make the learning personally meaningful and understandable?
- How will the student be actively engaged in learning?
- How can students use their learning preference or strongest intelligences to work with the new information?

2. Study and assess the plan to be sure the most beneficial strategies and activities are in place for each student.

Use the following questions as a guide to assess the plan:

- Does the strategy or activity use the best technique or approach to teach the learner?

- Will the learner be able to build on prior knowledge and experiences?
- Do the activities promote transfer of learning?
- Will the new learning become personally meaningful for the learner?
- Does the plan use the learner's strengths?

Planning During and After Teaching the Unit Information

1. Teach the information.

Teaching is the process of guiding students to understand new information or a skill so it can be mastered and used with automaticity. It is important to remember in this phenomenal process that the student's brain is being wired or programmed during each experience.

- How will students know the purposes or objectives for the lesson?
- How am I going to hook the learners into yearning to work with this new information?
- Can students sense my enthusiasm and genuine desire for them to learn?
- Do the students have an opportunity to demonstrate an understanding of the directions?
- Are new vocabulary words and phrases clear and easy to understand?

2. Use flexible grouping and assess changes to meet needs.

In a differentiated classroom, teaching takes place in total groups, as well as individual and small group activities. Sometimes the learners need to move from one group to another because of growth, misplacement, or a diagnosed need. Therefore, the grouping placement is fluid. Here are some questions to consider during instruction:

- Are the groups fulfilling the set goals? How?
- Am I using the best grouping designs and scenarios for the cognitive learning?
- How are the groups getting along socially? Why?
- Which students need to remain in the group?
- Which learners need to change to a new group? Why?

3. Assess during learning.

It is essential to assess during learning to keep students on track in each lesson. Everyone needs to understand the value of ongoing assessment. Individuals, partners, and small groups need to know how to use assessment tools during learning so they can monitor themselves and make corrections as needed.

- What does each student know?
- What is each student doing to demonstrate that he or she is learning?

- How will I stay aware of the student's needs during the lesson?

  ___Observations

  ___Checkpoints

  ___Self-checks

  ___Appropriate questions

  ___Anecdotal records

  ___Notes

  ___Other

- Which actions will become a recorded grade?
- How will the learner's needs be addressed during learning?

4. Readjust instructional strategies and activities as needed.

- Does the student need to review information or skills?
- What are the gaps?
- Which gaps need to be filled in order for the student to learn the grade-level information?
- Is the student ready to move to a more challenging activity?
- Do I need to gather a group of students together for reteaching, an academic contract, or a separate menu?

5. Assess after learning to develop new plans.

Assessment is a never-ending process. The results of the assessment after learning are addressed in the upcoming lesson design.

- What assessment tools do I need to use?
- Which parts of the lesson can the learner self-assess to see mistakes and make corrections?
- Did the learner master the standard or skill?
- Is the student able to use the new information independently?
- What segments of the lesson need to be reviewed or identified for reteaching?

A PLANNING GRID FOR DIFFERENTIATED INSTRUCTION

The following is a planning tool to use in differentiating curriculum. Use the grid to plan a successful unit of learning. This initial planning is a guide to working smarter earlier so the students work harder and eagerly on tasks that are strategically selected for their individual needs.

Remember, assessment drives curriculum plans.

Figure 6.2

Unit Topic _____ Date From _____ Through _____

I. What Will You Teach?

As a results of this unit, the students will learn:

Standard	Content	Skills	Concepts

Objectives:	

II. Preassessment tool(s) _____

Date administered _____

Analysis of Preassessment Data

A. **Total Group Needs**

B. **Small Group Needs**

Level 1: Readiness (identified needs to develop background knowledge)

What do they know?

What do they need next?

Level 2: Approaching mastery (on grade level)

What do they know?

What do they need next?

Level 3: High degree of mastery (knows most of the information, concepts, and skills)

What do they know?

What do they need next?

C. **Individual Needs**

Student's Name	Knows	Needs
1.		
2.		

III. Content to Be Taught

To total group

To small group

To individual

(Continued)

Figure 6.2 (Continued)

Student

	Level 1	Level 2	Level 3
1.			
2.			

IV. Resource Selection

Total Group

Resources
1.
2.
3.

Small Group

Group	Resources to Use
Level 1	
Level 2	
Level 3	

Individual

Student	Resources to Use
1.	
2.	

Individual Assignments

Total Group Plan

Assignment	Time	Multiple Intelligences Addressed	Groups TAPS/Type	Materials	Assessment Tools
1.					
2.					
3.					

Differentiated Small Group Plan

Group	Assignment	Time	Multiple Intelligences Addressed	Groups TAPS/Type	Materials	Assessment Tools
Level 1						
Level 2						
Level 3						

Student	Assignment	Time	Multiple Intelligences Addressed	Groups TAPS/Type	Materials	Assessment Tools
1.						
2.						

V. Evaluation: Summative Analysis Report and Reflections

A. End-of-Unit Assessment(s)

1.

2.

Total Group on Grade-Level Evaluation Analysis	
Mastered	
Needs Next	

B. Individual Needs

Student's Name	Mastered	Needs Next
1.		
2.		

C. Comments: Things to Remember and Reflections

PROACTIVE PLANNING: CREATING A TROUBLESHOOTER'S GUIDE

Proactive planning provides you with tools to provide seamless instruction. A troubleshooter's guide identifies the predicted, instructional dilemmas that may be encountered with each class with suggested solutions for each situation.

Complete your own troubleshooter's guide for planning during the first few weeks. Use information derived from an analysis of cumulative records, as well as conferences with the student, parents, and other teachers. Observe, observe, observe. Fill in the blanks with the name of the individual or group. Here is an example of the form. Customize it for your group of students and adapt it to the learner's needs throughout the year.

Figure 6.3	
Projected Trouble Spots	*Possible Solution*
_____ rarely ever has materials for class.	• Post a list of materials needed for class on the entrance way outside of the classroom: "Materials for class today!" • Establish routines. For example: 　　Each day you need ____. 　　Every Wednesday you need ___. • Occasionally, verbally reward those who have their materials. • Be careful not to use this as an excuse to get out of class. • Have some extra materials. Establish if it is being done as a convenient way to get you off subject matter.
_____ is easily distracted.	• Assign the student a spot that has the fewest distractions. • Use proximity and reminders. • Create buy-in with high-interest assignments! • Use a timer. • Say, "If you complete ___, you can___."
_____ needs more time to complete the work.	• Give specific, verbal praise for being on task and for work completed. • Do not assign too many tasks at one time. • Model in detail what is supposed to be done. • Use a timer. Challenge the student to complete the work before the bell rings. • Break tasks into small segments or shorter time frames.
_____ knows an upcoming topic.	• Give the student an exemption and move on to another topic. • Do an in-depth study into an area of interest within the topic. • Prepare an academic contract for a research project. • Let the student design a new game about the topic. • Choose an area to study and present learned information to the class.
_____ has trouble following directions.	• Give the directions in smaller chunks. • Give the learner time to explain the directions to someone. Receiving directions: listening, reading before beginning to work. • Use the student's favorite method to demonstrate procedures. • Assign a personal consulting partner. • Vary the style used in giving the directions: written, oral, or both.

Managing Diverse Cultures in Today's Classroom

Remember!

Children develop language by interacting with others.

Oral language develops before written language or reading a language.

Daily involvement in activities that promote language in reading, writing, speaking, and listening allows a student to learn a new language and have better academic success.

Realize that students often experience confusion and mixing of the languages.

Remember, the more the learner is around people using English, the faster the student will learn English. Their language is still honored.

Tips

Post environmental print with signs, labels, students' names, and directions.

Survey family members to find out ethnic customs and cultural backgrounds.

Know the desires of family members for the student to address individual needs and concerns.

Use flexible groupings so the students are exposed to the diversities.

During the transition time, from their native language to English, allow students to mix the languages or express themselves in their own language to show what they know. Many times, the student knows more about what is shown because of the language barrier.

Questions to ask yourself about diversity

Do I keep a foreign-language dictionary handy and available for students and for me?

Am I providing directions in the learner's modalities and learning styles?

Am I providing literacy experiences that reflect a variety of cultures?

Do I research and learn all I can about the cultures and heritage of my class members?

Do I know about the learner's special days or holidays?

What aspects of the student's cultural background do I need to explore?

Managing Time

Managing Personal Time

1. Meet time guidelines and due dates. Write a reminder for the deadline a couple days earlier on your calendar.

2. Be a list maker and prioritize the items. Check off or mark through completed items. Place activities, due dates, appointments, and other important events on a desk or wall calendar. Avoid crowding too many expectations or overlapping tasks in one time period.

3. When asked to give a commitment, say, "I will get back to you." Check your calendar and be sure this is something you want to do.

4. Arrive at school early enough to prepare for the day and gather your thoughts.

5. Find time for yourself.

Managing Class Time

1. Establish and teach routines for daily activities and transitions. Time each one for two to three days so you know the amount of time for each routine.

2. Plan! Plan!

3. Have instant sponge activities ready for difficult moments.

4. Use focus activities.

5. Give clear directions.

Figure 6.4	
Timewaster	*Ways to Save Time*
Repeating yourself	1. Privately record your teaching and listen for repetition. 2. Identify patterns and become aware of when it is happening. 3. Make a list and check off completed items. 4. Do not procrastinate! Complete the task while it is fresh in your mind. 5. Ask an observer to note your repetitions.
Telephone	1. Cluster outgoing calls. 2. Use an answering machine to screen incoming calls. 3. Use a timer to limit amount of time on the phone. 4. In a polite way, let callers know when you are busy. 5. Talk to a friend as a reward after completing a task or following a major accomplishment.
Getting off task	1. Become aware of what pulls you off task. 2. Make a checklist of tasks and prioritize it. Check each item off as completed. 3. Use agendas, lists, a PowerPoint presentation, or an outline.

Timewaster	Ways to Save Time
	4. Do not let bird walking questions and comments pull you from the lesson's flow. Address those after completing the task. 5. Tell students to hand you notes with questions that are unrelated to the study.
Looking for lost items	1. Everything needs a place. Return each item to its home after using it. 2. Keep supplies and materials near your work space. If you have more than one work area, place supplies such as pens, notepads, paper, stapler, and paper clips in each one. 3. Create your own filing system. 4. Ask yourself, "Where did I have it last?" 5. Gather needed instructional materials and supplies early so last-minute searches are avoided.
Correcting papers	1. Establish a way for students to correct many of their own papers. This needs to be done promptly to provide feedback and immediate intervention. 2. Only correct the necessary assignments. Remember that every paper does not require a grade. Some work is designed for practice. 3. Grade the work immediately instead of letting it pile up. 4. Have students keep corrected papers in a folder or portfolio. They can use them to talk about what they are learning or need next. 5. Involve students in some peer editing and sharing.
Becoming overwhelmed	1. Prioritize! Accomplish one thing and then move to the next. 2. Set a deadline. Complete one segment and celebrate! 3. Take a break. When you return, it may not be as overwhelming. 4. Complete the most difficult task first. Relax your mind. Then move to the easier ones. 5. Obtain assistance from someone else. Delegate and share the responsibility for work.
Having a full calendar	1. Realize how much you can do! 2. Do not take on more responsibilities than you can handle. 3. Prioritize. 4. Keep an appointment calendar with you at all times. 5. Complete scheduled tasks before taking on another responsibility.
Procrastinating	1. Remember, do not put off tasks you can do today. 2. Set a new goal when one is reached. 3. Get the most dreaded items out of the way first. 4. Celebrate and move to the next task or assignment. 5. Place deadlines on segments of the task.

(Continued)

Figure 6.4 (Continued)	
Timewaster	*Ways to Save Time*
Not delegating to others	1. Share responsibilities. 2. Form committees with members to help. 3. Delegate! 4. Use the talents of other people. 5. Friends, coworkers, and parents are usually eager to assist, especially if they know students will benefit.
Unorganized materials	1. Everything has a place or a home where it belongs. Teach students to return items to their "homes." 2. Place color-coded labels on the place where the material is stored with the same color on the material. 3. Organize things by categories. 4. Teach students to clean up. Post reminders such as, "If you mess up, you clean up." 5. Discard materials that are no longer needed.
Collecting and distributing papers	1. Use "In/Out" baskets, folders, or containers. Display them in the same place daily but not on the teacher's desk. 2. Find a place for the materials needed for the day's or week's assignments. At the end of the day, remove extra items. Gather materials for the next day and make them accessible. 3. Color-code folders by subjects or levels of tiered assignments. Consistently use the same colors for independent assignments or center activities. 4. Assign a student to be a materials manager. 5. Designate areas for answer sheets so students can check their own papers.
Not able to concentrate	1. Practice active listening. Focus all of your attention on the individual who is talking, so you hear what he or she says. 2. Probe with questions and restating for more details and clarification. 3. Restate the learning. 4. When confused or stressed, take a break and come back to it. 5. Unclutter your mind, reduce tension, and then listen.
Classroom movement	1. Be visible. Keep moving among students. 2. Never form a walking pattern. 3. Stand on the opposite side of the room when a student is speaking. Students usually focus on the teacher when talking or presenting to the group. 4. Use nonverbals to get messages across and send signals. 5. Place yourself at eye level and on the same side of the paper, book, or artifact so the students view you as a helper. In this position you see the information from the same view as the student.

Timewaster	Ways to Save Time
Controlling off-task behaviors	1. Use student names in context. 2. Use positive remarks: "I like the way. . . ." 3. Keep a calm voice for upsetting circumstances. 4. Use voice inflection while presenting content to show your passion. 5. Omit sarcasm. (See the "SCARcasm" section on page 15.)
Stressing out!	1. Take a deep breath. 2. Walk away for a minute. 3. Pat yourself on the back for reaching so many students! 4. Name the many ways you reached students today! 5. Don't sweat the small stuff!
Fearing change	1. Look for support by finding colleagues or someone who is a believer in differentiation. 2. Examine your beliefs and opinions. 3. Confront your fears and barriers related to change. 4. Explore and learn about new ways to reach individual learners. 5. Remember that change often comes gradually. Identify the strategies and activities that you currently use and want to keep. Start changing by implementing the segments or ideas that are the easiest and most comfortable for you.

Identify Time Savers

Eleven Reminders to Ensure Success

1. Familiarize yourself with the standards.
2. Vary your instructional strategies and activities.
3. Create a learning climate.
4. Exhibit "with-it-ness."
5. Provide a wide variety of material and resources.
6. Learn the students' likes, dislikes, strengths, and weaknesses.
7. Assess before, during, and after learning.
8. Adjust assignments when necessary.
9. Plan student-focused opportunities.
10. Use flexible grouping designs.
11. Realize that change is gradual.

PLANNING A PROFESSIONAL LEARNING STUDY FOR DIFFERENTIATED INSTRUCTION

What Is a Professional Learning Study?

A professional learning study can consist of everyone in the school—all stakeholders in the students' success—including the teachers, administrators, and staff members. Each study session is designed to focus on improving teaching and learning for differentiated instruction.

What Are the Educational Benefits of a Professional Learning Study

- Student learning is always in the spotlight.
- There is purposeful professional development and training.
- Each member is aware of the expectations and support that personally exist during and after school.
- The community works collaboratively to ensure the success of each student. When a learner is at risk, not motivated, or failing, all available resources are used.
- Participants engage in professional development opportunities, reading, brainstorming, and discussions. They continually seek new ways to grow in new knowledge to affect student learning.

Administrator's Role

- Guide the faculty and staff to create a vision for each learner's success.
- Select schoolwide goals and objectives that focus on the needs and strengths of individual students.
- Get staff input on the topics and book choices for professional study. Read the selection.
- Provide professional development opportunities that support differentiated instruction.
- Have an administrator attend each meeting. When strategies are implemented in the classroom from study, the support is there.

Demystifying the Professional Learning Study

Let students know that each study session involves teachers and others who want to improve teaching and learning. Explain that everyone involved is learning how to help students be more successful.

Teacher's Role

- Commit and buy into the study! Learn for your personal growth so you can be a better teacher for your students.
- Join the sessions to read, discuss, question, find answers, share, and debate.
- Emphasize the value of learning in lessons and daily routines. Realize that every teacher is an expert and is a member of the team. Respect and value each contribution.
- Refer to the different ways individuals learn. Keep thinking, "How can I use what I am learning to plan better and meet the individual needs of my students?"
- Keep students and parents informed when members of the support team are involved in professional planning or training to improve learning.

**FIVE (STAR) MANAGEMENT TIPS FOR ESTABLISHING
A PROFESSIONAL LEARNING COMMUNITY**

1. Identify the needs of the staff with regards to differentiated instruction. Give team members a voice in selecting the topics related to their professional needs. Discuss and prioritize the suggestions. Come to consensus on the study's goals and purposes.

2. Develop a timeline for the goals.

3. Select the book, article collection, Web sites, video series, or other resources to use during the study.

4. Ask each group member to commit to being present and accountable at the meetings.

5. Establish team roles.
    a. Select a leader to take charge and conduct the meetings.
    b. Assign a liaison from the administrative level to be a team member. This individual provides support and a voice from a higher level of control.
    c. Share responsibilities and assign roles so each person makes a valuable contribution.
    d. Assign a team captain and recorder for each study meeting.

Example

Suggested Session Procedures

1. Involve members of the team to select or have an active voice in the selection of the professional development topic.

2. Provide a time for members to sign up for a section of the study, such as a chapter of the book or an article. Some sections are best researched by a group, rather than an individual.

3. The study team discusses and comes to consensus on the goals and the purposes of the study. A timeline is developed around the goals.

4. After selecting the topic and establishing the goals and the purposes, the team selects the book, article collection, Web sites, video series, or other resources to use during the study.

5. Each group member needs to commit to being present at the meetings. As a team member, each member needs to be accountable.

6. Establish roles.
    a. Assign a team liaison. This individual can encourage, share information, and clarify rules or regulations as needed.
    b. Have a member leader to conduct the meetings and be in charge. Assign a captain and recorder at each meeting. Rotate these roles to different group members each meeting so that every participant leads the team at least one meeting and is the recorder for at least one study session. At the first meeting, provide a sign-up sheet for the volunteering of the night each member is the leader.
    c. Each team member needs a role so the responsibility is shared and each member feels a vital part of the study.

7. Allow time for the groups to read, discuss, and plan presentations of their sections. Each meeting, one individual leads the discussion and guides the lesson. Questions and lead-ins for discussion are presented for the group to discuss, learn, and adapt the information from each session assignment.

8. Review where each group is on the timeline. Revamp and adjust additions and deletions as needed.

9. Review previous learning. Discuss and list personal and group impacts, values, and timewasters.

10. Provide time for members to share how they are using the learned information.

11. Learn the new information. Plan times for the introduction, as well as novel ways to present and discuss the information. The group in charge gives thought-provoking lead-ins and questions to keep discussions challenging, exciting, and useful.

12. Engage members in a reflection period. Give assignments, advertisement blurbs, and logistics for the next sessions.

Examples of Professional Learning Studies in Action

Example A: Book Study Team

The team agrees to study a book of interest. A meeting calendar is distributed with scheduled reading assignments. Each member signs the schedule as the recorder or team leader for specific meeting dates. The goals are set as the group identifies what everyone wants to gain from the study.

During the meeting, the readings and discussions are valuable because the team is learning together, and each individual member can use what is learned in their various job roles.

Example B: Studying a Video Series

A video series is carefully chosen for viewing portions and discussing what is seen and reflecting how the learning transfers to each participant's situation.

Example C: Personal Taping Series

Each team member videotapes a portion of his or her teaching. Each signs up for a night of stardom to head the group and show his or her contribution. At an assigned meeting segment, the star of the meeting shares with the group what they will be viewing. The clip is shown and discussed for growth for all.

Self-Analysis of Progress in Establishing a Differentiated Instruction Classroom

Periodically assess yourself as a teacher who is establishing a differentiated classroom. Use the following implementation checklist (Figure 6.5) to identify the components of differentiation you currently use and highlight areas to improve. In addition, check areas you need to explore to challenge more students.

Figure 6.5

Phases for Implementation		
Phase 1	*Phase 2*	*Phase 3*

☐ Teach students and standards with the most effective resources and materials.
 	
☐ Teach with varied instructional strategies around the different modalities, styles, and intelligences.
 	
☐ Realize that people learn differently.
 	
☐ Use effective assessment tools for assessing learning during and after the learning.
 	
☐ Survey students to get to know them.
 	
☐ Create a brain-compatible climate.
 	
☐ Establish rituals and routines.
 	
☐ Use novelty to challenge learners.
 	
☐ Use critical and creative thinking. Be an effective questioner.
 	
☐ Group by student's interests and ability.
	☐ Create work zones for student-focused activities using centers, stations, and labs.
	
	☐ Give choice for students to show what they know.
	
	☐ Realize that assessment drives curriculum.
	
	☐ Use student-focused activities.
	
	☐ Establish centers, stations, or learning zones.
	
	☐ Use flexible grouping, including TAPS.
	
	☐ Survey students to discover interests, habits, and knowledge base.
	
	☐ Use leveled computer programs.
	
	☐ Use a variety of graphic organizers.
		☐ Assess before, during, and after the learning using informal and formal tools. Use data effectively to plan for individual needs.
		
		☐ Use flexible grouping by moving students as needed.
		
		☐ Grade using a blending of grade-level assessments and materials on knowledge level.
		
		☐ Implement the models:
		1. Tiered, adjustable assignment
		2. Curriculum compacting
		3. Problem-solving model
		4. Project-based model
		5. Contract model
		
		☐ Using
		  ○ Agendas
		  ○ Choice boards
		  ○ Cubes
		
		☐ Level activities for centers and independent activities.
		
		☐ Teachers work smarter, not harder!
		
		☐ Students are more responsible for their learning.

Where are you in implementing differentiated instruction?		
Phase 1	Phase 2	Phase 3

←——————————————————————————————————→

INTRODUCING A DIFFERENTIATED OBSERVATION TOOL

Use the sample observation form (Figure 6.6) to assess differentiation in action before, during, or after implementation. It may be adapted to meet the needs of a school or a classroom.

This observation tool is designed to be use by the following:

Peer-to-peer coaches	Mentors	Administrators	Curriculum specialists
Supervisors	Teachers	Professional developers	

Figure 6.6

The Differentiated Classroom
Observation Form

Teacher_____   Grade Level/Subject Area_____

Observer _____   Date_____

EVIDENCE

Physical Environment	Often seen	Sometimes occurs	Little or no evidence
1. Presents an inviting, relaxed environment for learning			
2. Provides comfortable desks and work areas			
3. Contains individual, designated personal spaces for extra books and other items			
4. Is designed for quick and easy groupings of tables and chairs			
5. Is arranged for teacher and student movement during work sessions			
6. Provides work areas for individual needs, including knowledge/ability levels			
7. Reflects current content or skills through student displays and artifacts			
8. Showcases learning with a print-rich environment			

Feedback

Strengths
Recommendations

EVIDENCE

Teacher Behaviors	Often seen	Sometimes occurs	Little or no evidence
1. Works with total groups, individuals, and small groups			
2. Monitors individuals and small groups			

Teacher Behaviors	Often seen	Sometimes occurs	Little or no evidence
3. Uses a variety of ongoing assessment tools such as checklists, surveys, and anecdotal records			
4. Applies assessment information to guide instruction			
5. Addresses academic, emotional, social, and physical needs of students			
6. Provides time for students to actively process information			
7. Gives specific feedback to individuals and/or small groups			
8. Exhibits excitement and enthusiasm for the standard, topic, or skill			

Feedback

Strengths
Recommendations

EVIDENCE

Materials/Resources	Often seen	Sometimes occurs	Little or no evidence
1. Include a variety of reading levels			
2. Are accessible to students			
3. Support the standards and topic			
4. Are age appropriate			
5. Are up-to-date			
6. Are available in an adequate number for the class size			
7. Contain appropriate resources and reference materials			
8. Include a variety of manipulatives and hands-on materials			

(Continued)

Figure 6.6 (Continued)

Feedback

Strengths
Recommendations

EVIDENCE

Instructional Strategies	*Often seen*	*Sometimes occurs*	*Little or no evidence*
1. Uses a variety of assessment tools before, during, and after learning			
2. Uses a variety of instructional strategies to teach standards			
3. Meets the diverse needs of learners			
4. Engages students in flexible grouping designs			
5. Presents information using varied appropriate strategies and activities			
6. Uses centers and/or stations for individual and small group instruction			
7. Engages students with projects and/or problem-solving activities			
8. Presents students with choices in learning activities			

Feedback

Strengths
Recommendations

Example A: Pass Response

The selected headings are placed on separate pieces of paper, and the faculty groups are sitting at tables. Distribute one heading to each table. The table group reads the question or statement, and a recorder writes the responses. The session leader gives a signal for the groups to pass the papers. They continue reading the questions, responding and passing the papers when signaled until all papers have been passed.

Example B: Self-Assessment of Differentiated Instruction

Give each teacher the form for a personalized self-assessment of implementing differentiated instruction. Ask participants to fill in each section and then meet with a partner, department, grade-level group, a team, or interest group to compare and discuss their notes.

Example C: Carousel Gala

The following carousel gala (Figure 6.7) is an effective activity for a professional development session. The data gathered shows which areas of differentiated instruction are being implemented, viewed, and interpreted by the group. The following examples present various ways to use this grid.

1. Select the items that are appropriate for the group's stage of implementation or interest.

2. Place each selected item on the top of a piece of chart, poster paper, or large wipe-off board. Place these items around the room like a carousel.

3. Groups of three to five are assigned to each statement or question.

4. The group reads the question or statement, and a group recorder writes the group responses.

5. After the group presents some answers, the session leader gives a signal for the groups to move to the next poster in the carousel.

6. At the next chart, the group reads the question or statement and the last group response. This group now adds to the response. This procedure continues until the posters are filled.

Figure 6.7

1. Name your favorite preassessment tools for students. *Informal* *Formal*	2. List effective assessment tools to use during the learning. *Informal* *Formal*	3. List useful, evaluative tools to use at the end of the learning. *Informal* *Formal*	4. How do you get to know your students?
5. Brainstorm components of an effective learning environment.	6. How and when do you use flexible grouping?	7. Name ways to move students into groups.	8. How do you challenge gifted students?
9. Name management tips for using a variety of assignments to meet individual needs.	10. List various activities for independent work assignments.	11. Provide tips for using academic contracts.	12. Brainstorm effective ways to provide choice.
13. What do you need to remember when assigning projects?	14. How do you motivate students to learn?	15. How do you teach students to think on their own?	16. How will differentiated instruction help you with curriculum mapping?

Carousel Gala

How do you differentiate curriculum?

MANAGING THE SUPPORT ROLE

1. Remember that change happens gradually.

- Become familiar with all aspects of differentiated instruction so that your knowledge base is accurate. For example, one myth related to differentiation is that the teacher must have groups throughout the class period. Group instruction is only *one* way to implement differentiated instruction.

- Differentiate professional development to guide teachers on their paths to differentiation. Each teacher is unique in professional knowledge, experiences, and interest in implementing this philosophy.

- Realize that educators often go through a state of dissonance when they are asked to abandon teaching beliefs and replace them with new approaches. In this state, they cling to familiar, successful practices as they become aware of their need to change.

- Teachers readily embrace a new program or strategy when they see the value in its effectiveness, and they are convinced that it is better than "their way."

- Everyone is already differentiating to some extent, so start by "tweaking" the effective strategies and activities, then add new ones. Help teachers see and celebrate what they are already doing without even realizing it. Guide them to see that they don't have to change everything.

2. Provide support.

- Make newsletters and morning announcements that highlight teacher successes.

- Present highlights and kudos for teachers who are implementing differentiation in their classrooms by writing about activities, strategies, assessment tools, models, or strategies that work successfully in the classroom.

- Encourage teachers to submit their own newsletter article or morning announcements.

- Submit happenings, articles, and pictures to the local, state, and national papers and journals.

- During morning announcement times, let students share what they are learning individually or in small groups.

- Spotlight a teacher! Select a DI Teacher of the Month and showcase the ways differentiated instruction is addressed to meet the learners' needs.

- Encourage parents, local business, and community members to attend events that showcase differentiation.

- Have the students share their portfolios with their parents and peers.

- Schedule sharing times to brag about a growth spurt, a new activity, or a funny story.

- Compile lists of improvements made by individual teachers, grade-level teams, subject-area teams, or pod partners. When teachers share what they are doing to benefit learners, they become a professional learning community.

- Provide time at faculty meetings, professional meetings, and/or grade-level meetings for group sharing.

- Place signs around the school promoting increased achievement for every student.
- Display and showcase artifacts that represent the information students are learning. Place the artifact displays in hallways, media centers, and other common areas.
- Host a "Sharing Party." Teachers like to get ideas from each other.
- Host an expert breakfast so everyone can share what is working and what is not working. Remember to only address problems that you can solve. The other problems kill momentum and waste time.

3. Conduct classroom visits/morning classroom walk.

- When visiting rooms for a pop-in visit, leave a sticky note of how you saw the differentiation instruction theory practiced.
- Walk in every classroom every day so the students and the teachers see you. It is important to be visible and speak to everyone on the staff.
- Remember, when giving suggestions for improvement, talk about the things that you saw working well before and after you identify a weakness.
- As you tour the school, identify spots that are alive with creativity and stem from outstanding teaching creativity. Praise the teacher.
- Create a school scavenger hunt. Teams are formed to go on the hunt at a faculty meeting. Assign several things from those notes you made on your tour, and ask your teachers to locate them around the school. They must identify the place they located the item and how they could use the idea to promote student learning in their own classroom. Give teachers a chance to share and celebrate the activity.

4. Provide quality professional development opportunities.

- Strategic planning/curriculum mapping
- Professional learning community
- Ongoing professional development
- Faculty meetings, workshops, inservices, retreats
- Team and grade-level planning

5. Be a catalyst for differentiation.

- Plan strategically using the most effective tools.
- Believe you can make a difference for learners each day.
- Tweak or adapt your management strategies for the unique needs of learners.
- Believe in the philosophy that all students CAN learn.
- Share your success with differentiated management strategies with colleagues.

KEYS TO DIFFERENTIATED MANAGEMENT

The following acrostic provides a way to view the key components of differentiated instruction. Staff developers can personalize this list by allowing time for grade-level teams or interest groups to develop an acrostic that describes their differentiated classrooms.

Determine the standards and concepts to be taught.

Identify student needs with strong assessment tools before, during, and after learning.

Formulate lesson plans that link the targeted standards with individual needs.

Find effective strategies and activities to teach the information.

Engage students in activities that employ their interests and the ways they learn.

Relate learning to the students' worlds.

Encourage risk taking with wise choices.

Nurture the social and emotional aspects of the students.

Target the learners' needs with flexible grouping designs.

Ignite each student's desire to learn.

Adjust assignments to match the learner's abilities, knowledge levels, and interests.

Tailor lessons with student-focused activities.

Entice and ignite lifelong learners!

CONCLUSION

Put on your captain's hat! You are ready to chart your course, assess the strengths and weaknesses of your crew, and use their talents in meaningful, intriguing ways. Remember that a key to learning is engagement. If you can teach students new information and skills while engaging them in the process, you will have a happy—and productive—crew!

OUR HATS ARE OFF TO YOU!

REFERENCES

SOURCES

Barkley, S. (2005). *Wow! Adding pizzazz to teaching and learning.* Allentown, PA: Performance Learning Systems, Inc.

Gardner, H. (2006). *Multiple intelligences: New horizons in theory and practice.* New York, NY: Perseus Books Group.

Goleman, D., Kaufman, P. , & Ray, M. (1993). *The creative spirit.* New York: Plume.

Gregory, G., & Chapman, C. (2007). *Differentiated Instructional Strategies: One Size Doesn't Fit All* (2nd ed.). Thousand Oaks, CA: Corwin Press.

Jacobs, H. (1997). *Mapping the big picture, integrating curriculum and assessment K–12.* Alexandria, VA: Association for Supervision and Curriculum Development.

Joyce, B., & Weil, M. (2004). *Models of teaching, 7th edition.* Boston: Allyn & Bacon.

Sousa, D. (2006). *How the brain learns* (3rd ed.). Thousand Oaks, CA: Corwin Press.

Sternberg, R., & Grigorenko, E. (2007). *Teaching for successful intelligences: To increase student learning and achievement,* (2nd ed). Thousand Oaks, CA: Corwin Press.

Tomlinson, C. A. , & McTighe, J. (2006). *Integrating differentiated instruction and understanding by design.* Alexandria, VA: Association for Supervision and Curriculum Development.

Tomlinson, C. A., Kaplan, S. N., Purcell, J. H., Leppien, J. H., Burns, D. E., & Strickland, C. A. (2006). *The parallel curriculum in the classroom, book 2: Units for application across the content areas, K–12.* Thousand Oaks, CA: Corwin Press.

RECOMMENDED RESOURCES

Beattie, J., Jordan, L., & Algozinne, R. (2007). *Making inclusion work: Effective practices for all teachers.* Thousand Oaks, CA: Corwin Press.

Bishop, P. A., & Pflaum, S. W. (2005). *Reaching and teaching middle school learners: Asking students to show us what works.* Thousand Oaks, CA: Corwin Press.

Blankstein, A. M. (2004). *Failure is NOT an option: Six principles that guide student achievement in high-performing schools.* Corwin Press and Hope Foundation.

Chapman, C. (1993). *Developing the multiple intelligences classroom: If the shoe fits.* Arlington Heights, IL: Corwin Press.

Chapman, C., & Freeman, L. (1996). *Multiple intelligences centers and projects.* Thousand Oaks, CA: Corwin Press.

Chapman, C., & King, R. (2003). *Differentiated instructional strategies for writing in the content areas.* Thousand Oaks, CA: Corwin Press.

Chapman, C., & King, R. (2003). *Differentiated instructional strategies for reading in the content areas.* Thousand Oaks, CA: Corwin Press.

Chapman, C., & King, R. (2004). *Differentiated assessment strategies: If the shoe fits.* Arlington Heights, IL: Corwin Press.

Costa, A. (2007). *The school as a home for the mind: Creating mindful curriculum, instruction and dialogue* (2nd ed). Thousand Oaks, CA: Corwin Press.

Harmin, M., & Toth, M. (2006). *Inspiring active learning: A complete handbook for today's teachers* (2nd ed). Alexandria, VA: Association for Supervision and Curriculum Development.

Haynes, J. (2007). *Getting started with English language learners: How educators can meet the challenge.* Alexandria, VA: Association for Supervision and Curriculum Development.

Jensen, E. (2005). *Teaching with the brain in mind* (2nd ed). Alexandria, VA: Association for Supervision and Curriculum Development.

Marzano, R. J., Gaddy, B. B., Foseid, M. C., Foseid, M. P., & Marzano, J. S. (2005). *A handbook for classroom management that works.* Alexandria, VA: Association for Supervision and Curriculum Development.

Marzano, R. J. (2007). *The art and science of teaching: A comprehensive framework for effective instruction.* Alexandria, VA: Association for Supervision and Curriculum Development.

Nunley, K. F. (2006). *Differentiating the high school classroom: Solution strategies for 18 common obstacles.* Thousand Oaks, CA: Corwin Press.

Schmoker, M. (2006). *Results now: How we can achieve unprecedented improvements in teaching and learning.* Alexandria, VA: Association for Supervision and Curriculum Development.

Sousa, D. (2006). *How the special needs brain learns* (2nd ed). Thousand Oaks, CA: Corwin Press.

Sparks, D. (2007). *Leading for results: Transforming teaching, learning and relationships in schools* (2nd ed). Thousand Oaks, CA: Corwin Press and National Staff Development Council.

Sprenger, M. B. (2006). *Becoming a "wiz" at brain-based teaching: How to make every year your best year* (2nd ed). Thousand Oaks, CA: Corwin Press.

Sylwester, R. (2007). *The adolescent brain: Reaching for autonomy.* Thousand Oaks, CA: Corwin Press.

Tomlinson, C. A. (2004). *Differentiation for gifted and talented students.* Thousand Oaks, CA: Corwin Press and National Association for Gifted Children.

Wiggins, G., & McTighe, J. (2006, March). Examining the teaching life. *Educational Leadership, 63*(6), 26–29.

INDEX

**CORWIN
PRESS**

The Corwin Press logo—a raven striding across an open book—represents the union of courage and learning. Corwin Press is committed to improving education for all learners by publishing books and other professional development resources for those serving the field of PreK–12 education. By providing practical, hands-on materials, Corwin Press continues to carry out the promise of its motto: **"Helping Educators Do Their Work Better."**